Guiding

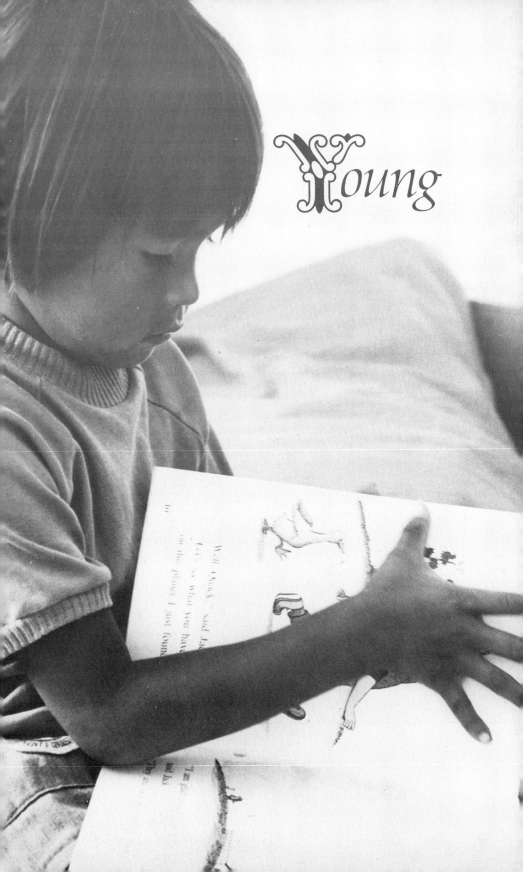

Young

Children

Verna Hildebrand Ph.D.

MICHIGAN STATE UNIVERSITY

Macmillan Publishing Co., Inc.
NEW YORK

Collier Macmillan Publishers
LONDON

Macmillan Publishing Co., Inc.
866 Third Avenue, New York, New York 10022
Collier-Macmillan Canada, Ltd.

Library of Congress Cataloging in Publication Data

Hildebrand, Verna.
    Guiding young children.

    Includes bibliographies.
    1. Education, Preschool.   2. Teacher-student
relationships.   3. Children—Management.   I. Title.
LB1140.2.H52   372.21   74–481
ISBN 0–02–354230–6

Printing: 6 7 8 9   Year: 8 9 0 1 2

Dedication

I wish to dedicate this book to my husband, John; to our children, Carol and Steve; to the many children from whom I have learned so much in the day care centers, nursery schools, and kindergartens with which I have been associated; but, especially, to *all* children of this planet we share as a home. As communicated so beautifully in the following poem by Mamie Gene Cole, the quality of life tomorrow on our planet will be determined by these children.

I am the Child

I am the child.
All the world waits for my coming.
All the earth watches with interest to see
*   what I shall become.*
Civilization hangs in the balance,
For what I am, the world of tomorrow
*   will be.*

I am the child.
I have come into your world, about which
*   I know nothing.*
Why I came I know not;
How I came I know not.
I am curious; I am interested.

I am the child.
You hold in your hand my destiny.
You determine, largely, whether I shall
*   succeed or fail.*
Give me, I pray you, those things that
*   make for happiness.*
Train me, I beg you, that I may be a
*   blessing to the world.*

—*from* "Child's Appeal," Mamie Gene Cole

Preface

Guiding Young Children is designed to be a suitable textbook for classroom use in any of the departments at community colleges or universities that offer courses in child care or in early childhood education. The emphasis is on the process of guiding and teaching young children—the interactional opportunities of caregivers, teachers, parents, and children themselves to develop the human potential of children.

Throughout this country and in other countries, too, there is growing pressure to provide more nursery facilities for infants and more nursery and day care centers for preschool children. There is also a pressing need to improve the quality of many of the present programs, making them fulfill social-psychological and educational needs of children. As the number of children increases, more and more qualified teachers and caregivers are needed. In addition, there is a growing cadre of volunteers who give their time and talent in working with young children.

Whether working in small groups of children as in day care homes or in larger centers, these newcomers to the child care tasks are seeking help. They are asking about ways to handle the ordinary routines, about handling behavior problems, and about teaching concepts to young children.

Guiding Young Children offers the student, teacher, assistant, or volunteer basic lines to follow in guiding and teaching infants and preschool children. It offers help in understanding the commonly observed behavior of young children. Suggestions are made for guiding children during all the routines and during the typical learning activities of the school—art, science, literature, language, music, dramatic play, and outdoor play.

For additional information on some related curriculum matters, the reader may wish to refer to portions of *Introduction to Early Childhood Education,* an earlier textbook by the same author and publisher. Instructors will notice that *Guiding Young Children* has been written to complement the earlier textbook. It has been organized so that it can effectively precede, serve with, or follow the earlier textbook in a sequence of course work or stand by itself as a complete textbook for a particular course. The author's *Laboratory Workbook for Introduction to Early Childhood Education* also offers, for classroom instructors and students, many ideas and guides for meaningful observations and discussions appropriate for most topics in both textbooks.

Parents and individuals involved in courses in parenting will also find helpful suggestions throughout the book.

Developmental principles and research findings are the bases for guidance suggestions. This book grew out of many years' experience teaching in day care, nursery school, and kindergarten and in guiding college students and Head Start teachers in learning and practicing principles and techniques. It answers questions posed in consultations with day care teachers and directors.

V. H.

Acknowledgments

I owe a debt of gratitude to many individuals. For the insights gained from Leone Kell, Kansas State University, who was my first child guidance instructor, for the inspiration of Catherine Landreth, University of California at Berkeley, who enlivened her classes with anecdotes from lively children in the nursery schools where I was a graduate assistant, and for the support from Virginia Messenger Stapley, Oklahoma State University, who supervised this young instructor in a comfortable fashion that left much room for creativity in developing programs for young children, I am truly grateful.

I am indebted to Helen Hostetter, Kansas State University, who encouraged my early writing of information for the practitioners of the art and science of early child development and education. I wish to thank Estelle Wallace of Texas Tech University and Kenneth Cannon of Brigham Young University and formerly of Texas Tech University; Jessie Bateman Barns and Dora Tyer of Texas Woman's University; and Beatrice Paolucci, Margaret Jacobson Bubolz, and Linda Nelson of Michigan State University, who have also encouraged my writing.

To colleagues, professors, students, children, and parents at these various universities, those of the public day care program and kindergarten of Albany, California, and those at Michigan State University and Texas Tech University where I have taught a variety of courses and groups of children in the laboratory nursery schools and kindergartens, I express my thanks for a stimulating environment.

Recognition is due a number of colleagues who have read and reacted to all or portions of the manuscript. They are Rebecca Hines, University of

xiii

Houston; James Walters, University of Georgia; William E. Martin, Purdue University; Sandra Morris, Mississippi State University; Phyllis Lueck, Dearborn Public Schools; and Janice Altadonna, Bernice Borgman, Vera Borosage, Margaret Bubolz, Mary Gray, Frances Kertesz, Beatrice Paolucci, and Lillian Phenice, Michigan State University.

I am further indebted for photographs to directors, teachers, students, parents, and children in several children's groups. I want to thank photographers Ed Breidenbach, Lee Butcher, Donna Creasy, Mary Gray, Roberta Hay, Eddie Hildreth, Rebecca Hines, Joe Kertesz, Connie Lisiecki, Mary Odell, William Mitcham, James Page, Margot and Gerald Seelhoff. Also, Flemmie Kittrell's contribution of pictures from a project at Howard University is gratefully acknowledged.

V. H.

Contents

XV

Developing Human Resources

"Daddy, Daddy," shouted Barbara. She was happy to see her father, who was picking her up at nursery school. "Daddy, come here and see what I can do," she called. Mr. Baker smiled and followed his little daughter to the climbing bar. Barbara said, "Watch me!" She expertly grasped the cross-bar and held tight while she flipped her legs over the bar, then dropped her arms and swung by her knees. She smiled at her father from her upside-down position. Watching closely, her father said, "That's great, Barb. I didn't know you could do that. Do it again, will you?"

MR. BAKER'S human resources of interest and praise encouraged Barbara's development of motor skills. These skills became resources or means for Barbara to achieve the more difficult skills she would soon be learning, such as bike riding and roller skating.

Try thinking of resources as intermediate goods required for making other goods or as means for achieving other goals. For example, you can think of steel as a resource for making automobiles, wheat as a resource for making bread, physical coordination as a resource for walking, and spelling ability as a resource for writing.

We are accustomed to think of common resources such as money, fuel, and food, which often make the headlines. However, people and the talents they are developing are the most important resources. Without people's abilities, skills, interactions, and communications, society would be a major loser.

1

Love is an important human resource. (Nazarene Child Care Center, Lansing, Michigan, Gerald Seelhoff, Photographer.)

You are in the process of developing your personal human resources in order to guide young children more effectively. More high-quality child care services will build human resources that this country needs badly.[1]

[1] For a sensitive essay in which Evangeline H. Ward, president of the National Association for Education of Young Children, the nation's largest association dedicated to young children's development, care, and education, speaks out on priorities of the nation in relation to young children's services, see Evangeline H. Ward, "From the President," *Young Children*, Vol. 29 (Mar. 1974), 130–132.

HUMAN RESOURCE DEVELOPMENT— THE GOAL

Developing human resources is the goal of education from infant schools to classes for senior citizens. Through reading, study, and practice your personal competence will blossom. You'll find you have abilities that perhaps you are unaware of at this moment. These are your resources, your human bank account for the future.

What are your talents? What are your strengths? What do you know? What can you learn? Your talents, strengths, knowledge, skills, and potential to learn are your human resources. Human energy

Good mental and physical health are interacting human resources for teachers and children. (William Mitcham, Michigan State University Staff Photographer.)

Older children are resources for younger ones, sharing their ideas and energy. (Southern University, Baton Rouge, Louisiana, Eddie Hildreth, Photographer.)

is the basis of all human resources. These resources will give you the means to achieve some goal. Money is the most familiar resource. It is a material or nonhuman resource that can be spent for some desired object or service—that is, goal. Human resources can also be "spent" and are means for achieving some desired goals. Lucky for you, though, your human resources don't become depleted like money, but will become enhanced with use. The more you use them the more you'll have.

As each goal is reached it can become a stepping-stone or resource for achieving additional goals. For example, with development of your potential abilities for guiding young children you can become a more effective teacher or parent. Or, if you have special aptitude for music or mathematics, you might develop these resources and become a musician or a mathematician.

Two aspects to look at when we consider human resources are that they are both *utilized* and *devel-*

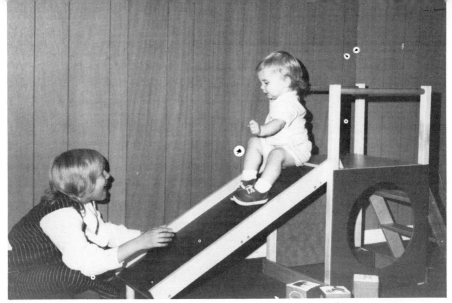

"Come baby, you can do it!" the little girl says, encouraging the baby to use the slide—a combination of human and nonhuman resources. (What's New in Home Economics, *Donna Creasy, Photographer.*)

oped in the school and in the home. For example, in this text I have utilized my energy, knowledge, and experience to help you in the development of your teaching and parenting skills. You, in turn, as a teacher or parent will sooner or later utilize your energy, knowledge, and experience to develop little children's human resources—their abilities and skills —in the best possible way.

In addition to utilizing and developing human resources, the helping professions call for the *exchange* of human resources. "Two heads are better than one" is an old adage that is at work when an individual interacts with and is helped or challenged by another person as he solves a problem.

Person-to-person interaction on the educational scene can promote the exchange of human resources. The interaction can be teacher-child, child-child, parent-child, teacher-parent, or interaction with an important person, sometimes called a "significant other." Of course, interactions can have a negative impact on the involved individuals, but with skill, knowledge, and a firm ethical position on the part of teachers and parents the interaction can assure positive results for children and adults.

Individuals learn from each other through interaction and communication. We can note the exchange of resources of skill, knowledge, and encouragement for the resources of friendship, respect, and love in the following: a teacher shares an idea for a bulletin board with her colleague down the hall; a farmer asks the extension agent for advice in selecting seed wheat; a grandmother pats her grandchild's head and says, "You're real pretty." In each interaction both the giver and the receiver are strengthened through the exchange. Though the resources given or received are intangible, they are valuable nonetheless.

As educators, we are concerned with the human resources of intellectual abilities, physical skills, creativity, and the motivation to put resources to work to achieve goals for the individual and for society at local, state, national, and global levels.

Building such human resources as love, trust, empathy, and loyalty is important, especially in this day of stress on cognitive abilities, programmed learning, and concept cartridges. Person-to-person interaction and communication need to be nurtured in the home, school, and community. Humans need other humans regardless of the material comforts and gadgets they possess.

Think of Bea, a young nursery school teacher, who still vividly recalls a day many years ago when she was only four. She came running into her grandfather's little grocery, saying excitedly, "Grandfather, Grandfather, I can write my name." She remembers how his eyes lit up with interest as he tore a strip of paper from a roll of butcher paper, sat down with her by the counter, and asked her to "show me." She produced the letters bold and clear. He complimented her generously on her accomplishment and placed the little paper in his wallet. "He carries it to this day," she reports. It symbolizes to her his support, at an effective moment, for achieving an education.

As teachers and as parents, we utilize both human and nonhuman energy resources for reaching the goals we set for individual children. Nonhuman resources include funds, facilities, equipment, supplies, and materials. Human resources include health, energy, ideas, motivation, mental and physical abilities, and the emotional support and help we freely give and accept from others. Children, siblings, parents, teachers, and other professional and lay individuals of the community all possess human resources capable of being developed, utilized, and exchanged in the process of educating young children.

All should appreciate the possibilities of contributions by the custodian, the cook, or the bus driver to the process of education. The attitudes and helpfulness of secretaries, as well as the professionals, in agencies serving individuals and families can make valuable contributions to human resource development. For example, Anna, a foreign-born woman, may be seeking help in learning to speak and write English. She phones the basic education office. The answer can be courteous, communicating, and un-

A teacher, some play-dough, and some tools combine to help a child grow in her manipulative and social skills. (Michigan State University Laboratory Preschool, Connie Lisiecki, Photographer.)

derstanding, which will assure Anna's participation in appropriate classes. A single negative comment might frighten her away for a long time, thereby inhibiting her resource development.

Humans both *create* and *transform* resources, both human and nonhuman resources. Creating and transforming abilities must be preserved and strengthened in each individual. The children of today will be the leaders of the twenty-first century. They will face situations that neither their parents nor teachers can totally predict.

Teachers as Resources for Children

The teacher is a decision-maker, selecting goals and setting the stage for children to utilize both nonhuman and human resources to achieve goals. The allocation of both types of resources is part of every decision the teacher makes.

A teacher who possesses resources of good mental and physical health, lots of energy, and emotional stability is able to help children in ways not possible if these resources are lacking. Teachers who possess excellent mental ability and are well informed, and those who have high motivation and are well prepared, surely achieve more goals for children than those without these resources. A teacher with the ability to relate to each child, to empathize with him, and to love him may be expected to develop more of these characteristics in children. Children gain from teachers who utilize or set in motion the human resources that are available in other teachers, parents, and community members.

Teachers also need the ability to marshal the nonhuman resources for the teaching and learning tasks at hand. Even as you study this course you have books, paper, classrooms, libraries, and money that have been allotted toward a goal of preparing you to guide young children. Teachers endeavor to increase human and nonhuman resources to enhance the learning experiences for students. Teachers of preschool children are noted for their resourcefulness in expanding resources through use of volunteers (human resources) or through "found" materials (nonhuman resources) such as scrap lumber for carpentry or odds and ends for art projects or play materials.

Children share a clown game with their teacher by pasting spots on her face. (Michigan State University Laboratory Preschool, Connie Lisiecki, Photographer.)

Children as Resources for Other Children and for Teachers

The idea of encouraging older children to help the younger ones creates in some people a nostalgia for the one-room school of the American pioneer era. The British Infant School and the Open Classroom are modern-day examples. This concept is in operation when sixth graders assist in the kindergarten. One child operates as a resource for another in any class where a child who is already skillful shows another how to do something. Children learn many of their new skills as they watch and imitate others

Children are resources for other children as they work together in the center. (Michigan State University Laboratory Preschool, Connie Lisiecki, Photographer.)

in the nursery school and kindergarten. If admitting ignorance were not so discomforting, demonstration and idea exchanges would operate at upper age levels more frequently and with greater ease.

Teachers receive energy from children as well as give energy to them. Many of us who have worked with children over a period of time know how much about life and learning these children have really taught us. Our motivation to continue teaching depends a great deal on the positive response children give our efforts. Children really are a resource for the teacher, giving her love, respect, and friendship as she shares her knowledge and skills with them.

Parents as Resources for Both Children and Teachers

Most parents want to be a resource for their child's education. Many do an excellent job of utilizing both nonhuman and human resources to provide a stimulating educational environment in their homes. This advantage has been referred to as the "hidden curriculum" of the middle-class child. Parents may need to be guided, and sometimes reassured, as they strive to use their resources to help their children during the school years. Nowhere in the long process of education is the parent's contribution more important than in the preschools. Involving parents in order that they can truly contribute must be the goal of every school program.

Mothers' energy resources have traditionally been tapped for serving on bake-sale and carnival committees, as room mothers, or as drivers on field trips.

An interested father is a resource for his daughter and for another child through conversation and assistance. (University of Houston, Rebecca Hines, Photographer.)

However, we need to keep in mind that traditional stereotyped roles are no longer binding for women. The many talents of women are now being widely applied. Major benefits to women and to society are indeed apparent. Though some mothers may have little time or interest in baking cookies, they may be helpful to the teacher in other ways.

Fathers, too, can be a valuable resource. Remember how Mr. Baker encouraged Barbara in our little story that opened this chapter. Fathers' visits and participation in the school scene should be encouraged. They can also share their vocational or avocational skills. For example, a carpenter father may supervise room renovation, a contractor father may help with new trike paths. Parents with a talent such as playing a musical instrument can perform for and lead children in a musical experience. Either fathers or mothers may offer resources for field trips or special demonstrations at their place of work.

Teachers as Resources for Parents

The teacher's role becomes one of guiding parental resources so that they can contribute toward reaching goals. Building the parents' ability to help their children grow, develop, and learn is usually part of the school's parent-education program. Because the school can achieve little success without support from parents, the parent-education or parent resource-building aspects must be undertaken simultaneously with educational programs for the child.

Teachers provide consultation to parents. They may furnish reading materials, or direct them to community services that will support needs of the child and the family. In this mobile society the teacher may become the advisor to the family, because she may be more interested in the child than is any other individual outside his family.

Volunteers as Resources for Children

Volunteers of various types can be recruited to help children during and after school. Such exchanges of resources can be mutually beneficial. Programs that organize such volunteers as foster grandparents, cadet teachers, college students, and classroom aides all help put human resources to work benefiting children. Planning for, guiding, and rewarding volunteers are essential tasks of the teacher if this wealth of human resources is to be effectively utilized for children.

MEASURING GOAL ACHIEVEMENT

Building human resources is the goal of education. Efforts are being made to measure the outcomes of education by means other than grades derived exclusively from paper-and-pencil tests. You will often hear the terms *competency-* and *performance-based criteria.* Under such a scheme you, as a teacher, may be judged by your performance in the classroom with children as well as by what you can say or write on paper about teaching children.

Attempts at defining the desired outcomes of education for young children have been made for many years and are still being worked on throughout the country. When public monies are being spent there is increased concern that desired goals be met. Therefore, standards of performance are being set that apply to children, to teachers, and to some extent to parents.

There is a real hazard that some individuality and humanism may be lost in this evaluating process, and we should be on guard to prevent this. However, it is clear that human resources are not well developed in the substandard custodial-type child care found in some early childhood education programs. Substandard programs cannot be tolerated in a literate and rich country such as ours. Our children are our greatest resource for the future; their potential must not be wasted.

Child care services along with other human services have become important consumer items for families and for society in general. When we buy something and pay good money for it, we want to be sure we are getting the quality we pay for. We can take back the jeans if the stitching rips. Public interest groups are forcing manufacturers to make higher-quality products. But in human services, such as child care, the outcomes are far more serious when quality control is lacking. We can't toss out the product and start over.

The Office of Child Development in the Depart-

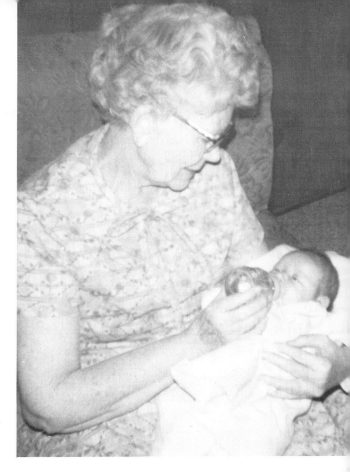

A *grandparent's skills,
experience, and love
can be valuable re-
sources for care of chil-
dren.* (*Lee Butcher,
Photographer.*)

ment of Health, Education, and Welfare in Washington recently published *Guides for Day Care Licensing.* The publication suggests model regulations for states to use in establishing or revising their regulations related to day care and other child development programs. These guidelines, developed by child development professionals and licensing specialists, offer important minimum standards for good-quality child care.

CONCLUSION

We in child development and early childhood education must take the lead in the movement for high-quality in child care. Our goal is to develop optimum personal competence in all children, and we must marshal the human and nonhuman resources for the task.

15 *Conclusion*

APPLICATIONS

(In all applications at the end of each chapter be sure to identify the ages in years and months of all children discussed.)
1. Assist two children in a home or a school. Note examples of exchanges of human resources. Explain what happened. How were the children's resources helped or hindered?
2. Recall a point in your own experience when one individual used his resources in a way that supported your human resource development. Explain what happened.
3. Analyze one of your own skills. What are the skills that this new skill is built on? At what age did you begin developing the original skill?
4. Select a child for a special case study. Be prepared to keep cumulative records on a single child throughout the course so that you can write a final report.

INDEPENDENT STUDY

Some colleges may have appropriate independent study or community service project courses where capable students can properly receive extra degree credits for providing tutorial help on a scheduled basis to some child (perhaps their case-study child) or to some child care center where help is needed. This can be an important service in a community and a stimulating real-world learning situation for a college student.

SUGGESTED FILMS

Why Man Creates   Color   25 minutes
Emphasizes the place of creativity in the world, the relationship of ideas to institutions. A view of the process of developing new ideas. Kaiser Aluminum Film Distribution Center, Kaiser Center 864, Oakland, California 94604.
The Precious Years   Color   30 minutes
An ABC documentary that examines the curriculum of the Institute for Early Education in Chicago. Film footage concentrates on three teachers in real-life situations at preschool centers in the Chicago area. ABC Merchandising, Inc., 1330 Avenue of the Americas, New York, N.Y. 10036.

FOR FURTHER READING

ALLEN, SALLY, et al. *Perspectives on Child Care*. Washington, D.C.: National Association for the Education of Young Children, 1972.

BIBER, BARBARA. *Challenges Ahead for Early Childhood Education.* Washington, D.C.: National Association for the Education of Young Children, 1970.

COMBS, ARTHUR W. *Educational Accountability: Beyond Behavioral Objectives.* Washington, D.C.: Association for Supervision and Curriculum, 1972.

DITTMAN, LAURA L. *What We Can Learn from Infants.* Washington, D.C.: National Association for the Education of Young Children, 1970.

DOWLEY, EDITH M., and ROSE M. BROMIVICH. "The Role of Curriculum in Early Childhood Development Programs." In Dennis N. McFadden (Ed.). *Early Childhood Development Programs and Services: Planning for Action.* Washington, D.C.: National Association for the Education of Young Children, 1972.

HILDEBRAND, VERNA. *Introduction to Early Childhood Education.* New York: Macmillan Publishing Co., Inc., 1971.

HILDEBRAND, VERNA. "Two Heads Are Better Than One: Building Human Resources." *Education,* Vol. 94, No. 3 (Feb./Mar. 1974), 279–281.

HYMES, JAMES, JR. " 'Childhood' in Early Childhood Education." *Theory into Practice,* Vol. 12, No. 2 (Apr. 1973), 72–76.

KEISTER, MARY ELIZABETH. *The "Good Life" for Infants and Toddlers.* Washington, D.C.: National Association for the Education of Young Children, 1970.

KEYSERLING, MARY DUBLIN. *Windows on Day Care.* New York: National Council of Jewish Women, 1972.

KLEIN, JENNY. "The Child Development Associate." *Childhood Education,* Vol. 49, No. 6 (March 1973), 288–291.

LANDRETH, CATHERINE. *Preschool Learning and Teaching.* New York: Harper & Row, Publishers, 1972.

OFFICE OF CHILD DEVELOPMENT. *Guides for Day Care Licensing.* Washington, D.C.: Department of Health, Education, and Welfare, Government Printing Office, 1973.

PIERCE, CHESTER. "Becoming a Planetary Citizen: A Quest for Meaning." *Childhood Education,* Vol. 49, No. 2 (Nov. 1972), 58–63.

WARD, EVANGELINE H. "From the President." *Young Children,* Vol. 29, No. 3 (Mar. 1974), 130–132.

17 *Conclusion*

Valuing as a Basis for Actions

"Oh, there you are, Dana," Miss Stevenson said to a shy little girl who was arriving late to the nursery school after the activity was well under way. "We've been hoping you would come to help us make the applesauce." Dana smiled and went to remove her coat. Miss Stevenson spoke quietly to Dana. She understood that this shy little girl needed quiet recognition and did not want attention drawn to her from all the children.

INDIVIDUALIZED and personalized teaching were very high in Miss Stevenson's hierarchy of values. She felt that it was important for each child to be recognized and spoken to as he arrived each day. The quiet yet warm greeting assured Dana that she was very important to her teacher, Miss Stevenson.

TEACHING—ART OR SCIENCE?

Teaching is often referred to as an art, and credit is sometimes given to intuitive or creative teachers for the exceptional programs they devise. However, in addition to possessing intuition and creativity, teachers should be able to process rapidly (1) knowledge of child development, (2) knowledge of individual children's needs, (3) knowledge of guidance techniques and alternatives, (4) knowledge of curriculum and materials, and (5) knowledge of their own and others' experience. With such knowledge, coupled with intuition and creativity, teachers should be able to make on-the-spot decisions and

18

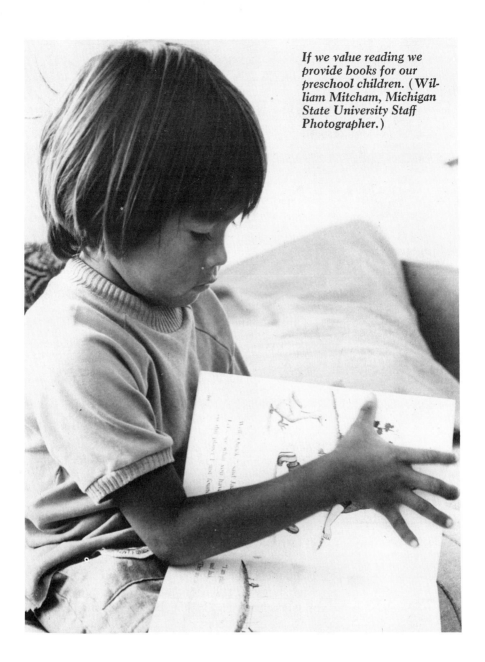

If we value reading we provide books for our preschool children. (William Mitcham, Michigan State University Staff Photographer.)

implement those decisions in a satisfactory and growth-producing manner for all concerned.

Decision-making in the nursery school, in the day care home or center, and in the home can be person-centered and in keeping with the human resource development ideas proposed in Chapter 1.

19 *Teaching—Art or Science?*

When we value perceptual development we support children's exploration of new materials. (Howard University, Flemmie Kittrell Project, Fred Harris, Photographer.)

VALUE BASIS OF DECISIONS

Your decisions regarding what to do with children will be based largely on the *values* you hold. Values are concepts of the desirable. They are the "oughts" or "shoulds" that guide our actions. Your values are reflected in your behavior and determine the goals you set and the actions that grow from your goals. Many values may be unconscious until you work at bringing them to the level of awareness, or search for the implicit values on which your actions or the actions of others are, in fact, based.

Where do values come from in your own scheme of things? Actually, you've been acquiring them all your life, from your family, your friends, and your community, including your schooling. Values get firmly set early in life and are difficult to change.

They relate to such things as family, religion, economics, politics, work, play, health, freedom, individuality, order, and beauty. What are the "oughts" or "shoulds" related to each of these concepts that immediately come to your mind?

You, as a teacher, hold values, the parents whose children you serve also hold values (and these may be different from yours), and the children are developing their values. These three viewpoints must be considered if you are to provide the best guidance for young children.

VALUES INTO ACTION

"Do values really make that much difference?" you may be asking. Following are nine stories about nine hypothetical teachers. These stories were developed for and are part of some research being conducted by the author. Each story is designed to illustrate a particular value orientation. Can you identify and label what value orientation is uppermost in each story and in the decisions the teacher is making in her class? In real life, a teacher is probably a combination of several "stories." Which one illustrates for you the most important focus of a teacher's decisions? Which is most like you? Least? Pick out the first- and second-ranking stories and the lowest-ranking story. Can you explain your reasons for ranking the stories the way you did? If you can discuss the stories with a few parents, you may find that their views differ from yours. Where do these differences arise? How can you mediate the differences if you have their children in your classroom?

1. Teacher A thinks it important for children to learn to get along with others. She feels children learn to get along, to help each other, and to share by having freedom to interact. Her classroom is usually a beehive of activity. She willingly puts off a science lesson if there is a spontaneous group activity in progress at the moment. Teacher A makes friends with children and parents and arranges situations so that each child will know and make friends with all the others. When difficulties arise, she prefers to let children work out the problem, interven-

When we value nature we teach children to appreciate the out of doors. (William Mitcham, Michigan State University Staff Photographer.)

ing only as a last resort. She sometimes helps parents arrange their children's play groups during weekends or vacations.

2. Teacher B believes that children should be well prepared for "real school." Her classroom schedule is arranged so that she gets lots of basic learning material covered each day. She avoids getting sidetracked during a class project; therefore, she is able to carry out lesson plans completely. She believes she must teach children a good deal of information, including ABCs, colors, shapes, and numbers. Her children frequently achieve above average on standardized tests, which indicates to her that they are

When we value knowledge we take time to inform children about the world around them. (University of Idaho Laboratory School, Ed Breidenbach, Photographer.)

When we value inde-
pendence we take time
to help children use
tools. (Nazarene Day
Care Center, Lansing,
Michigan, Gerald Seel-
hoff, Photographer.)

learning the material. Her talks with parents focus on children's preparation for first grade. She participates in lectures and seminars to enlarge her own learning whenever available.

3. Teacher C is concerned that children develop a sense of morality and good judgment. She often discusses with them how they ought to behave. She tells them her own views and introduces religious stories and ideas to the children. The children are taught what is right and wrong and are expected to behave accordingly. Manners and saying "please" and "thank you" are stressed. Teacher C discusses any topic that is of interest to children, especially if she feels it will aid their character development. She encourages them to correct each other if they feel someone is doing something wrong.

4. Teacher D keeps her classroom looking attractive at all times. She takes special care that the colors are harmonious and that various artifacts are displayed in the room. Children's art objects and paintings are carefully mounted and labeled. Creative movement and music, including works of the great composers, are a part of the program. Well-written children's literature is used regularly. Teacher D wears colorful and fashionable clothing. She helps children arrange their hair and clothing to look their best.

5. Teacher E's schedule and activities are outlined by the school's director, and she carefully follows these guidelines. She is grateful for the leadership of her school's director and values the opinions of

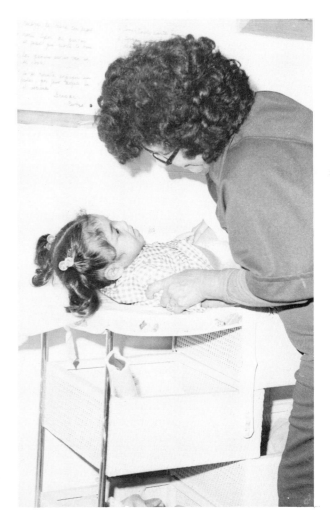

When we value communication we talk with children in friendly, helpful tones. (University of Houston, Rebecca Hines, Photographer.)

fellow teachers and parents. At the beginning of each year the director distributes a list of policies and regulations that gives Teacher E a guide for administration in her classroom. She believes that the director is a competent administrator and knows a lot about running the class. She is pleased when the director brings in new learning programs for her to use.

6. Teacher F likes for children to have lots of fresh air and sunshine. She carefully checks to see that the children have sufficient light, correct temperature, and chairs and tables of suitable height. Each morning she checks up on their habits of good breakfast, daily bath, tooth brushing, and proper rest. She checks throats and chests for signs of contagious disease and has children taken home when they seem ill. Routines of toileting and hand washing are frequent in her schedule. Nutritious foods are always available for snacks.

7. Teacher G feels that children should really plan their own program. She avoids thinking ahead about what children will be doing each day, but brings toys out as children arrive and indicate their interests. She may choose an activity because she particularly wants to do it that day. She tries to respond to children's needs of the moment and avoids pushing them into organized learning tasks. She emphasizes spontaneous learning, picking up on some project that the child seems interested in. Her schedule is completely flexible, and rarely do the children follow the same schedule for two days in a row.

8. Teacher H believes that each child learns in a different way. She considers the child a person first and a student second. Her program is arranged so that each child can express his individuality. A supportive atmosphere prevails that allows the child to feel free to venture into new experiences, but at the same time it is not one of indulgence. Teacher H strives to plan a rich variety of experiences with fresh views of familiar scenes, excursions to new places, or walks in parks. She uses many methods of motivation and novel ways of sparking children's imaginations.

9. Teacher I stresses protecting the school property and conserving materials. She teaches the children to use supplies such as paint, paper, and glue sparingly. She searches for "found" materials to supplement her supplies and utilizes all volunteer services available. She shows children how to use all their paper for a picture even if they paint a small spot and start to leave. Teacher I is also concerned with saving time, works at being efficient, and expects to teach children these traits. She thinks education is a way of improving one's station in life and a way of making a good living.

In these nine situations the primary value orientation in each story is

1. Socialization
2. Intellect
3. Morality
4. Aesthetics
5. Authority
6. Health
7. Freedom
8. Individuality
9. Economics

Each teacher places certain values in higher priority than others and therefore in decision-making situations chooses alternatives that reflect these values. For example, if the children have unloaded the entire shelf of blocks in the classroom a teacher who places a high value on order may be upset. However, she may be reconciled to the behavior when she notices that the blocks are being used in a creative manner, because creativity is a "good" in her value system. In the moment between when the teacher almost scolded the children for unloading the blocks and when she actually compliments them for their interesting structure she must weigh several value-based alternatives.

RECONCILING VALUE DIFFERENCES

When several teachers work as a team, as is typical of most preschool classrooms, frank discussions about values must be held so that the short-term and long-term goals can be established for the group and for each child. Teachers' values are not likely

Valuing as a Basis for Actions

When we value humor we encourage children's enjoyment of each other. (University of Idaho Laboratory School, Ed Breidenbach, Photographer.)

to be identical, but the teachers must come to some level of agreement; otherwise, conflicts arise and children and parents will be predictably confused. If Miss Laissez-faire and Miss Highly Structured are assigned to the same classroom, results may be damaging to children unless compromises are worked out.

Conflicts over values may arise between parents and the teachers. Should teachers teach a white child to love a dark-skinned child when that is not the accepted value of the community? Should teachers teach views that parents do not agree with? Should teachers teach children to be "better" or different than their parents? A serious acceptance of each other's rights to differing views and a willingness to mediate the conflicts are essential for resolving problems.

Given demands by parents or others to teach content or to use methods unacceptable from a personal-professional value base, the teacher's ultimate resort is to quit the teaching position, unless parents or others can be convinced that the teacher's value position has validity and are willing to compromise. The teacher must live with herself. Working day after day in a system that defies one's values would not only harm the teacher psychologically but might also harm the children.

For example, a striking value conflict arose when a new teacher began working in a day care center. She discovered that caregivers regularly disciplined children by spanking their bare buttocks with rulers. She protested that form of discipline to the caregivers and to the director. However, failing to get the practice modified, she said, "I quit. I've got my own conscience to sleep with." When she left the day care center she picked up the rulers, took them to the social service authorities responsible for licensing, and reported the case.

State and national values are translated into laws and into policies resulting from laws. These provide guidelines for teachers to follow and may protect the teacher by defining the number of children she can legally have in her class, the minimum space requirements for the school, the training that she is required to have before certification and so on.

The teacher's philosophy of life, of human development, of family dynamics, and of education will be reflected in the program that is developed for children and in the interaction that takes place between and among individuals.

Teaching styles develop out of the teacher's personality, knowledge, experience, and values. "Teaching style" denotes the unique way that the teacher makes decisions and interacts with the children in the class. For wholesome development to occur, the classroom management must reflect the teacher's understanding of the child's total existence. There must be a joint endeavor between home and school. Children may spend as many as nine hours a day in a child care center, but the child spends more hours away from the center than in it, though it is to be hoped that many are bedtime hours. A teacher may plan for as many as fifteen or twenty children and several assistants, which complicates the decision-making considerably. Enough adults should be available to preserve the person-centeredness philosophy of the center.

Value orientations are hard to change, but persons do change their values given adequate reasons and time to practice their new behavior. With increased knowledge of child development, teachers and teachers-to-be can learn to adjust their expectations to fit children's developmental levels. Given alternatives to authoritarian teaching styles, they can learn to be more democratic and person-centered. Or, given experience with a flexible schedule, a disorganized person can become comfortable when she learns to be more orderly. Most importantly, a better understanding of alternative value systems and implications for children is gained.

CONCLUSION

Value orientations determine the philosophy of education that teachers choose. Values determine the moment-to-moment actions of teachers. Through increased knowledge of and sensitivity to child development, teaching techniques, curriculum, and their own and others' experience, teachers will be

31 *Conclusion*

able to be assured that their intuitive teaching achieves a person-centered, intelligently planned, decision-making quality.

APPLICATIONS

1. Read the value stories in the chapter and rank the one you think is the most desirable focus of a head teacher's planning. List your second-place story. List the ninth-place story. Discuss or write an explanation of reasons for your ranking.
2. Write a little story describing another teacher who represents the kind of teacher you would like to be. Which values do you find that you have included?
3. Discuss with a parent what he or she feels is the most desirable focus of a nursery school program. Write a summary of the comments. Identify the values emphasized.
4. Make notes about the background of your case-study child.

SUGGESTED FILMS

Head Start to Confidence   Black and white   17 minutes
   A Head Start training film showing a group of four-year-old children with their teachers, who reach out to these children to convince them they are capable and worthy. Concludes with a case study of a little boy. Modern Talking Pictures, 1212 Avenue of the Americas, New York, N.Y. 10036. Head Start films are available free from this New York office or from any other Head Start office in your city or area.
Mothers and Toddlers   Black and white   22 minutes
   A Chicago program for both mothers and toddlers. Martin Luther King, Jr. Family Center, 124 North Hoyne, Chicago, Illinois. 60612

FOR FURTHER READING

BAUMRIND, DIANA. "Will a Day Care Center Be a Child Development Center?" *Young Children*, Vol. 28, No. 3 (Feb. 1973), 154–169.
BEREITER, CARL, and SIEGFRIED ENGELMANN. *Teaching Disadvantaged Children in the Preschool.* Englewood Cliffs, N.J.: Prentice-Hall, Inc., 1966.
CALDWELL, BETTYE M. "Can Young Children Have Quality Life in Day Care?" *Young Children*, Vol. 28, No. 4 (Apr. 1973), 195–208.
HILDEBRAND, VERNA. *Introduction to Early Childhood Education.* New York: Macmillan Publishing Co., Inc., 1971.

HILDEBRAND, VERNA, and BEATRICE PAOLUCCI. "The Value of Decisionmaking for Nursery School Teachers." *Journal of Home Economics,* Vol. 65, No. 3 (March 1973), 16–18.

KERCKHOFF, RICHARD K., and SHERRY C. TRELLA. "Teaching Race Relations in the Nursery School." *Young Children,* Vol. 27, No. 4 (Apr. 1972), 240–248.

MITCHELL, EDNA. "The Learning of Sex Roles Through Toys and Books: A Woman's View." *Young Children,* Vol. 28, No. 4 (Apr. 1973), 226–230.

MOSKOVITZ, SARAH. "Behavioral Objectives: New Ways to Fail Children." *Young Children,* Vol. 28, No. 4 (Apr. 1973), 232–235.

SOLE, JUNE SOLNIT. "Family Day-Care—A Valuable Alternative." *Young Children,* Vol. 28, No. 4 (Apr. 1973), 209–215.

WEBER, EVELYN. "The Function of Early Childhood Education." *Young Children,* Vol. 28, No. 5 (June 1973), 265–274.

Knowing Children as a Basis for Decisions

"Do all babies eat sloppily?"
"Don't you think a two-year-old can learn to stay out of the street?"
"How do you know when to discipline a child?"
"Will you teach my son to read and write?"
"Isn't he big enough to dress himself?"

TEACHERS FREQUENTLY are asked such questions by parents and by new employees and students who are learning about children as they work in a child care center. For teachers and parents to make appropriate decisions about interpersonal communication and guidance and about educational goals and strategies, a basic understanding of children's growth and development is necessary.

Who are these children you are going to teach? They are your children and mine, your sister's children, or your cousin's, or your neighbor's next door. They are rich children and poor, black children and white, happy children and sad. You'll be teaching children who desperately need a place to be while their parents work. You will be teaching children who have no parents or who are neglected by them. You will be teaching children whose parents have planned for them, cherish them, and want them to have a high-quality, enriching group experience.

KNOW CHILD DEVELOPMENT

Knowing children will be our major goal while we work with children. The science of child development is still in its infancy relative to other sciences. As teachers and parents, we can add to the science of child development the insights and un-

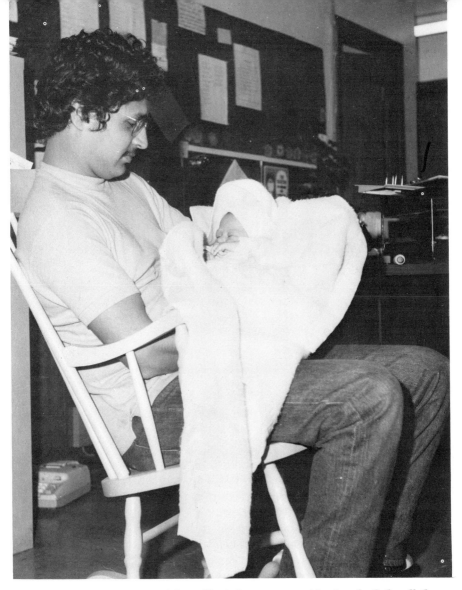

High-quality infant care provides for the baby all the comforts and tender loving care of home. (University of Houston, Rebecca Hines, Photographer.)

derstanding gained through direct experience with children. Though there is much written about children, you will note that often it has a tentative quality, because scientists recognize the inadequacies of our current knowledge. There are many theories. Some have been tested in laboratories but require much more study in the field before anyone can say

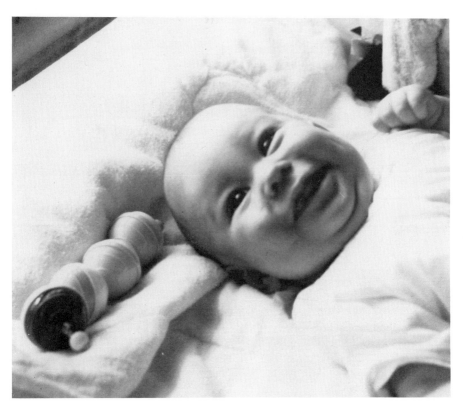

how much genuine insight they offer about how children grow, develop, and behave. However, we can use the theories to provide helpful points to observe in our work.

You, as a parent, teacher, or one who is becoming a teacher, through your daily contact with children can check out some of the theories and experiences of those who have gone before. This book is based on experience gained through working with children for many years. It is a sharing of experiences in the hope that you won't have to "rediscover the wheel," so to speak. It is hoped that this book will be helpful in making improvements for young children in homes and schools. That's where the action is.

INFANTS

There are the infants. Three months, six months, seven, and nine. Pablum spewing from their mouths. Mobiles tinkling over cribs. There is still much controversy about whether babies "ought" to be kept in day care centers.[1] Certainly if day care centers have our children, yours and mine, we'll declare that the center "should" be a good one, for infancy is one of life's critical periods. (Note the use of the value words *ought* and *should* and recall our discussion in Chapter 2.)

A number of factors are contributing to the need for infant care—either in home day care or in group care centers. Many mothers desperately need to work to keep food on the table and clothing on the family's back. All are not women without husbands. With the high cost of living, it may increasingly take two to make an adequate living. Some women maintain their jobs for "insurance," having seen what happens to families if the breadwinner is laid off work. Of course, some women work for personal fulfillment, and there is growing sentiment that this is their "right." Men, too, need child care, especially widowed men who want to keep their families together. Communities should provide high-quality centers for children no matter why the children are enrolled.

Good infant care is expensive. It takes lots of hands to feed, bottle, change, nap, amuse, stimu-

[1] See Phyllis T. Elardo and Bettye M. Caldwell, "The Kramer Adventure: A School for the Future?" *Childhood Education*, Vol. 50, No. 3 (Jan. 1974), 143–152, for an example of positive outcomes from a high-quality, multiage-grouping experiment.

"What's for dinner? I'm ready."
(James Page, Photographer.)

late, and love babies for many hours a day for five or more days each week. Currently some economists are attempting to define the "economics of the home" wherein the monetary contribution of a mother's time is calculated. When we look at high-quality infant care we begin to see the validity of their work. Cost estimates on demonstration projects of high-quality infant care come to about fifty dollars per week per child for only eight or nine hours for five days each week in a group setting. Mothers, of course, are on tap twenty-four hours a day, seven days a week, for the care they give.

Day care services for infants will be one of the issues that will be hotly debated in the coming years. As a teacher you'll be on the front line where the action is. What are the good points? What are the bad? What can be done?

One of the areas of greatest concern when parents send an infant to a center is that of health. Infants are particularly vulnerable to germs, so extra care must be given to protect their health. Cleanliness, isolation of babies who show symptoms of illness, and particular attention to the health of the caregivers are of vital importance. If you are going to work with infants, you will receive special training in health and sanitation from the health advisors for the center.

Another parental concern is whether separation from the mother and care by a series of different caregivers will harm the baby's emotional development. This is indeed an important concern and one that high-quality centers give their closest attention. In such centers one adult works consistently with the same small number of babies in small groups. Large groups are avoided. This way caregivers learn the special needs and signs of each child. Even very young babies show individual differences. They eat, sleep, wake, and socialize each in his own way.

Another parental concern is whether the child will learn as much and be as smart as he would be if he were home receiving his mother's "undivided" attention. "Undivided" is in quotes because even mothers at home cannot give undivided attention. There is work to be done, there are other children to attend, and the women's own personal diversions must take some time, too. Babies *can* learn as much in high-quality centers as at home, though some differences in what they learn naturally occur.

In high-quality centers there is a great deal of adult conversation and stimulation directed to the baby to encourage his language development. Talking to the baby, listening to his babbling, and other such responses to him are part of the interaction that goes on daily. There is a rich environment of interesting playthings and books and an opportunity for outdoor play, stimulation, and fresh air.

In a high-quality center for infants the child will be given innumerable opportunities to develop what Dr. Jean Piaget, a researcher of child development, calls the *sensorimotor stage*. The sensorimotor stage is the period from birth to approximately age two when the infant learns through handling objects, moving himself about, and in general exploring things with hands, body, tongue, eyes, and ears. This exploratory stage is the stepping-stone to later development, and it is important that the child fulfill his desires or needs to explore. A variety of playthings for his use and a safe environment for using them will encourage the child's thinking and doing. As caregivers we must allow the type of exploratory activity that a baby needs. We must encourage the baby to explore and use new skills.

Parents may be concerned that the baby will cry and miss them. Every effort will be made to satisfy the usual needs of infants that make them cry— being wet, hungry, lonely, tired, or bored. The small number of infants under one caregiver's charge will be arranged so that the caregiver can attend to all the children's needs adequately. The caregivers are people who love and enjoy babies, appreciate their individual differences, and sincerely appreciate the growth they see taking place each day. The center does not try to supplant the mother, but to substitute for her to the greatest degree it can during the hours she is away. The caregiver will try in every way to learn from mothers a baby's special habits and the ways the mother does things. This information will be utilized in routines whenever feasible. Caregivers will welcome a mother's participation in their routines so that she can know what the baby does each day and how the caregiver manages him.

Parents will worry about the baby's elimination, so they will receive a report on the regularity of the functioning of bladder and bowels during the day. Babies differ from each other in habits and types of movements. A change in bowel movements can be a sign of illness; therefore, parents need to receive reports of unusual changes.

Infants usually sleep several times a day. A regular schedule of sleep will help the child be rested and ready for his mother when she picks him up. A ritual may evolve around bedtime, just as it does at home —for example, a bath and a bottle given regularly before bedtime.

Babies' food needs are of primary importance during the first year, especially when formula and special foods are on the menu. Digestive upsets are common and can be serious, so special attention will be given to the sanitation of the food and to feeding the infant. Babies are held for feedings in high-quality centers.

Babies have need for mental and visual stimulation. Consequently, before babies can roll themselves over they will require the assistance of the caregiver to change position and have something new to look at from time to time.

Nothing panics a mother more than the bad news that her baby has become ill. Not only does she have concern for the baby, but also she feels that her job must go on somehow. Centers need some arrangements for taking care of sick babies during the day until the mother can get there. The health team—nurse and doctor—must be contacted. Mothers must also be encouraged to have arrangements made for backup care for a sick child in the home of a relative or friend. Mothers will then be able to deal more comfortably with this type of bad news.

The center needs specific policies about when it will care for a child who has what may appear to be a simple cold. Only with proper nursing care can a sick baby be cared for in a center without infecting other children and placing the child's own health in jeopardy.

Mothers of sick babies usually feel extremely guilty because often they must continue to work and leave their children to someone else. Caregivers should develop ways of communicating with parents to help them be effective in the parenting hours that remain each day after their babies leave the center.

Caring for infants during their first year is a very exciting experience. Growth and developmental changes take place very rapidly. The baby is more highly developed in the upper regions before he develops in the lower regions. You will remember this principle of development easily because you know that the baby does things with his hands—holds his bottle or shakes his rattle—before he can stand or walk. He sits before he stands.

Babies develop large, generalized movements before they learn specific small ones. For example, a baby can aim his arm toward the mobile over his crib long before he reaches with his finger and thumb and pulls at one of the objects to put it in his mouth. He learns how to grasp an object before he learns how to let go. He also kicks in large, gross movements before he uses his legs for creeping or walking.

Babies make cooing and babbling sounds that are the forerunners of the words they eventually use. An infant likes encouragement and responses to his verbalizations, although he practices them even when you leave the room. By nine months you'll hear familiar letter sounds.

Between four and six months, when his back is strong and his head quits wobbling, the baby likes to be propped to a sitting position to eat his solids and to watch the world go by. He may spend considerable time just looking at his newly discovered fingers. About this time he begins to use both hands in a coordinated way, closing in on an object he'd like to put in his mouth. For example, give him a graham cracker and watch him handle it with a whole-hand operation and eventually get it to his mouth to suck on.

Once he rolls over he'll discover his toes and even put them in his mouth. This feat will never be so easy again!

Between the fifth and eighth months most babies develop a fear of strangers, especially babies who have been home babies for the most part. It is a sign of growth that the baby knows the difference between his usual caregivers or mother and total strangers. When a baby is admitted to group care at this stage, caregivers should realize his anxiety is real but not unusual.

Between seven and twelve months the first teeth will appear. You'll note that the baby seems compelled to chew on anything he can get into his mouth. He will drool a lot. The teething may cause considerable discomfort, especially if several teeth come in at once.

Baby's creeping, pulling to standing, and walking will be exciting milestones in his development and should be reported to his mother so she can be watching for repeat performances at home. Babies normally begin walking between eight and fifteen months, with most of them taking their first steps around the twelfth month.

Other facts about infant development will be discussed in chapters related to guiding the child during his numerous routines and activities.

TODDLERS

Babies become "toddlers" when they begin walking. *Toddle* refers to the type of walk engaged in by young children between about twelve months and two and a half years. Of course, the mobile toddler is much more independent than the infant. In group care, as at home, caregivers must increase their vigilance, for now the child can get himself into more trouble than he could heretofore. He can get into the street but can't really understand that it is dangerous. He can eat the poison but can't distinguish the poison bottle from the water bottle. In a very real sense the child's physical development is ahead of his intellectual development. This is an example of how development is uneven.

The toddler moves at an unsteady gait across the room or yard. He often carries an object or two with him. If it is large, the object will be carried to his chest much as a football player carries the ball. He may fall down frequently, but bounces back with great confidence and continues the interrupted journey. He seldom hurts himself from the falls, having a low center of gravity and good padding from his diapers.

He shows beginnings of what psychologist Erik Erikson calls *autonomy* as he indicates his self-awareness and desire to do things on his own. He may seem big and independent one minute and afraid and dependent the next. The toddler, like most other children, enjoys looking at himself in the mirror, though without understanding that the other baby is himself.

Toddlers can often climb up stairs that they can't get down, or up on chairs from which they may fall. Therefore, they need watching, for falls from such distances can be dangerous.

The toddler begins to talk, too, along with all the other things he is learning. He can respond early to "Give Mommie the bottle," or the sock, or the spoon, but he will not be able to say a sentence for a while. Names of objects close to the baby and of people close to him are his first words. He adds verbs or action words in combination with the nouns such as "Go bye-bye," "Drink milk," or "Kiss Daddy."

He is beginning to say "No," which is a *negativism stage* that continues for the next year or so. You can expect him to say "No" earlier and oftener than he says "Yes." He may run away, kick, or just pull back. The more issue his behavior causes the more it continues. Thus good advice for parents and caregivers is to set the stage for desired behavior and make as little issue as possible over negative behavior.

Toddlers are learning many new things that keep their minds busy. These are related to language development and will be emphasized in later chapters.

Toddlers may seem like little satellites when you watch them at play. They move in their own orbits and may collide with other satellites momentarily, then move back to doing their own thing. They exhibit what has been called *solitary play*. Toward the end of the toddler period they engage in *parallel play*. That is, two children enjoy playing alongside each other but have little interaction save perhaps a smile exchanged. They each use whatever toys they have and make no plans for integrating their play

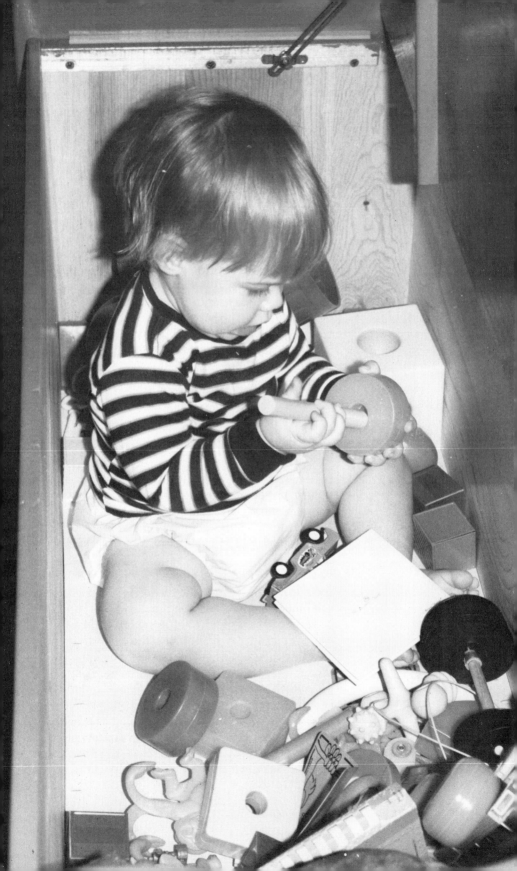

as they will when they are older. Even though a child at this stage is excited by the anticipation of "Let's go see Bobby" and seems to understand the possibility of a social outing, when the children get together he only plays along side (not *with*) the other child.

Toilet training is in its beginning during the second year. The child has much to get under control before he will really be toilet trained. According to studies of toilet training, once the child's muscles and understanding are mature enough the training will be accomplished quite easily. Many parents can testify to having rushed their first baby but allowed the later ones to "train themselves" and feel that the latter is the best in the long run.

In some babies there is a noticeable regularity of bowel movement—after breakfast, after lunch, after the morning nap, and so on. Once the baby can sit up comfortably, he may be placed on the toilet seat. If the schedule is indeed regular, the child may defecate in the toilet. The mother may feel that baby is "trained," but in reality it is she who is trained. "Training" implies conscious response to the signals, and that will be a long time yet. With care it can be partially accomplished by the end of the second year. The toilet seat should not become a punishing seat, or problems of far greater severity than washing a few extra diapers will be the result.

Bladder control comes much later than bowel training. Urination occurs more frequently, of course. It is wise to wait until close to the second birthday before real efforts are made in bladder training. When the toddler stays dry for longer periods, this is an indication that he is ready for training. At this point, his language is better developed, his motor skills or muscles are under better control, and he is interested in being independent. Also, learning generally proceeds more quickly than if started earlier. Summer is a good time for training because there are fewer clothes to get off and on and to get wet if accidents occur.

It should be noted that girls are usually trained earlier than boys. This is just one of a number of indications that girls mature earlier than boys, a fact that should be kept in mind when children of like

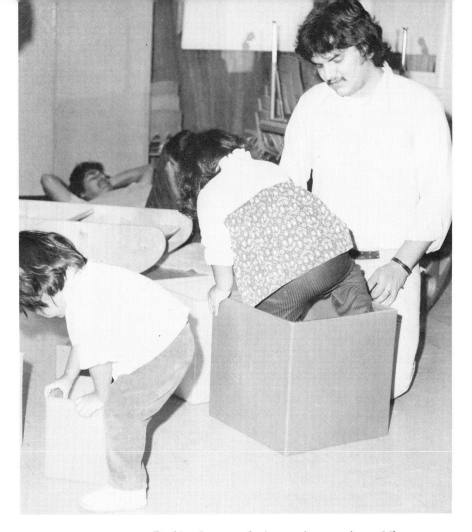

*Packing boxes make interesting toys for toddlers—
they'll climb in and out over and over. (University of
Houston, Rebecca Hines, Photographer.)*

ages are cared for in groups and thus might easily
be compared. It should be realized that there are
individual differences creating a range of weeks or
months when a child may mature. Daytime control
is earlier than nighttime control for both sexes.

In the early part of training little boys may sit on
the toilet to urinate just as girls do. Once they observe other boys they may prefer to stand. Standing
may help somewhat when they have an erection,
which is frequent when they are ready to urinate.
They will often have some difficulty in their ability

to hit the toilet, given the erection, the urgency accompanying the need, their inexperience with handling clothing, and so on. Therefore, caregivers are cautioned to be gentle when making demands for standards.

The less fuss that can be made over toilet training the better. If training is attempted and negative behavior results, then it is far better to drop the training plan for a while than to arouse the resistance of the child. Punishment should never become associated with toilet training.

The mother of a toddler being cared for in a group should be in on the training plan so that she and the caregivers are not working at cross purposes. From the use of a common phrase for the signal of need to the use of the same reward phrase, the cooperation of the two is important.

The toddler's eating procedure is becoming the self-help variety. Finger foods are especially useful; a child will readily consume bits of meat, fruit, vegetable, and toast if he is allowed to feed himself with fingers or fork. He also begins using his own cup clutched in both hands. Adults should remember to put a small amount in the cup if they want to avoid numerous mop ups.

TWOS AND THREES

Twos and threes usually have a slow, quiet pace in a nursery school. They still tend to be egocentric or self-centered, doing their own thing with little regard for interacting on any consistent basis with other children. They like the presence of others, may even shout at each other as they scale the slide and go down, but intricate cooperative play will come in the fourth and fifth years. Admonitions to "share" fall on deaf ears.

Twos and threes like climbing and sliding. They enjoy swinging but are still not coordinated enough to pump a traditional swing. They may have learned to ride a tricycle and may stick to that activity for quite a long period of time. They enjoy sand play, but may not realize when their sifting is blowing sand on a nearby friend or their spoon is heaping sand on another's foot. They like a little help in new ventures—a finger held as they climb a plank, an

Young preschoolers play side by side observing others as they do their "own thing." (Howard University, Flemmie Kittrell Project, Fred Harris, Photographer.)

adult nearby as they climb the slide or jungle gym the first time in the morning.

They use large strokes when they paint at the easel or draw with a crayon. The design comes out a scribble, random at first, then later somewhat organized with clear up-down or circular strokes. Scissors are hard to operate even for the threes. They like puzzles with four to six pieces and may choose the same puzzle for days at a time.

By three the child has a clearer understanding of language and follows directions more accurately. He enjoys practicing what he can say and may ask lots of questions—even when he knows the answers. If you will only turn the question back to him, he'll happily fill you in on the storehouse of information he has collected. For example, he may point out a cow, saying, "What's that?" If the adult says, "What *is* that?" the child may say, "It's a moo-cow." Perhaps his questions are merely a plea for conversation or reflect how adults talk to him.

Growth in physical size tapers off during the third year, with accompanying decrease in food intake. A small appetite often worries parents and teachers when they remember how "good" the child ate as an infant and toddler. They should remember that with slower growth his food needs are less and therefore avoid nudging him to eat more. He also has a growing need to decide things for himself, and he may focus on his food intake to make his autonomy felt. He feeds himself, but his slowness may make adults impatient. Dawdling also may show his lack of interest in food at this time.

Toilet training may stabilize around the late two- and early three-year period. There will likely be "accidents," but they will be less frequent now and he will know what it's all about. A matter-of-fact attitude is appropriate for accident times. A child may wet during his nap or at night, because control while sleeping comes after daytime control. A child who awakens dry should be taken to the bathroom immediately.

Twos and threes usually still need their afternoon naps, especially when they are fatigued from playing with other children in the neighborhood, nursery school, or day care center. Getting them to relax and sleep will demand skill and patience of the adults, but it is worth the effort, for the children wake refreshed, happy, and ready for new activities. Without naps they turn grouchy and difficult to cope with in the late afternoon and may fall asleep before they have had supper.

Twos and threes gain security from having the same people do things in the same way day after day. In nursery school groups a lot of time is spent in the routines of dressing, toileting, eating, and sleeping. The pace must be slow to meet their tempo and allow them to learn to help themselves with the routines. It is a period of growth and development, and the twos and threes are very charming as they learn.

FOURS AND FIVES

By age four children can cooperate on a mural or listen to an explanation from the teacher. (University of Idaho Laboratory School, Ed Breidenbach, Photographer.)

Fours are vastly different from threes. They are faster, more vocal, more independent, and more outgoing. They now crave the company of their peers. They have begun cooperative play, and though it may take a while to get organized the play can be intricate if allowed to continue for a time. Fours and fives need many new fresh ideas to work with each day. They are ready for field trips that stimulate their thinking or that serve to tie together some project for them. They enjoy larger groups and aren't as easily disturbed by continuous new faces, such as students or volunteers, as are the younger children. Fours and fives typically come to school with plans of what or with whom they are going to

Tools are handled by four-year-olds with guidance from adults to insure safety. (Michigan State University Laboratory Preschool, Connie Lisiecki, Photographer.)

play. If disappointed, they can express their displeasure loudly or through aggression.

Physically they are, of course, bigger. Their motor skills are more highly developed. They drive their tricycles fast and dangerously at times. The fives will graduate to two-wheeled bikes at home and tell their friends, gaining new status in their eyes. (Then the fours will hide the fact that they still have the learner wheels attached to their bikes at home!)

Cooperative play is the rule, with intricate role assignments taking place in the housekeeping corner, block corner, or play yard. With mature children, however, we see a type of individual activity that is different from the form noted during the toddler stage. At five they get very interested in a painting or project and may continue with it long after their friends have gone. This long interest span should be encouraged, as should the extension of projects that indicate a child's creativity. Often these children are secure in their social relations, feeling that they can enter the ongoing play anytime they feel like it.

Fours and fives are independent dressers if they

Four-year-olds like play-dough with tools "just like mother's." (Michigan State University Laboratory Preschool, Connie Lisiecki, Photographer.)

are given boots and zippers they can manage. They handle bathroom routines with skill and rarely have an accident if they are allowed to go to the bathroom whenever they need to. They eat well if served foods they like and a minimum of between-meal snacks. They are not fond of napping, and compromises are needed to avoid impasse over this requirement in some homes and centers. They are cooperative in clean-up routines if approached in a cooperative manner.

Especially when fours and fives have been in nursery school for several years, serious efforts will be required to plan a rich and varied curriculum. If a good program is lacking, these children will literally run the place in a chaotic manner. They may know the ropes better than a series of new or inexperienced teachers. Fours and fives are a decided challenge. However, many successes and satisfactions await the teacher who puts effort into a rich program of learning experiences for them.

ACCELERATED DEVELOPMENT?

Are fast growth and development necessarily desirable? "My five-year-old is already reading at the third grade level," proudly exclaimed a mother to the kindergarten teacher. Such comments are often coupled with a wish or even a demand that the preschool teacher contribute to this acceleration. However, teachers should keep in mind that scientific research gives no basis for concluding that faster than normal growth is necessarily desirable or that future success is thereby assured. The reverse could be true. In fact, the child just described and many similar children may not be helped in attaining any higher adult achievement level, but may even be injured by excessive pressure to exceed more normal developmental rates. Developmental stages and sequences are more important than chronological age. Later development and achievement must be built on a firm base of early development and practice. Consequently, a wise preschool teacher does not endeavor to pressure a four-year-old child to respond like a five, or fives to respond like sixes, and so on. Neither teachers nor parents should fall into a trap of pushing accelerated learning for which there is no adequate scientific support.

Young children, do, of course, differ in their readiness to learn certain skills. When interpreting a well-planned preschool program to parents, it is important to stress that learning, growth, and development are taking place in all domains—physical-motor, mental, social, and emotional. A reasonable balance must be achieved to develop the happy, fully functioning child for which we strive.

CONCLUSION

Besides knowing some general characteristics of infants, toddlers, and preschoolers as those presented above, the teacher must get to know children as individuals. In only a few days you can notice the individuality of each child. Each has his own personality, his way of doing things and behaving. These are challenges for caregivers to interpret.

Conferences with the parents, visits in the home, and participation of the parents in the program of the center are ways to get to know the child and his individual needs further. A total respect for what parents can tell and show teachers and caregivers is important. Respect is shown by sharing information, asking for advice, understanding differing points of view, responding to feelings and needs, avoiding blaming parents for things children do, and reporting happy and rewarding moments of a child's day.

Further points will be made regarding age differences and behavior throughout the various chapters. In addition, the interested reader is advised to pursue more in-depth reading of child development information in books listed in the bibliographies at the end of the chapters.

APPLICATIONS

1. Observe two young children. If possible, select two children who are several years apart in age. Compare the two on several developmental tasks such as eating, walking, running, talking, drawing, and type of play. Make a chart showing what you observe. Write a paragraph about what

conclusions you can draw about the differences you observe. Explain how they fit or don't fit the descriptions in the text.

2. Talk to parents of two children. Ask what their concerns are about the child at this time. Write a description of each interview and compare the two. What are the similarities? What are the differences? How can you account for the differences and similarities between the two sets of parents?

3. Talk to a teacher of young children. Find out what her views are regarding single age grouping and multiple age grouping. Write a paragraph about your interview.

4. Write a description of your case-study child and compare it to the appropriate description in your text.

SUGGESTED FILMS

Infancy: Development of the Child Series   Color   20 minutes
Covers human psychological development from birth through adolescence. Dr. Jerome Kagan presents two levels of developmental capacity of the young child. CRM Film Productions, 9263 Third Street, Beverly Hills, California 90210.

A Child Is   Black and white   22 minutes
Story of four Head Start children—so alike and so different. An intimate look at these children and the homes that influence them. Modern Talking Pictures, 1212 Avenue of the Americas, New York, N.Y. 10036. Free from any Head Start office.

FOR FURTHER READING

BAKER, KATHERINE READ, and XENIA F. FANE. *Understanding and Guiding Your Children*. Englewood Cliffs, N.J.: Prentice-Hall, Inc., 1967.

BRECKENRIDGE, MARIAN E., and MARGARET NESBITT MURPHY. *Growth and Development of the Young Child*. Philadelphia: W. B. Saunders Company, 1963.

DENENBERG, VICTOR H. (Ed.). *Education of the Infant and Young Child*. New York: Academic Press, Inc., 1970.

ELARDO, PHYLLIS T., and BETTYE M. CALDWELL. "The Kramer Adventure: A School for the Future?" *Childhood Education*, Vol. 50, No. 3 (Jan. 1974), 143–152.

HAMMERMAN, ANN, and SUSAN MORSE. "Open Teaching: Piaget in the Classroom." *Young Children*, Vol. 28, No. 1 (Nov. 1972), 41–54.

HILDEBRAND, VERNA. *Introduction to Early Childhood Education*. New York: Macmillan Publishing Co., Inc., 1971.

KEISTER, MARY ELIZABETH. *The "Good Life" for Infants and Toddlers.* Washington, D.C.: National Association for the Education of Young Children, 1970.

LANDRETH, CATHERINE. *Early Childhood: Behavior and Learning.* New York: Alfred A. Knopf, Inc., 1967.

MURPHY, LOIS BARCLAY. "The Stranglehold of Norms on the Individual Child." *Childhood Education,* Vol. 49, No. 7 (Apr. 1973), 343–349.

SMART, MOLLIE S., and RUSSELL C. SMART. *Children: Development and Relationships.* New York: Macmillan Publishing Co., Inc., 1972.

SPOCK, BENJAMIN C. *Baby and Child Care.* New York: Pocket Books, Simon & Schuster, Inc., 1968.

STONE, L. JOSEPH, and JOSEPH CHURCH. *Childhood & Adolescence.* New York: Random House, Inc., 1973.

TODD, VIVIAN E., and HELEN HEFFERNAN. *The Years Before School.* New York: Macmillan Publishing Co., Inc., 1970.

Guiding Children Indirectly Toward Self-direction

Kimmie came into the playroom and selected a puzzle from the puzzle rack. She put it on the table nearby and began to take it apart.

KIMMIE'S TEACHER deliberately stored the puzzles near the table, making it convenient and natural for the children to get out puzzles for use on the table. The arrangement gave them an inviting space to work with minimum interference. The puzzle pieces could be accounted for easily. Kimmie's behavior was being guided indirectly by her teacher. Guidance techniques of this kind have great merit and are widely used in professionally run centers.

Guidance is defined as all the adult does or says either directly or indirectly to influence the behavior of the child. Guidance is a consciously determined act based on carefully considered values and goals. The goal of all guidance is to help the child to become a happy, fully functioning individual who can make decisions and direct himself. The two types of guidance, indirect and direct, will be examined.

The word *discipline* could be used in place of *guidance*. However, in its common usage the word discipline often carries a narrow connotation of punishment that limits its use in a constructive discussion of helping children grow in independence and self-control.

INDIRECT GUIDANCE

Indirect guidance influences a child's behavior through management of the space, the equipment and materials, and the people in his environment. Indirect guidance does not deal with the child

57

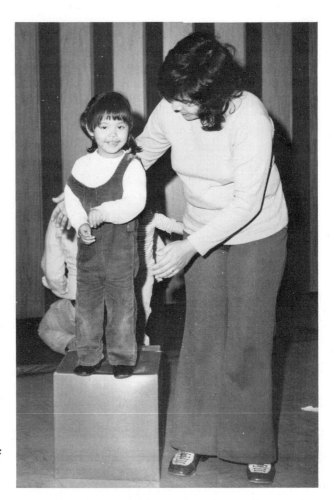

Availability and arrangement of equipment suggest action to children. (University of Houston, Rebecca Hines, Photographer.)

directly or specifically. It is the behind-the-scenes work and planning that pays off in big dividends in helping children become self-directed.

Although indirect guidance is one of the easiest methods of guidance to use, and probably as successful as many direct methods, it is often overlooked. Indirect guidance is promising because it deals with those elements over which the teacher has major control. Factors outside the child may be affecting the child, being largely responsible for the desirable behavior that the teacher or parent hopes will continue or the undesirable behavior that she hopes to eliminate. When searching for a solution to a child's behavior problem, indirect guidance is

Marching around the table helps the band members keep from bumping into each other. (Nazarene Day Care Center, Lansing, Michigan, Gerald Seelhoff, Photographer.)

the first place to turn. What are some of these indirect guidance techniques?

Balance the number of children and the age and sex composition of the group with the number and experience of the teaching staff. These factors are significant in the management of a group and in giving attention to individual needs of children. Schools have various admission policies. Some take all children who apply or are old enough. Others carefully select equal numbers of boys and girls with birthdays from each quarter of the year. The open school concept of mixed ages is popular in some schools. Whatever the policy, it will make a difference in guidance strategies.

The advisable ratio of children to adults depends on children's ages. The Office of Child Development in the Department of Health, Education, and Welfare in *Guides for Day Care Licensing* recommends minimum staff requirements for facilities serving 13 or more children as follows:

Children of age: 0 to 2 Staff: 1 adult to 4 children
2 to 3   1 adult to 5 children
3 to 5   1 adult to 10 children

Thus with 13 children age 0 to 2 the total adult staff present would need to be four, 13 twos to threes would require three adult caregivers, and 13 threes to fives would require two adult caregivers.

Large numbers of children in a single group prove excessively stimulating and fatiguing to each other. The younger a child the smaller the number of children that he should be required to interact with each day. For infants and toddlers the groups should be no larger than six. Three- and four-year-olds' groups should be kept under twenty to encourage friendships among children. Warehousing children in large masses without adequate adult loving care is a practice to be avoided.

Person-centered teaching can occur when the teachers deal with a few children and their families on a long-term basis. Mutual trust develops among teachers, parents, and children when the groups are kept small. Keeping children and teacher together as children mature, rather than promoting the children to a new group and teacher, helps avoid the problems accompanying adjustment to a new group. Teachers will also work harder to find solutions to problems when they know they will not be able to promote them to some other teacher.

The right toy for a toddler is one she can grasp with a hand and explore in her mouth. (What's New in Home Economics, *Donna Creasy, Photographer.*)

If part or all of the teaching staff is inexperienced, then fewer children should be assigned until experience has been gained. Directors and other experienced staff can also be helpful to inexperienced staff members. Planning of all kinds must be done in more detail when staff members are inexperienced, because they have fewer alternatives for coping tucked away in their memories.

To accommodate parents, children are often admitted on a part-time basis. These children often feel that they have missed something when enrolled with many all-day children. Where their numbers are sufficient, the school should assign them all to one group and assign a sensitive teacher who makes special short-range instead of extended week-long plans. If a child has an opportunity to wrap up a project on his day in the center, he'll feel good about coming back. If he feels that he's had to leave it midstream, he will be unsatisfied.

Some limits may logically be placed on part-time

participation, for example, only mornings, only afternoons, or only a Monday, Wednesday, and Friday sequence. Drop-in-after-school children should likewise be separate from the ongoing groups and should have special plans made especially for them. To get children to participate fully in a regular program, some directors provide a fee-incentive; for example, five days cost parents only a little more than four days. Thus children, parents, and school may all gain needed benefits.

Questions often arise regarding admission of children with special needs. Unless the staff size and expertise are adequate, it is unfair to both the child and the staff to admit such children. Special children often need very complex programs and the support of highly trained technical consultants. This consultation is now becoming more readily available with recent legislation designed to assist handicapped individuals. Parents and teachers are urged to seek the necessary assistance for handicapped children they know. Some states provide the service beginning at the child's birth.

Plan a schedule or sequence of events to suit the pace of the children. A scheduled sequence of events that is followed regularly with only minor changes gives children considerable security and knowledge of what to expect. Knowing what follows will give children clues as to how to behave.

Schedules are typically made up of blocks of time, a block of forty-five minutes to an hour for self-selected activities, thirty minutes for clean-up, snacks, and quiet time, and so on. The lengths of these time blocks can be longer or shorter to meet the children's needs.

Special consideration for the schedules the children's families maintain will be a determining factor. Children will be arriving in a nursery school or child care center at various hours. You may admit certain children within a few minutes of their waking-up time. Others may be hungry, having breakfasted early. Some are not brought to the center until midmorning. Others will be tired, having been up late at night. Some accommodation in the schedule and routine should be possible to allow for

A regular routine includes washing of hands, which preschoolers learn to manage capably. (University of Houston, Rebecca Hines, Photographer.)

individual needs of children. It is very likely that a child who is half awake, tired, or hungry will have little interest in normal play activities until his personal needs are met. If pressed to participate, he may be difficult to manage.

Playing out of doors meets the needs of many children early in the day. Teachers should consider allowing those who especially need vigorous activity to be supervised outdoors upon arrival. When this schedule is used, the parents can be requested to dress the child for outdoor play and can readily determine his clothing needs themselves, whereas if they expect the teacher to dress the child later they may "forget" essentials.

Arrange the space so there are clues as to appropriate behavior for that space. As he looks around the yard and rooms, the child should be able to tell whether a space is for noisy play, for solitary or group play, for active or passive play. Depending on how he's feeling at the moment, he may choose a certain part of the facility. Clues may be derived from the materials the child sees, pictures that are displayed, or the customary uses made of certain areas. Teachers may tell children, "You may drive the truck in the block room, we keep the trucks out of the art room because their noise bothers us." Because habits take time to develop, there is good reason to keep the arrangements stable for a while in order that children will learn what does take place in certain areas and, therefore, learn the appropriate behavior for that space. When multiple uses are made of space, such as when naps are taken in the playroom, lowered lights and dividers placed in front of the play materials will give children the clue that it is naptime instead of playtime.

Plan a rich and varied curriculum appropriate to the ages and experience of the children. If learning experiences are either too easy or too difficult, children may misbehave. However, boredom is one of the greatest causes of misbehavior. Children who have attended the same center for several years will require special plans because they will know the place inside out. Boredom can be the reason for a previously cooperative child turning mischievous. Also, if children attend kindergarten a part of the day, the center's efforts will need to go into planning activities that are different from those in kindergarten. Five-year-olds who are nearing six are ready for many curricular challenges and really warrant a special teacher who makes plans for them.

Arrange activities in an interesting way that invites participation. Having materials out and ready to go will stimulate children to become involved with little direct contact from adults. A child will sense the freedom he is allowed and will go to activities that attract him or to activities where friends he is comfortable with are playing. A child will know what to do with a waiting easel with paper and paints ready to go. Seating the dolls expectantly in the highchairs will entice children into the housekeeping area to continue the theme or alter it as they see fit. Having a costume garment displayed nearby may invite them to dress up. An open book in the library corner or a record placed on the open record player will invite their use. Order is part of this type of guidance, suggesting a planned, orderly use of the material. If equipment is displayed in a helter-skelter manner, it should be no surprise that children respond with like behavior.

Arrange materials and equipment so children can use them safely and with minimum help. Children like to feel "big" and independent. One often hears them say, "I did it myself." An inclined plane placed under the swing set allows a child who is learning to pump to manage his own starts. Preparing finger foods for snacks and meals, thereby making it easy for the child to feed himself, sets the stage for self-direction. Having a single-speed record player that fits the records supplied adds to the child's independence because he can operate it without adult help. Having toy shelves and the lockers for children's clothing at children's heights makes self-help easier. Arranging outdoor equipment away from fences discourages climbing on fences.

Store out of sight the materials you'd rather children did not use; materials considered dangerous MUST BE stored outside of children's rooms. Your extra supply of paper and paste fall in the first category. Each day you place at the children's level amounts you expect them to need. Then, if the extra supply is stored up out of their sight and reach, you can keep those supplies in a good, orderly condition and parcel out extra materials as needed. However, materials do need to be close by in case your early estimate is in error. Having to leave the room for supplies is a sure way to interfere with your management of a group.

Any dangerous materials such as cleaners should be kept completely inaccessible to children in another room or locked closet.

Arrange storage for toys and supplies near the area of expected use and near a surface appropriate for their use. For example, when the puzzle rack is on a shelf near a table, the habit of using the puzzles at that table will easily develop. The problem of lost pieces will be avoided more readily than if puzzles are carried to various parts of the room. If a table, comfortable chair, or pillow is near the library shelf, the children will easily make a habit of using the books in a place where they can concentrate and where they will be able to handle the books with care. Block storage that is in a carpeted area protected from cross traffic, near the storage for small animals, figures, or vehicles, will help block play go forward in a constructive way.

Attention to surfaces is worthy of note. Paints, water, juice, and food are more readily cleaned from hard surfaces, so arrangement of activities with such material on hard surfaces helps avoid overcautioning children. Children and even adults may spill liquids quite unintentionally, and there are far fewer admonitions and accompanying guilt feelings if the material can be hurriedly mopped up. Though carpets are advertised as "washable" and "moppable," repeated spilling leaves odors that become unpleasant after a while.

Heavy blocks, trucks, and carpentry that may mar woodwork or furnishings should be stored near where they can be used without overcautioning children about care of property. Carpeting is useful for these areas because it can reduce the noise level. Carpentry can be used outdoors to a good advantage because that takes out the noise, too!

Equip the room and yard with sufficient play spaces for the number of children in the group. It is a simple matter to count the number of possible play spaces to see how many your room or yard can afford. For example, given two tricycles, two swings, and a teeter totter, you have six spaces. Indoors you might have two at the easel, four in the housekeeping corner, and four at the puzzle table, making ten play spaces. There should be about fifty per cent more spaces than children in order to provide freedom of choice and suitable alternatives if one activity isn't working out for some reason. For sixteen children, then, there should be a minimum of twenty-four play spaces. Sufficient well-operating equipment that provides adequate play spaces will help keep harmony among the children.

Arrange learning centers so that the number of seats available suggests the number of children appropriate at a given time. The best teaching can usually take place with four or five children involved in an activity, so when setting up the space the teacher should place only four or five chairs around the table. Children will generally take the hint and pass by an activity when there is not an empty chair. If not, they can be asked to return when a seat is available. It does not help children to try to squeeze in more in a given learning center than your working space will accommodate comfortably and the teaching staff can help adequately. For example, a harried teacher trying to keep up with eight or ten fingerpainters surely cannot give the desired assistance or reinforcement that is characteristic of effective teaching. More satisfaction comes from keeping the number manageable and repeating the popular activity on ensuing days.

Observe children when others can be responsible for them in order to gain basic information about each child's behavior and needs. This enables you to collect objective data relative.to a child's behavior. When involved with such observations, you may miss significant points if you must also divert attention to other children. From such baseline data provided by observations, you can help develop firmer strategies for guiding the child.

Confer with parents to develop a fuller understanding of the child's total experience and to gain assistance in deciding on guidance strategies. Parents and teachers both need to know what the other is doing with the child. By learning from parents more than can be observed at school, and by sharing information with parents, you can often substantially help with a child's behavior.

CONCLUSION

These twelve techniques of indirect guidance just discussed will be listed again for your convenience. They are to be carried out, for the most part, when the children are not at school. Time must be set aside when teachers are not responsible for children to enable the staff to do the *thinking* and *doing* that these techniques require. It is simply not enough to plan on the run, as is the custom in some centers, or to squeeze planning into children's naptimes. There must be planning time, conference time, arranging-the-room time, evaluation time, and seeing-parents time. All child care teachers need a chance for feedback from their peers, for sharing ideas and insights, for charting the new directions, and simply for knowing each other as people with concerns other than the job. Children generally suffer when planning time is catch-as-catch-can.

Without planning and evaluation, guidance becomes a haphazard act rather than a consciously determined act based on carefully considered values and goals as is proposed here. Time and thought given to indirect guidance will help insure the success of the direct guidance techniques to which we now turn in Chapter 5.

TWELVE TECHNIQUES OF INDIRECT GUIDANCE

1. Balance the number of children and the age and sex composition of the group with the number and experience of the teaching staff.

2. Plan a schedule or sequence of events to suit the pace of the children.

3. Arrange the space so there are clues as to appropriate behavior for that space.

4. Plan a rich and varied curriculum appropriate to the ages and experience of the children.

5. Arrange activities in an interesting way that invites participation.

6. Arrange materials and equipment so children can use them safely and with minimum help.

7. Store out of sight the materials you'd rather children did not use; materials considered dangerous MUST BE stored outside of children's rooms.

8. Arrange storage for toys and supplies near the area of expected use and near a surface appropriate for their use.

9. Equip the room and yard with sufficient play spaces for the number of children in the group.

10. Arrange learning centers so that the number of seats available suggests the number of children appropriate at a given time.

11. Observe children when others can be responsible for them in order to gain basic information about each child's behavior and needs.

12. Confer with parents to develop a fuller understanding of the child's total experience and to gain assistance in deciding on guidance strategies.

APPLICATIONS

1. Observe a preschool child in a home or school setting. Explain how the arrangement of equipment or supplies makes it hard or easy for the child to behave appropriately.
2. Observe a preschool child in a home or school setting. In what ways can you discover whether the child is aware of the schedule or sequence of events? Explain.
3. Observe a preschool child in a home or school setting. Find out what materials are kept strictly out of the child's reach. Explain.
4. Practice using indirect guidance. Report to your class what happened.
5. Observe the mother or the teacher guiding your case-study child. What indirect guidance seems to be effective?

SUGGESTED FILMS

Setting the Stage for Learning   Black and white   22 minutes
Affirms the importance of play as a valuable and indispensable resource for learning during the early years. Churchill Films, 662 North Robertson Boulevard, Los Angeles, California 90069.

Organized Free Play   Black and white   22 minutes
Depicts the elements of a Head Start center, the equipment, program, and teaching techniques. Zoned areas of activity for group and individual activity are illustrated. Modern Talking Pictures, 1212 Avenue of the Americas, New York, N.Y. 10036. Free from any Head Start office.

69 *Conclusion*

FOR FURTHER READING

HILDEBRAND, VERNA. *Introduction to Early Childhood Education.* New York: Macmillan Publishing Co., Inc., 1971.

LANDRETH, CATHERINE. *Preschool Learning and Teaching.* New York: Harper & Row, Publishers, 1972.

MARSHALL, HERMINE H. "Criteria for an Open Classroom." *Young Children,* Vol. 28, No. 1 (Oct. 1972), 13–19.

RAMBUSCH, N. *"Learning How to Learn: An American Approach to Montessori.* Baltimore: Helicon Press, Inc., 1962.

TODD, VIVIAN E., and HELEN HEFFERNAN. *The Years Before School.* New York: Macmillan Publishing Co., Inc., 1970.

Guiding Children Directly Toward Self-direction

Cindy is trying to roll out her cookie dough and is rolling it to pieces. The teacher says, "Let's roll it soft and slow, like this," as she places her hand on Cindy's hands and demonstrates. "Good," she says with a smile as Cindy begins to respond to the guidance.

CINDY'S TEACHER was using techniques of *direct guidance* as she helped Cindy with the cookie making.

DIRECT GUIDANCE

Direct guidance is used to influence a child's behavior through dealing with the child specifically, as contrasted with indirect guidance, which deals with the environment, as discussed earlier. The goal of the adult's involvement is to help the child to become a happy, fully functioning individual who can make decisions and direct himself. For discussion purposes, direct guidance is here divided into *physical, verbal,* and *affective guidance.* The example at the beginning of this chapter demonstrates all three forms. Direct guidance encompasses all of the interpersonal interactional communication processes. Through direct guidance the adults' human energy resources are transmitted to children to help them develop skills, knowledge, and self-direction.

PHYSICAL GUIDANCE

Physical guidance includes all the techniques where we use physical contact or physical proximity to influence the child's behavior. Some of these techniques are helping, demonstrating, leading,

71

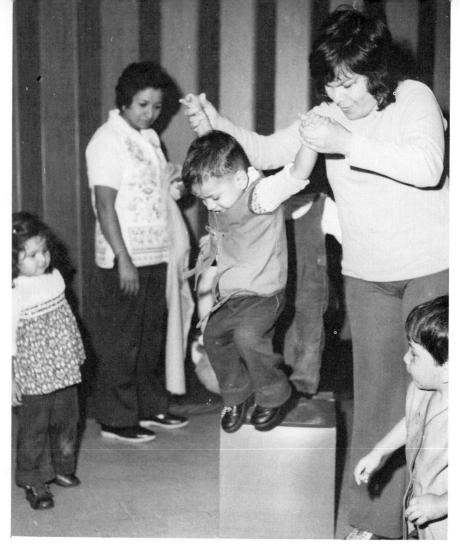

A helping hand encourages learning a new skill while friends look on admiringly.
(*University of Houston, Rebecca Hines, Photographer.*)

restraining, removing, and punishing. The physical proximity of an interested adult is significant in children's following rules and in their sustained interest in some learning activities. Left to do some activities alone, a child will leave. If an adult is present, then the child is more likely to stay.

Children's needs vary as to the amount and type of physical guidance that is appropriate. Helping in the two-year-old group means giving a hand as a

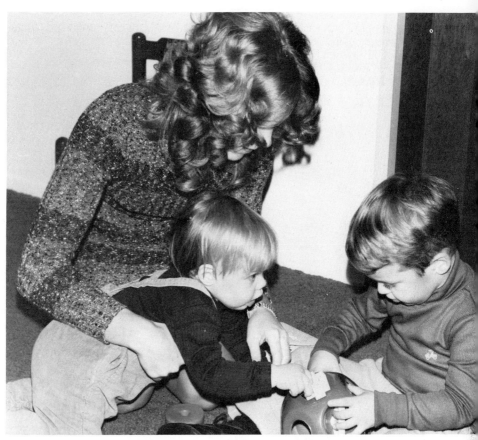

A toddler is curious about the toy the three-year-old is using. The older child will show him how the toy works —another example of resource exchange. (Frances Kertesz, Photographer.)

child takes his first voyage up an inclined plane, or climbs the slide, or takes to the swing. As a four- or five-year-old the same child would feel belittled if the teacher even offered her hand, more so if she insisted. Children will gradually grow in independence and less in need of help in most of the activities of the nursery school. The challenge to teachers is to know what kind and how much help is needed for each child and to step out of the picture as the child shows he can do things alone. Research indicates a wide variation in independent behavior among children who are even the same age. Also, individuals may backslide even when they've been doing something independently for some time.

Demonstrating or modeling for the child encourages him to imitate the desired behavior. "See, you

An adult is often needed to simplify a game for preschoolers. (Southern University, Baton Rouge, Louisiana, Eddie Hildreth, Photographer.)

do it this way" and "Now you try it" are comments the teacher often makes as she demonstrates. Perhaps she is showing the children how to flush the toilet, how to use a spoon, how to latch the gate, or how to step on the scales. Time and time again, if she does it first then they will quickly follow. They understand actions better than words, though we don't omit words and stay quiet just because this is true.

Children watch other children and imitate them. They learn through this imitation. Watch them at the art table, in the music room, at the lunch table. They may first imitate, then do it their own way. Adults do the same thing when they find themselves in a new situation—we watch others for clues as to the appropriate behavior.

Leading is a technique that gets children going in the desired direction. Perhaps you realize from various clues that a two- or three-year-old child needs to go to the bathroom. Take his hand and lead him over the most direct route. (Of course, go slowly enough that you don't scare him, but you usually don't have long to ponder!) If a group is going on a field trip, the child in front especially needs someone to take his hand and move toward the goal, to stop at the appropriate corners, streets, or things to see. Children gain comfort and security from holding the hand of a teacher or helper. Wanting to hold hands can be a sign of "I'm feeling lonely," or tired, or scared. Not wanting to hold hands can mean "I feel big enough to go alone."

A child should be restrained where necessary to protect him or others. Restraining, removing, and punishing are three types of physical guidance. If other aspects of a good program fall into place, then these negative types of guidance should seldom, if ever, be necessary. Restraint may be a simple act of putting your hand on a child's arm to slow him down on a stairs or actually keep him from hitting or kicking you or others. It has a legitimate place when the child is out of control and needs someone to help him. Other people, the learning environment, and the child himself must be protected. By taking him by the hands and sitting him down beside you for a quiet minute, the child who is out of control can be helped to regain his composure before he really acts out in a way that he may feel guilty about. Even play therapists do not knowingly allow a child to hurt them, so teachers should not feel that a child "needs" to hit them. Certainly he can be given objects to work off his need to hit such as boxing gloves, a Bobo clown, even hammer and nails (under supervision, obviously). If a child repeatedly requires restraint, then an analysis should be made of his behavior to plan more appropriate strategies in keeping with his needs.

Removing him from the group sometimes helps a child who is having trouble accommodating to group rules. The child may only need to be removed from the center of his trouble to a place where he can calm down and compose himself. The teacher can sit near him, providing a loving, nonpunishing attitude. A frequent cause of aggression is fatigue, so some effort to rest the child may be called for. At a later time you can take a look at the child's schedule to see if he is getting sufficient rest. A child might learn that being removed is more fun than staying with the group. A conscientious teacher will take a look at what she is expecting of the group if this seems to be the case.

Punishment that is meant to hurt or humiliate has no place in the education of the young child. It builds resentments, fears, antagonisms, and timidity instead of the healthy, happy child we hope to rear. In our work with children we must continually seek ways to guide children toward the learning of desirable behavior. In their studies, psychologists have found that punishment is not consistently successful in inhibiting aggressive behavior.

Getting down to eye level and using meaningful gestures helps children understand your guidance. Getting down to the child's level helps him know that directions are meant for him. Using gestures helps if he doesn't quite understand all your words. If you've ever been in a foreign country, you'll recall how much you depend on gestures and the context or immediate setting to give you clues to what's being said. It is well to get in the habit of sitting on a low chair or squatting or kneeling during much of the guidance you give. Remember how you must appear to tower over small children.

You can give children messages through body language. You can show interest, eagerness, or approval through activity of your body, just as you can show lethargy, reluctance, or disapproval. After being acquainted with you for only a short time, children will know when you are tense, irritable, relaxed, in a hurry, loving, and so on. Your stance, your face, how you hold your hands, and how you walk all tell others how things are going for you. This is one reason it is so important that teachers of young children get sufficient rest. If you're rested you'll find ways to cope, but if you're tired you'll get irritated and it will inevitably affect the children. Children of preschool age may indeed be better at reading your nonverbal clues given through body language than in understanding your verbal ones.

Physical proximity of an adult can influence the behavior of a child significantly. If the teacher is close to John and Jerry when they are having a big argument, they will know that she knows what has been said and done. If they are unable to solve the problem themselves, she'll know how to arbitrate fairly. Even though the rules are not stated, the boys will be reminded of them by her presence.

If a teacher moves into the vicinity of an argument, the children often calm down. Sometimes it is because just her presence has a calming effect on them, they do relax when she is there. Or they may be reminded of the rules that they had momentarily forgotten and begin putting them into effect. For example, two children are banging each other's tricycle, each trying to push past. The teacher walks near by. "Oops," says one, "I'm supposed to go this way." The teacher's presence reminds him of the direction traffic is supposed to flow on the one-way trike path.

VERBAL GUIDANCE

Verbal guidance is the use of words to influence the child's behavior. Through talking we expect to communicate with children. We want them to develop standards of taking care of themselves, standards of relating to teachers and children, standards of using learning materials. Many of these standards will be communicated verbally. We must remember that young children's language development is in a primitive state when we get them in nursery school, and, of course, when we admit infants to our centers we will be privileged to observe their language as it develops almost from the beginning. Children are just learning to talk and to understand when others talk. They may communicate quite effectively at home. It may come as considerable cultural shock to have to try to understand teachers who have different types of talk than their parents and siblings. Following are eleven guides that you will find helpful in guiding children through verbal means.

Speak directly to the child as you make eye contact with him. Be sure the child knows you are speaking to him, if you want him to follow your directions. It is never effective to call out directions across the yard or room. Unless you have the voice of a top sergeant, you won't be heard or heeded. Also, children tend to imitate the yelling.

Use short sentences about like the ones the child uses until you are sure he'll understand more complicated ones. Only the essential words are needed, such as, "Inside now," or "Clean-up time," or "Hold tight."

Use positive directions, telling the child what to do instead of what not to do. Using "don't" phrases leaves the child suspended and uncomfortable. Remember how you feel if you are driving along a freeway and one of your passengers says, "Don't drive so fast." You probably leave your foot on the accelerator while you look around for the reasons for the advice. Telling a child what to do helps him respond quickly, and usually that is what your "don't" commands are designed to do. For example, "Don't spill your milk" or "Don't step on Johnny" or "Don't urinate on the toilet" are often used to get quick results, that is, stop the behavior for whatever reason you feel it shouldn't go on. Next time such instances occur, try "Hold your milk straight, Janet," "Step over here," or "Raise the seat before you urinate, Jimmy."

The "don't" habit is difficult to break for many adults, but you will find that it is worth the effort, because "do" directions help the child become self-directed sooner. A calm, positive phrase helps the

Moments of physical closeness with the caregiver help solve many problems for young children. (William Mitcham, Michigan State University Staff Photographer.)

child correct his behavior and go on. Some adults say that they don't have time to think of the "right" way to phrase guidance, but in practice we usually have more time than we may think before anything really disastrous happens. In fact, taking time to give clear directions is important. Exactly what do you want to happen? Some guidance isn't clear even to an adult listener.

Place the action part of your guidance statement at the beginning of your statement. "Hold tight" is better than "You might fall out so be sure you are holding the swing tight." The child may lose interest before you get to the important part. In the earlier example, if you say "Raise the seat" to Jimmy just as he moves to the toilet to urinate, you may catch him before it's too late. If you give a long discussion he may have either urinated in his clothing or on the seat.

Give directions one at a time, if possible, and no more than two at a time. The younger the child the fewer the number of directions that should be given at a time. If you say "Scrape your boots and take them off, hang up your coat and put your mittens on the register to dry," you should anticipate that you'll be repeating at least the last part if not all of the guidance several times before it is done. The child may forget all of it by being bombarded with so much. Children process directions slowly and need the context to suggest next steps; therefore, give directions one at a time, or no more than two at a time.

Give children directions at the time and place you want the behavior to occur. Children don't keep things in mind for very long, so directions that are in context and of current interest are more likely to be heeded. For example, wait until you are outdoors before giving directions about safety on the playground.

Give only the directions the child really needs and avoid being overdirective and bossy. Having set the stage for behavior through indirect guidance techniques referred to earlier, use a little patience

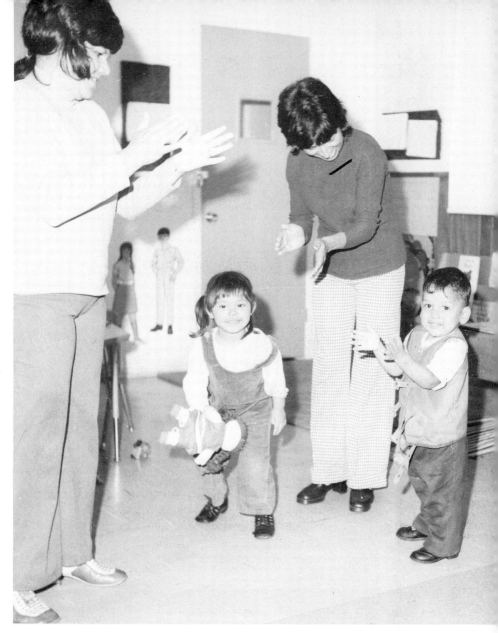

"Monkey see, monkey do, the monkey does the same as you." (University of Houston, Rebecca Hines, Photographer.)

and faith that children will behave acceptably without a steady barrage of "do this," "do that" directions. Stop talking and watch. See if they really need you to tell them what to do. You may be surprised at how self-directed they already are.

Make it clear whether the child has a choice or not. For example, some adults have a habit of saying,

81   *Verbal Guidance*

"Would you like to come in?" Now, this question should indicate to a child that if he prefers to stay outside the teacher will permit it. If she really expects the children to enter the classroom, then a more honest statement is "Come inside now." Watch such statements as "Would you like to take a nap?" or eat lunch, or go home. They usually are not meant as a choice for the child. "Would you like to paint or play with clay?" surely is a reasonable choice, and the child's decision would be acceptable to the teacher whichever way it went. Children should be given opportunities to make choices, but they should not be confused and disappointed by having choices offered and then refused after they make a choice. When you just want to offer suggestions, then have a take-it-or-leave-it approach, saying, "you could," "you might," "perhaps you would like."

Give logical and accurate reasons for requests. Children need to learn why requests are made of them. It is legitimate to say, "I want you to come to group time because I like to have everyone together" or "We will all go outdoors because there is no teacher to stay indoors with the children who want to stay in." In the long run we want children to be able to reason out new situations that have unique elements not in the situation we help them with. Arbitrary "I told you so" statements are not reasons. If you make requests or state rules that you cannot validly explain to a child, there is serious question about whether you are justified in making them.

Keep competition to a minimum by motivating the child through helping him set new personal goals for achievement. You can tell or show him a skill that is logically next in his learning. For example, if the child can make letters, you can say, "Before long you'll be writing your name." If he can make the swing go with help, you can say, "Before long you'll be pumping the swing all by yourself." It is not advisable to pit him against his friends to motivate him to do the tasks. Deciding to learn something for one's own reasons is growth. A steady increase in skills will help the child reach his fullest potential. We want him to be happy, not anxious. Competition breeds anxiety. It also thwarts friendships, because people with whom he is highly competitive are seldom a child's best buddies. The father who came to lunch and cajoled his son to "Eat more like Jimmy across the table" gave the teachers a clue to some of the boy's fears. They envisioned the family dinner table with the young preschooler being pressed to "eat like" the two older brothers. Perhaps here was one reason why he was such a finicky eater and was frequently constipated.

Competition will come soon enough, heaven knows, but let's allow our preschoolers a year or two when they can build their self-images without being challenged to climb higher, run faster, eat more, sing louder, dance faster, or read better than the other children.

Children know when they have succeeded. They are thrilled to zip their own zipper all the way the first time. They call "Teacher!" from the top of the jungle gym when they have conquered their Mount Everest. They take Daddy by the hand to show him how they can do a flip on the monkey bars. These successes are great because children have accomplished skills that yesterday or last month they didn't have. They don't work hard because they are competing with a peer. They work hard because it is fun to grow in some ability. To be able to share an accomplishment with someone who cares is important.

Praise children for jobs well done. Praise and approval should be sincere and given for merit—even if small. When you label some behavior as "a good job," the child learns what you like and he will try to repeat that behavior again. Likewise you should clearly disapprove of an act you do not want repeated so the child will realize the status of that act, too. Focus should be on the tasks rather than an approval or disapproval of the child per se. For example, when the child accomplishes taking off his boots and putting them in his locker, say, "You did a good job of taking off your boots and putting them away, Jonathan," rather than "You are a good boy for putting away your boots." Pleasing the teachers and learning and growing in confidence are the usual rewards in preschool. Some special children require special rewards to help them learn. Expert consultation is needed when teachers feel they have children who do not learn by the usual inherent rewards of a good preschool experience.

AFFECTIVE GUIDANCE

Affective guidance includes interactions between the child and the teacher that are especially related to emotions. The word *affective*, of course, has the same stem as *affection*. Affective guidance particularly helps develop the child's positive self-concept. Affective guidance is part of all the techniques that have been suggested, but because it is important it deserves separate discussion.

Affective guidance is a reflection of genuine feeling. We may give a quick and joyous hug to a child, or we may let a child cry on our shoulder when he is hurt. We can feel free to participate with children in laughter and joy, or we can console a sad or hurt child without making him feel embarrassed or small.

Giving positive feedback on other occasions than when a child follows directions helps keep teachers from just being "the boss." Sometimes when a child is "doing okay" a smile or a word helps him know you like him and approve of what he is doing.

Giving attention before the child demands it helps the child know you know he is there and that you are keeping his needs in mind. Some children who seem to be misbehaving to attract attention can be helped by well-timed doses of attention and positive feedback.

Reflecting the feeling the child is expressing and giving it a label help children understand their feelings. You might say, "You really feel good about climbing way up there, don't you?" or "I know how sad you feel, you really wanted that toy." The ability to reflect a child's true feelings comes with observation and practice in being sensitive. Empathy, the ability to feel as others feel, is important. It requires understanding, takes practice, and is essential for needed sensitive relationships at home, school, community, national, and international levels.

Observing helps you get to know a child better if you find yourself feeling negatively toward him. This happens occasionally, and you should cope with this feeling as quickly as you can. It usually helps if you understand the child better. What does he do that bothers you? What are his strengths? How can you build on his strengths to improve his relationships with you?

Perhaps a teacher's negative feelings may come from a child who exhibits one of her own weaknesses. For example, if you were whiny and unpopular as a child, then children with these traits may now bother you. Realizing the source of negative feelings can help you plan ways to respond to the child's needs. In every way, try learning more about such children and confer with others to get assistance.

CONCLUSION

Guidance is defined as all the adult does or says either directly or indirectly to influence the behavior of the child. Guidance is a consciously determined act based on carefully considered goals and values. The goal of all guidance is to help the child to become a happy, fully functioning individual who can make decisions and direct himself. Direct guidance includes all of the interpersonal communication processes.

Three types of direct guidance have been discussed. Physical guidance includes touching, leading, demonstrating, and the like. Verbal guidance includes techniques for communicating with young children through vocal means. Affective guidance includes techniques in the feeling realm. The reader will find further elaboration of these techniques throughout the text. These are important techniques to become acquainted with and to practice. However, knowing techniques is only the beginning. Techniques are no better than the abilities and judgment of people using them. You should try hard to become sensitive to the individual child's needs and to apply the techniques in a humanistic and person-centered way that will really be helpful to the child.

TECHNIQUES OF DIRECT GUIDANCE

Physical

1. Give help based on the individual child's need.

2. Demonstrate or model the desired behavior or skill.

3. Lead the child by the hand to give direction, reassurance, or assistance.

4. Restrain the child where necessary to protect him or others.

5. Remove the child from the scene to help him relax and regain composure.

6. Use no punishment that is meant to hurt or humiliate the child.

7. Get down to eye level and use meaningful gestures.

8. Use your body language to help the child feel good about himself and comfortable in school.

Verbal

1. Speak to the child eyeball to eyeball.

2. Use short sentences.

3. Use positive directions, telling the child what to do instead of what not to do.

4. Place the action part of your direction at the beginning of your statement.

5. Give no more than two directions at a time, preferably only one.

6. Give the child directions when it is the time and place you want the behavior to occur.

7. Give only the directions the child really needs and avoid being overdirective and bossy.

8. Make it clear whether the child has a choice or not.

9. Give logical and accurate reasons for requests.

10. Keep competition to a minimum by motivating the child through helping him set new personal goals for achievement.

11. Praise the child for jobs well done.

Affective

1. Give positive feedback for other occasions than when the child follows directions.

2. Give attention before the child demands it.

3. Reflect the feeling the child is expressing and give it a label.

4. Get to know the child better if you find yourself feeling negatively toward him.

APPLICATIONS

1. Practice guiding a preschool child in a home or a school. Give an example of using a form of physical guidance with the child. What was it? How effective was it? Explain.
2. Practice guiding a preschool child in a home or a school. Give an example of using a form of verbal guidance with the child. What was it? How effective was it? Explain.
3. Practice guiding a preschool child in a home or a school. Give an example of using a form of affective guidance with the child. What was it? How effective was it? Explain.
4. Observe the mother or the teacher guiding your case-study child. What direct guidance seems to be effective?

SUGGESTED FILM

Discipline and Self-Control   Black and white   25 minutes
Discusses the problem of discipline as one of teaching and living with young children. Shows how the teacher can establish control in a friendly climate and prevent disciplinary problems. Modern Talking Pictures, 1212 Avenue of the Americas, New York, N.Y. 10036. Free from any Head Start office.

FOR FURTHER READING

GOLAMBOS, JEANNETTE. *A Guide to Discipline.* Washington, D.C.: National Association for the Education of Young Children, 1969.

HILDEBRAND, VERNA. *Introduction to Early Childhood Education.* New York: Macmillan Publishing Co., Inc., 1971.

HYMES, JAMES, JR. *Behavior and Misbehavior.* Englewood Cliffs, N.J.: Prentice-Hall, Inc., 1955.

LANDRETH, CATHERINE. *Preschool Learning and Teaching.* New York: Harper & Row, Publishers, 1972.

READ, KATHERINE. *The Nursery School.* Philadelphia: W. B. Saunders Company, 1971.

REIF, THOMAS F., and GARY E. STOLLAK. *Sensitivity to Young Children: Training and Its Effects.* East Lansing, Mich.: Michigan State University Press, 1972.

TODD, VIVIAN E. *The Aide in Early Childhood Education.* New York: Macmillan Publishing Co., Inc., 1973.

TODD, VIVIAN E., and HELEN HEFFERNAN. *The Years Before School.* New York: Macmillan Publishing Co., Inc., 1970.

Being a Significant Adult in Children's Lives

The children had just finished listening to a record about rockets. The teacher was discussing it with them. Diana moved over by the assistant teacher and snuggled up very close to her. They exchanged glances that indicated feelings of mutual love and affection.

ALL ADULTS who perform services for children are significant adults in their lives. It is important to believe that the things you do, even a seemingly simple exchange of human warmth such as between Diana and the teacher in this anecdote, really make a difference in the total development of the child.

Whether you are a parent, teacher, assistant teacher, or volunteer in a home, in a family day care home, or in a nursery school or day care center, you will have the opportunity to help children develop their human resources in the process of your interaction.

In making the moment-to-moment guidance decisions that help children become self-directed individuals, you will first apply your general knowledge of children's development such as we discussed in Chapter 3. Second, you must gain information about the individual children in your group—the Johnnies and Marys and their very personal needs. Third, you will find useful the principles of indirect and direct guidance described in Chapters 4 and 5. Fourth, your values and goals, as discussed in Chapters 1 and 2, must be consciously applied to each decision you make.

Guiding children to help them reach their fullest

89

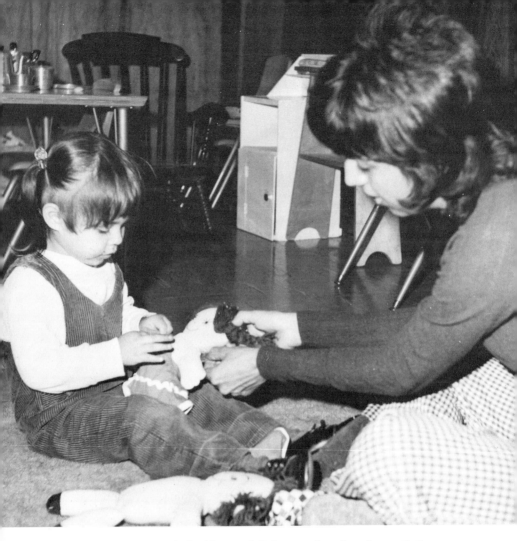

A significant adult is one who takes time to help you dress your doll. (University of Houston, Rebecca Hines, Photographer.)

potential requires the pooling of much information on your part, then acting with warmth and personal concern for each child. Even with a great deal of experience you will be saying, "There is so much I don't understand," so you must keep your mind open to learning more.

There are a number of personal attitudes that will help you make the decisions and become the most effective and significant adult that you can become. Discussion of these attitudes follows.

BEING A MODEL

To do your teaching and caregiving job well, you must be a model of the type of a person you'd like the child to become. If you want him to be kind, then you must be kind. If you want him to be loving, then you must be loving. If you want him to be smart, then you must use your intelligence. Children do imitate those around them, and when you have the opportunity and responsibility to be with children on a regular basis then you can expect them to pattern their behavior after yours.

BEING SELF-CONFIDENT

You should be confident of yourself and of your ability to cope with your responsibilities. Confidence is not built overnight, but little by little. In your assignments in nursery schools and day care centers, you will be given opportunities to develop your skill gradually. At the same time you should look for opportunities to be useful to the children and to the adults who work with you. There is always so much to be done that a helpful person who doesn't need to be told every task to do is a real asset.

Confidence grows when you find time to get down on the children's level and laugh and enjoy them. When you are warm and accepting of both children and their parents, they will be warm and accepting of you. Confidence grows when you feel you are a friend of coworkers, when you find opportunities to praise a job well done as you hope they will praise yours. Comments such as "That was a neat painting project" or "I wish I could lead music like you can" cost nothing, but mean a great deal to the person who hears them. These are, of course, examples of human resource exchange.

Confidence grows from knowing what is expected. Time used for getting clear directions from those in charge, or giving clear directions if you are in charge, is well spent. Posting some directions and communicating others in staff meetings and through individual contacts are means for knowing what is expected. Being alert and keeping your mind on the situation help you know what is expected. It is your responsibility to ask, seek, and be assertive if you do not have enough information to do your job well. In the immediate environment it may mean appropriately questioning a director, head teacher, co-worker, or parent. In the larger sense it may mean reading books, going to class, or attending workshops.

Your confidence will grow as you feel that you measure up to the standards you raise for yourself, to the standards raised by your administrator—whether director, principal, or parent board—and to the standards raised by the profession as a whole. The last are communicated through books such as this one and through the journals published by our professional organizations. (See the list at the end of this chapter.)

BEING DEDICATED

You should be dedicated to your role of serving children, or you really should look for some other occupation. Children deserve people who like them and enjoy working around them, not people who are just working until something better comes along. If children get on your nerves, then caregiving and teaching are not for you. If you think children are out to beat you, then these roles are not for you. But if you find real satisfaction in serving children, in seeing them smile, grow, learn, walk, and run, then teaching and caregiving may be for you.

If you are dedicated, you will try to learn as much as you can about your tasks. Dedication doesn't necessarily mean that you sacrifice your life to this career, because we can play many roles in our lives. You will actually be a better teacher or caregiver if you have interests outside your job that are very different from your career tasks. For example, at parties you can talk about politics instead of children. You can join art, music, or sports clubs instead of child study clubs just to give your own personality an opportunity to grow in other directions at the same time that you are devoting many of your hours to learning about and working with children.

One positive outcome of the feminist movement is that you aren't going to be hemmed in to the previous female roles of teaching and child care unless you want it that way. Discrimination against women is subsiding. Career opportunities are opening up in everything from applied mechanics to zookeeping.

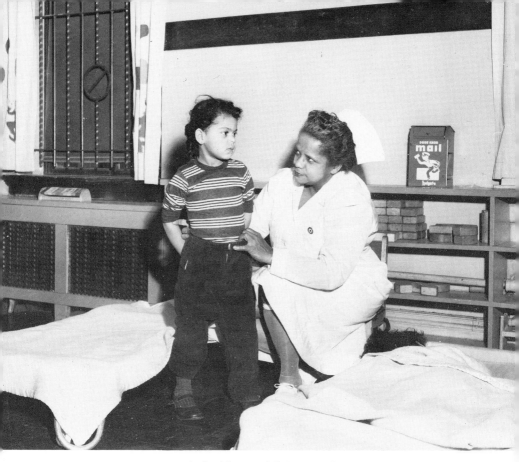

A significant adult is one who takes an interest in your health and general well-being. (Howard University, Flemmie Kittrell Project, Scurlock Photographers.)

Therefore, the women who might formerly have been locked into careers in child care can happily look elsewhere for their mode of livelihood, service, and self-expression. Gone are the days when mothers counseled all their daughters to go into teaching. Therefore, only men and women who are sincerely dedicated to the development of human potential need to find themselves pursuing an early childhood career.

HAVING CONFIDENCE IN PEOPLE

You should have confidence in people. Try hard to believe that people are basically good. Recognize that behavior has meaning and seek ways to discover the meaning of the behavior, whether in a child or an adult. If you feel a dislike for a child, then seek out more information about him immediately. What is his background? Has he a health problem? What are his strengths? What does he do well? Think how you might be if you had had the same things happen to you that have happened to him. Use time in staff meetings to share, in a professional discussion, the knowledge various members have about individual children and families. "Staffing," as this sort of briefing is sometimes called, must be done in a professional manner. Information communicated as gossip can be harmful to the child, to the parents, and even to the reputation of the school. Remember that the intimate facts and feelings that parents may share with you to help you more fully understand their children should be kept in confidence.

BEING STRONG, HEALTHY, AND ENERGETIC

You need to be strong, healthy, and energetic if you are to work effectively with young children. There is no use kidding that ours is an easy job. You are up and down dozens of times a day. You are on your feet indoors and out. You lift and carry equipment and sometimes children. You need patience when all children seem to need you at once. The requirements are not superhuman, of course, but simply demand a good constitution supported by proper diet, rest, and attention to your health. Proper shoes, boots, and other comfortable attire will be important to the way you feel.

It is disconcerting to children, not to mention administrators, to have their "teacher" absent frequently for health reasons. If you find yourself even considering calling in sick on anything like a frequent basis, then this may not be a career that will be suitable for you. Either you really don't have the physical stamina required, or your health is an excuse for avoiding a job that maybe you unconsciously don't like. Mental health is, of course, as important as physical health. The ability to keep life on a even keel is very important when you deal with children on a day-to-day basis. For example, if things are going badly with you and your husband, boyfriend, or roommate, then the pressure will eventually affect the children in your group. You may lose interest in them, fail to plan for them, or fail to respond to them with patience and understanding. People with their own problems should not attempt to deal with vulnerable people such as infants and young children.

KNOWING CURRICULUM

You will need to know about the curriculum of schools for young children and realize what possibilities are available in equipment and experiences offered to the children. When children are provided a rich and varied curriculum, they keep productively busy. The author's book, *Introduction to Early Childhood Education,* listed in the bibliography at the end of the chapter, is a source of detailed information on curriculum. It can help teachers plan a rich learning environment. With the book as a base, the creative teacher will be able to plan a program that is highly challenging to every aspect of a child's development. Knowing about curriculum, equipment, and supplies is very helpful in planning the guidance of children. Behavior problems can be dealt with effectively through expert knowledge and use of curriculum.

BEING A SCHOLAR AND A PROFESSIONAL

Your scholarship should go well beyond the subjects you will teach children. Your reading should help you understand the political, social, scientific, and aesthetic world that you and the children and their families live in. Knowledge of the implications of education in a democratic society is important for teachers. And, of course, your scholarship should include study of human growth, development, and behavior to help you develop and achieve the expectations you hold for children under your care.

As you work you will be developing your own teaching style, which is your own way of working with children that is effective and meets standards of the profession and yourself.

USING YOUR VOICE EFFECTIVELY

Your voice is a teaching tool. It can be effective for helping children know what to do. The firmness in your voice can give the children confidence. They will know that you expect them to comply with your directions by the way you tell them to do something.

A significant adult is one who shows you how to work a toy and has patience while you practice. (University of Houston, Rebecca Hines, Photographer.)

Of course, if they do not do what you ask, you will patiently lead them through the desired behavior so that next time they will know that you expect them to comply. You will speak in a normal voice directly to children rather than using a "to whom it may concern" approach. Speaking in a quiet manner is more effective than loudness. If you observe a class-room where loud or shouted guidance is being used, you can predict fearful children, unheeded guidance, or both.

SETTING LIMITS FOR CHILDREN

As a significant adult in children's lives, you must set limits on behavior at times. It is your responsibility to make the decisions children can't be expected to handle, while encouraging other decisions by children. For example, you may decide *when* art materials are to be used, children may then decide *what* materials they want to use. Children should not be overloaded with decision-making.

Limits must be set that (1) protect the children from each other, (2) protect the learning environment, and (3) protect the equipment. Firm decisions about what behavior can and can't be allowed should be discussed in staff meetings, then limits should be fairly maintained.

Some teachers are confused about setting limits. They feel a permissive atmosphere is best. These are, of course, value positions that must be reconciled. One might say that one child's limit is another child's freedom. For example, if I can't hit you, then you are free from being hit. If I can't knock your puzzle on the floor, thereby destroying your learning environment, then you are free to learn as you put your puzzle together. If I can't knock over the highchair, breaking it and the doll, then you are free to play with the doll for days and weeks to come.

It seems that these three types of limits are fair if children are to live together in a group and if children are to be prepared for life in the larger social world. Limits can be clearly stated to children. Opportunities to knock and hit can be provided in legitimate areas of the school, thereby allowing the children to get rid of the feelings indicated by such behavior. These outlets will be discussed in more detail in Chapter 20.

BEING ALERT TO HEALTH AND SAFETY

As the responsible adult, you have to be constantly alert for children's health and safety. You will always stand or sit where you can keep an eye on the portion of the room or yard that has been designated your responsibility. You will not leave that responsibility unless you advise another teacher or there is no child there. You will be conscious of cleanliness, contagion, and drafts, which affect health.

You will get tuned in to the sounds of a smoothly running school just as a mechanic knows the sound of a smoothly running automobile. If voices are raised or crowds gather, you'll sense that something is amiss. You'll act to alleviate a problem before it becomes serious. Perhaps you'll change the schedule, add a new piece of equipment, use a personal touch of physical or verbal guidance, whatever is called for to ease the situation.

Timing is of crucial importance. If such changes are made after children have come to blows, then they are not nearly as helpful. Skill in teaching is knowing when to step into a situation and acting on that knowledge.

BEING A TEACHER INSTEAD OF A SUPERVISOR

Teaching is more than supervising. You are playing a teaching role, whether in the classroom, at home, or on the playground. This means that there are many opportunities for children to learn and for you to facilitate learning. You are there, alert, interested, and knowledgeable about the situation. Teaching calls for interacting, enriching, observing, and planning for interaction with each child in the group. It is far more than supervising. If you were only a supervisor, you might rest at ease until trouble broke out, and you might not expect to deal with the consequences of your negligence, as a teacher must.

BEING A DECISION-MAKER

Social Decisions

The interaction decisions that make up the major portion of your guidance are called *social decisions*. In social decisions the alternatives are often not clear-cut. Each decision results from mediation of alternatives. That is, you may do the best you can for the moment knowing that it is not completely satisfactory to many. There may be a conflict in values or goals. For example, a child wants to stay inside to finish a painting. The teacher and the child both value completing work started. However, she and all the children value outdoor play, the other children are ready to go outside, and no teacher is available to stay indoors with the child. The teacher decides and tells the child that he can leave his work out to finish when they return inside.

Sometimes a compromise must be worked out whereby individuals tolerate parts of all the conflicting factors. Such a situation arises when several children want to be leader. Choosing the one who the teacher thinks asked first may be only a tolerable solution, not a happy one, for most children.

Sometimes the decision-makers behave as though the conflicting factors did not exist, which, of course, may mean that they behave in an inconsistent manner. This happens if a child's needs or feelings are ignored, perhaps when a child prefers to be active and the teacher asks him to listen to a story.

Educational Decisions

A teacher also makes many educational decisions. These are technical decisions related to choice of curriculum, goals, and content. They also include choice of teaching technique and choice of educational resources for achieving goals. Educational decisions should be based on knowledge, research, and experience.

Resource Decisions

Resource decisions are made when the means for achieving goals are allocated. Teachers and adminis-

A significant adult is one who provides lots of materials and helps you make something pretty. (Nazarene Day Care Center, Lansing, Michigan, Gerald Seelhoff, Photographer.)

trators of child care and nursery school programs are continuously allocating both human and nonhuman resources for the achievement of the program goals. In Chapter 1 you read a discussion of these concepts. These decisions should be made on a thoughtful basis when children are not present.

In making decisions or choices, the decision-maker must have enough information to recognize the alternatives. There is no opportunity for choice unless there are at least two alternatives. The consequences of classroom decisions will last a long time. Each decision may not seem earth-shaking in itself, but the cumulative effect can be. Material or nonhuman resources are expendable and must be replenished. Though human resources aren't used up, the optimal time for their development and utilization may pass. An opportunity for an exchange of human resources once passed may never reoccur again in the same way—for example, when a child's enthusiasm is squelched instead of praised.

CONCLUSION

Being a significant adult in children's lives means being a decision-maker. Being the decision-maker means you are the one who weighs alternatives and carries the choice into action. As a teacher you are assuming responsibilities for human encounter—an ongoing process that demands commitment and involvement. Your values will be tested over and over again as you work with parents to make the best possible life for their children.

All decisions should be given conscious thought. Without such thought, some decisions get made by default, and the people involved are buffeted along, much as the tide along the coast sloshes a piece of driftwood. Preferred goals are seldom achieved under such circumstances.

APPLICATIONS

1. Make a list of the various headings in the chapter. Observe and talk to either a mother or a teacher to learn how she is fulfilling the suggested aspects of being a significant person in a child's life. Report.
2. Make a list of the various headings in the chapter. Make an analysis of

yourself to determine where you stand on becoming a significant person to a child. Make a chart or write a short narrative showing the results of your self-analysis. List the goals you think are next for you to achieve.
3. Explain how limits are set in a home or school setting where you can observe. What are the limits? Who sets them? Do you think they are consistent over time? How do you think the children feel about the limits?
4. Record several episodes where you have interacted with your case-study child.

SUGGESTED FILMS

John—17 Months   Black and white   45 minutes
Filmed in a British Infant Center where care is given to infants around the clock. The film shows John, who remains for nine days. It shows regressive behavior of a happy little boy when subjected to a new situation and many caregivers. New York Film Library, 26 Washington Place, New York, N.Y. 10003.

Person to Person in Infancy   Black and white   20 minutes
Stresses the importance of human relationships between infant and adult. It shows that in group care as well as at home there is a considerable range of warmth and adequacy of relationships. Modern Talking Pictures, 1212 Avenue of the Americas, New York, N.Y. 10036. Free from any Head Start office.

PROFESSIONAL ORGANIZATIONS

American Association of Elementary-Kindergarten-Nursery Educators. 1201 Sixteenth Street, N.W., Washington, D.C. 20036. Publishes *Educating Children.*

American Home Economics Association. 2010 Massachusetts Avenue, Washington, D.C. 20036. Publishes *Journal of Home Economics.*

Association for Childhood Education International. 3615 Wisconsin Avenue, N.W., Washington, D.C. 20016. Publishes *Childhood Education.*

The Day Care and Child Development Council of America. 1012 14th Street, N.W., Washington, D.C. 20005. Publishes *Voice for Children.*

National Association for the Education of Young Children. 1834 Connecticut Avenue, N.W., Washington, D.C. 20009. Publishes *Young Children.*

Organisation Mondiale pour l'Éducation Préscolaire and the United States National Committee for Early Childhood Education. 81 Irving Place, New York, N.Y. 10003. Publishes *International Journal of Early Childhood.*

FOR FURTHER READING

BOWMAN, BARBARA T. "Role Models and Social Change." *Childhood Education*, Vol. 49, No. 4 (Jan. 1973), 180–183.

HILDEBRAND, VERNA. *Introduction to Early Childhood Education*. New York: Macmillan Publishing Co., Inc., 1971.

HILDEBRAND, VERNA, and BEATRICE PAOLUCCI. "Management and Decision Making in the Nursery School." *Journal of Home Economics*, Vol. 66, No. 4 (Apr. 1974), 9–13.

KATZ, LILIAN G. "Teaching in the Preschool: Roles and Goals." *Children*, Vol. 17, No. 2 (March 1970), 42–48.

LALLY, J. RONALD, ALICE S. HONIG, and BETTYE M. CALDWELL. "Training Paraprofessionals for Work with Infants and Toddlers." *Young Children*, Vol. 28, No. 3 (Feb. 1973), 173–181.

MARSHALL, HERMINE H. "Criteria for an Open Classroom." *Young Children*, Vol. 28, No. 1 (Oct. 1972), 13–19.

MOORE, SHIRLEY. "The Training of Day Care and Nursery School Personnel." In Dennis N. McFadden (Ed.). *Early Childhood Development Programs and Services: Planning for Action*. Washington, D.C.: National Association for the Education of Young Children, 1972.

QUILL, JEANNE. *One Giant Step—A Guide for Head Start Aides*. Washington, D.C.: National Association for the Education of Young Children, 1968.

TODD, VIVIAN E. *The Aide in Early Childhood Education*. New York: Macmillan Publishing Co., Inc., 1973.

WILLIAMS, C. RAY, and THOMAS F. RYAN. "Competent Professionals for Quality Care and Early Education: The Goal of Child Development Associate." *Young Children*, Vol. 28, No. 2 (Dec. 1972), 71–73.

# Introducing a Child to a New Group of Children

It was Bradley's turn to have his throat checked.
When the nurse started to look at him he tore away
from her and cried, "No, no. I want my mama."
His face turned red and his bottom lip puffed out.

NEW CHILDREN frequently resist routines. They often cry. It takes a while for a child to become accustomed to the routines of a nursery school, but the main problem was that Bradley was not accustomed to having his mother leave him at the school.

In the following pages you will learn some methods for easing the child into the nursery school situation so he will be comfortable and happy. Bradley's mother was one who had time to help with his introduction to the group situation. However, some children are brought to day care centers "ready or not," as children say in games of hide-and-seek. When a mother has committed herself to a job, then the child goes to the center "ready or not." Of course, it would be better for the child, the mother, and the center if the child were prepared in advance for the new experience of entering a group. Children who are anxious may not eat or sleep. They may have setbacks of long-standing duration in toilet training and socialization. Some of the following suggestions will help you help the child make a satisfactory entry into his new group.

PARENT VISIT

Many parents believe that if a center advertises child care someone has stamped "approved" on that center. This may not be true. There are some regulations in nearly every state, but most regulations are minimal; therefore, parents should visit a center to see if it meets their standards. Even after they enroll their child they should be alert to shifts in compliance. One mother placed her child in a center when she began her teaching job. The first day when she returned to pick up the child the entire group was asleep without any supervision. She dressed her child, then looked for someone to advise

A new child with an engaging smile is readily welcomed into a group. (Mary Gray, Photographer.)

that she was taking the child. She finally found the director in a second-floor room. She told the director that it was the last day her son would be coming to the center for she felt the supervision was not sufficient to keep him safe.

Centers should invite prospective customers in for a visit. One or both parents should go with the intention of staying several hours to "just watch." First, the director will likely brief them on program and procedures. She will be aware of the standards that the center should be meeting and will discuss them with parents in a confident manner, having been through this interview numerous times. After a tour of the facility, parents should ask to sit in the back of the classroom or nursery where their child will be spending most of his time. Here they may be able to gain some insights into the type of care that children are given. They can note the children's freedom, the interactions among adults and children. Of course, teachers and caregivers may behave differently under observation than they may when visitors are absent, but if the parents stay during several routines they should be able to get a fair idea of the operation.

They can notice if teachers are kind, if children enjoy school, if there is a minimum of crying and aggression. They should also look for cleanliness and for provisions for emergencies such as fire. They should look for children with signs of illness.

The child should not accompany his parents to the centers while they are investigating the center. The presence of the child can be very distracting for parents. Instead of looking at the center discriminatingly, they will be concerned with needs of their own child.

For three- or four-year-olds the premature visit to the center may cause him to be fearful, even rebellious. The children who are enrolled may make what appear to be unfriendly comments to the visitor. The child and even the parents may then conclude that they don't like the center. Once the choice has been narrowed, the center can be introduced as "your nursery school," then the child may be brought for an introductory visit.

Babies and toddlers, too, should be taken for pre-

Being new in a group can be a sobering experience. (William Mitcham, Michigan State University Staff Photographer.)

liminary visits to their new home-away-from-home before they are left. The steps outlined here can be followed for them as well.

HOME VISIT

When teachers and caregivers make a visit to the homes of newly enrolled children, they are setting the stage for a comfortable and happy introduction of the new child into the group. The child will be getting acquainted with one or two new persons on his own ground. The teachers can observe how the mother and child interact, what the child's place is relative to other children in the family, and how the physical surroundings seem to be influencing him.

The child will feel comfortable with his own toys around him. He will remember these new people when next he meets them at his "new school." The fact that the teacher knows where he lives will give him confidence and security as he becomes adjusted to the new situation.

Parents, too, will be more at ease in their own home. Appointments are naturally made with indications that the home visit is part of the routine procedure prior to a child's enrollment. The reason for the visit is to get acquainted with the child on home base and to discuss the school program and any concerns the parents have regarding their child's adjustment. When the visit is made before the child really enters school, the parents need not worry that their child has been misbehaving or has a problem, as they may later on if an appointment for a home visit is made. At the early date parents are the ones who know the child and have information to give.

Parents of young children are surprisingly easy to talk to once you get acquainted with them. They are happy to find a person with sincere interest in the development of their child. Many are isolated from relatives and from friends who are interested in children, so they welcome the teacher who will talk about the child's concerns. Working mothers have limited time for neighborhood kaffeeklatsches where some commiserating with other women might take place. Therefore, they welcome the interested teacher who is concerned about their child.

If this sounds like a pep talk to teachers and children's caregivers to make home visits, it is. The benefits will be many, and you will readily discover them by making your first home visits. Visits do take time, but are well worth the effort in the long run. The initial visit need not be long, a half hour will do, and with careful routing you can visit several homes in an afternoon. Children will frequently say, "You came to my house" or "You know where I live, don't you?" indicating increased confidence in teachers whom they have met on their own ground. Of course, subsequent visits besides this initial one are important, and you will note increased rapport with children and parents as a result.

SCHOOL VISIT

A visit to the school facility prior to attending gives children a further feeling of confidence in the new situation. They can explore the room a little at a time with mother staying as close as needed. It is helpful if the visit can take place when other children are not there or perhaps while they are out in the play yard, for the new child can survey the physical setting before becoming involved with the people environment. The child can discover where his locker will be—his own personal space. He can even try out the bathroom, which may hold some anxiety for him if he is only now getting accustomed to using one. The sleeping room and cots may also be shown to him. He should be allowed to enjoy the play yard and to try out the equipment there.

FIRST ATTENDANCE

A first big step toward independence is the child's first introduction to school. The child's first attendance may be with an ongoing group where he is the only new child. It may be with a newly forming group. In the ongoing groups a new child is taken in stride as he fits into the routines. He may stay for a short time the first few days, and his mother is usually encouraged to remain to give him support where he needs it.

In new groups the teacher may choose to start only a few children at a time so there will be ample time for her and the assistants to interact with each child individually, showing him the routines and equipment. Parents may stay if needed. Parents may tell their child they are leaving and leave, thus giving their child practice in handling himself for a while. After each group has had its day or two of introduction, then the teacher brings the entire group together on a regular basis.

These procedures may sound like idealistic ways to introduce the child to his first school experience. Because this is such an important new step, it is well to make it as free of anxiety for as many children as possible. There are families who have time for this casual introduction to nursery school if the teacher wants to plan it this way.

However, there are also the working mothers, many without funds to pay for part days of nursery

"This is our new friend, his name is Bobby," says the teacher. (Michigan State University Laboratory Preschool, Connie Lisiecki, Photographer.)

school or the time to take from their work to introduce the child in this casual manner. Their children may have been accustomed to numerous babysitters prior to entry into group care. Teachers and caregivers can expect to be presented children who indeed will be left "ready or not." It is wise to have the mother simply wave goodbye, so the child knows she is really gone. It is unwise to allow a mother to slip off from the child, because when he discovers her absence he may be more upset than ever. Once the child knows she is gone, he often adjusts rather quickly.

ROLE OF HELPERS

Helping the Child

As a helper you can play a significant role in the introduction of new children in the group, whichever of the situations just discussed apply. For example, one assistant consoled a quietly withdrawn but anxious child while the lead teacher carried through with routines. The assistant sensed the child's need to have someone nearby and responded to that need.

Another time the new but confident student teacher carried on with a group while the teacher was tied up with a child who cried so loudly that the teacher could not even get away to call the child's mother. The child was one who had had years of experience with babysitters, so no one had predicted that he would react so violently to being left at school, where he had already visited.

On another occasion a mother entered the parent cooperative nursery school with her own child and observed the teacher being overwhelmed with a sobbing child who was unhappy at having been left. The mother's child went happily about her playing and allowed her mother to help the teacher with the sobbing child. After a period of walking and consoling, the child accommodated to the school enough to finish the day playing.

Teachers, as they become acquainted with children on home and school visits, will make estimates of how various ones will adjust. They will take these estimates into account as they plan the learning experiences for the first few days. The estimates will affect the assignment of responsibilities to coworkers. Even so, the helpers will need to be particularly sensitive to children's needs and step in where needed. When the home visits and school visits have been made as suggested, the child who is deeply unhappy will be a rare exception.

There are some things to try when children are unhappy as they enter school. Stay close to the child and console him. Frequently it is better to hold him or hold his hand. Some monologue-type conversation may alleviate anxiety if you don't press for answers to questions.

The younger children, infants and toddlers, are usually easily distracted by just showing them something new such as a toy or a bus passing by outside. A cracker, a drink, or a walk may be a good diversion for an unhappy child, helping him get his mind on something else. Occasionally, you can get another child to include the child in his play, thereby alleviating the situation. Reminding the child "Mother will come back" or "Mommies always come back," may be helpful. Acknowledging that you know he's sad but that everything will soon be all right may help.

Taking the child away from the group to "help" you with some project may work, provided it is possible for you to be away from the group. By helping with cleaning up the kitchen or bathroom, the child may regain his composure. Some children will relax if they hear a story or record. Others may find painting relaxing. Water play is often good, especially in the kitchen or bathroom setting—this makes the parallel with the home evident.

You will want the new child to feel that school is an interesting and protecting place. Consequently, your guidance should support, and not blame, him while he makes his initial adjustment to the new place and people and to the absence of his mother.

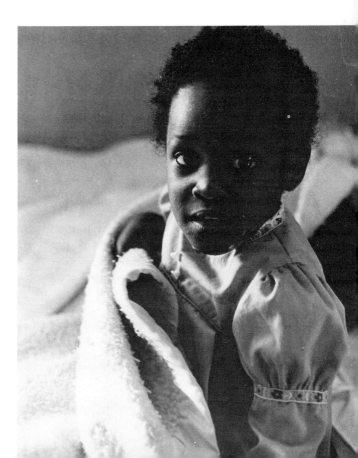

A new child has to learn about the rest routine and develop trust in the caregivers if relaxation and sleep are to come easily. (Michigan State University Spartan Day Care Center, Connie Lisiecki, Photographer.)

All your knowledge of the child, his family, and their needs must be combined to help you decide what course is best during these crucial days.

When a child has been absent for vacations or because of illness, some of the same anxiety about being left may be revived. Generally this anxiety will be overcome far easier than was the original anxiety.

It is a rare child who can tell his parents that he is ready for them to leave the school and leave him alone. Therefore, it is better not to put the child into a position of making this decision. The teachers and parents should make the decision, anticipating as many of the rough spots as possible, then dealing with the situation decisively when the time comes. Often parents who hesitate or delay departing may leave their child more upset than necessary.

It would be unfair to assume from the time we've spent discussing helping unhappy children that the majority have difficulties entering nursery school. If the preliminary steps have been taken carefully, choice of nursery school, introduction of the teacher to the child at home, and introduction of the child to the school, then the first days generally go in a fairly comfortable way for most children. In this aspect, as in all others, there are individual differences among children.

A contrasting type of child bears mentioning, too. This is the fellow who seems to have confidence and moves into play groups with gusto. He, too, may need your help, because if the children are in already formed play groups he may be rejected by the oldtimers. Far wiser is the newcomer who looks the situation over and somewhat cautiously finds his niche little by little. In only a few days he is likely to be playing with the leader of the group.

A mother sometimes apologizes for her child's hesitancy about participating with the other children. Some parents don't like to see a child hold back, perhaps riding a trike alone instead of playing with the group. They may explain it as "unusual" behavior and feel that the child is not happy or is not going to participate as they want him to. The teacher's role is to reassure the parents that the child knows best, that he will participate with the larger group as he feels ready, and that she will help him as he indicates an interest.

The overconfident person is usually a boy, but girls have a problem, too. Especially in late four- and five-year-old groups, girls begin forming "best friend" pairs, and a new girl may have some difficulty if she is chosen as a "best friend" of a leader or if a leader decides to reject her. The teacher's role is difficult. I once tried to talk to kindergarten girls about how it felt to be left out. They verbalized about how it was "bad" to leave someone out, that you "shouldn't" do it, and so on. The conversation was very hypothetical, and they never really understood that the situation applied to them.

ALTERNATIVES FOR PARENTS AND CENTERS

Parents can agree to introduce their child to an early childhood education program on a trial basis. This is acceptable to many centers. Centers also may exercise some options regarding admission of children.

Sometimes when a new center is opening the staff gets so anxious about numbers that they eagerly take all children—often without regard to age balances, facilities, and staff talents. A few weeks later they may have a waiting list that includes children who would have balanced their classes and operation plans in a far more reasonable manner. There are children handicapped to various degrees whom a particular center definitely should not try to serve because of space, staff, or program limitations. These should be explained to parents frankly.

The center should offer space to a family on a tentative basis. "You try us out, and we'll see if your child likes our school and if we can give him the program he needs. If either of us feels our school isn't effective for your child, we'll help you locate a more suitable child care service." Such a policy can save many problems and hard feelings for all concerned.

Helping the Mother

The mother whose child is going through this introductory stage may also need help. A mother may have a hard time adjusting to leaving the child regardless of the reason she gives for enrolling him.

She may feel rejecting enough as it is, so it is better if the child blames you for having to stay rather than blaming his mother. Through the home visits, conferences, and school visits, mothers gain confidence in the teacher and her assistants. If they can become confident that the school is a good place to be, then leaving the child can be less painful.

Sometimes a child can be happily adjusted if his mother brings him to school but will be very unhappy if left by his father or a car-pool mother. Fathers may jump to the conclusion that the child is not enjoying school or that the child is ill.

In cases of difficult separation, the teacher who has the best rapport with the child should step in to ease the situation and help get the child occupied with something he likes. At this point, a new and strange teacher who tries to help can only compound the problem.

Volunteering to telephone the parent later when the child settles down can help the parent's day go more smoothly. The call can reassure the parent that the child is not ill and that he is now relaxed and playing happily. It can help alleviate the parent's guilt feelings for having left him in such a state.

CONCLUSION

The first days of school are of utmost importance for each child. This is often his first experience as an individual separate from his family. Up to this point he may have been carefully protected from social contacts that would have helped him make this new step with confidence. The teacher's role is to take as many steps as feasible to introduce the child to the center in a gradual way. If this is impossible and the policy of the school is still to admit the child, then the teachers must cope with the child as best they can. Some suggestions have been made. It is important to impress on parents that time should be allowed for this introductory process before they go to work.

Throughout this introductory phase, the child will be accepted and loved by parents and teachers even though he is having difficulty becoming independent. He will never be called a baby or be threatened or shamed for his behavior. On the contrary, the adults will give him love, understanding, and support as he takes this first important step alone out into the big wide world.

APPLICATIONS

1. Discuss with parents of a nursery school child the reasons they have for sending their child to school. Find out what steps they took to decide on the school the child is enrolled in. Write a report of your discussion.
2. Discuss with the preschool teacher the methods used to introduce a new child to the center. Write a brief report of your discussion.
3. Observe a new child or a group of children being introduced to a center and report on the problems encountered. Which suggestions in your text were being followed, if any?
4. Discuss with others or recall and record how your case-study child was oriented to a new group.

FOR FURTHER READING

HILDEBRAND, VERNA. *Introduction to Early Childhood Education.* New York: Macmillan Publishing Co., Inc., 1971.

READ, KATHERINE. *The Nursery School.* Philadelphia: W. B. Saunders Company, 1971.

TODD, VIVIAN E. *The Aide in Early Childhood Education.* New York: Macmillan Publishing Co., Inc., 1973.

TODD, VIVIAN E., and HELEN HEFFERNAN. *The Years Before School.* New York: Macmillan Publishing Co., Inc., 1970.

Arranging Space
for Learning
and Self-direction

*Todd was showing his grandmother his nursery
school. "This is my locker," he said. "This is where
we go to the bathroom. These are our blocks. This
is where my teacher tries to make us sleep, and I
don't like that too much."*

TODD WAS PROUD of his nursery school and
indicated a comfort and security about it as he
showed his grandmother his home-away-from-home.

The arrangement of the space of the children's
facility can make a difference in how easy it will be
for children to learn and become self-directed in the
activities we plan for them each day. As the child
leaves the car or bus that brings him to school,
enters the school, goes through the self-care routines and learning activities, and leaves for home,
the physical setting in which he finds himself will
be having its effect on his behavior.

A carefully planned environment will support the
growing child and his development and learning.
The space and its arrangement can make the child
feel confident or afraid, competent or incompetent,
interested or uninterested, intelligent or dumb, in
control or controlled. In this chapter you can gain
some perspective on how the organization of the
space can contribute to learning, to the child's feelings of competency, and to the teacher's methods
of guidance.

LIFE SPACE

When the child enters his first nursery, nursery
school, or child care center, he is extending his life
space or home range. According to Dr. Leon Pastalan, a Michigan sociologist and architect concerned

with human environments, "At infancy one's home range scarcely extends beyond the body. If the infant is warm and well fed and reasonably comfortable, his world literally does not extend beyond the skin. He is almost totally unaware of what is occurring around him. He is primarily concerned with his immediate environment. However, as a child develops physically and intellectually his home range begins to expand. For instance, the child begins to make sense out of his surroundings in his crib, his nursery, and so on. He begins to sort out the various arrangements of objects and spaces that he can see and relate to. As soon as the child begins to develop his ability to walk, his home range expands even further, going beyond the crib, his nursery, out into the other rooms of the house, and soon the child is exploring not only spaces within the dwelling unit but outside as well and begins to sort out and respond to his immediate areas outside the dwelling unit. Then as

Interesting decorations in the room make a stimulating environment. (Michigan State University Preschool, Connie Lisiecki, Photographer.)

Learning zones are planned to provide for both quiet and active play. In cold climates the indoor climbing apparatus is an important resource. (University of Idaho Laboratory School, Ed Breidenbach, Photographer.)

he increases in age and development he continues to expand his home range until he reaches maturity where he has almost an unlimited home range in the sense that there can be a large number of spaces, objects, and people with sensed relationships that he experiences."[1]

How will the child respond to his new life space of the nursery or of the nursery school? What will be the meaning of this environment to him? According to Pastalan, "Environment is organized as intricately and systematically as any spoken language. It has a system of cues that tell us how to respond to a particular stimulus."[2] He says there are at least

[1] Leon A. Pastalan, "The Simulation of Age Related Sensory Losses: A New Approach to the Study of Environmental Barriers," Mimeo.
[2] Leon A. Pastalan, "How the Elderly Negotiate Their Environment," a paper prepared for *Environment for the Aged: A Working Conference on Behavioral Research, Utilization and Environmental Policy*, San Juan, P.R., Dec. 17–20, 1971, Mimeo.

three dimensions on which the environment needs to be organized. They are (1) organized space as mastery, (2) organized space as orientation, and (3) organized space as stimulus.

ORGANIZED SPACE AS MASTERY

Can the child master the relationships in the space—that is, the school? Will he feel secure and confident? Can he hope to control his environment?

All individuals and even small children need some *personal space* that is theirs to claim and defend, according to Pastalan. In the nursery school this is usually the locker holding the child's personal belongings, his coat and boots, and his paintings. It probably is also important that he be given *a* place at the lunch or snack table and *a* cot in a certain spot as his personal sleeping spot. It is Pastalan's idea that it should be very difficult for others to infringe on the individual's personal space. He suggests that "possession of a tangible piece of space seems almost essential for one's identity."[3]

With respect to this point, the day care center where no lockers are provided and the children's belongings are simply piled in the director's office must be violating the children's sense of personal space. Or the teacher who put a five-year-old's toy from home on a "too-high" shelf violated the child's personal space when she removed it from the child's locker.

Territoriality is an important space concept. In the nursery school, territoriality means a child's specific claim to a learning environment—the place at the easel, in the sandbox, or on the carpet with the blocks. We often say to nursery school children if there is a conflict over a piece of equipment or a space on the floor or in the sandbox that it is "yours while you are using it." This rule surely may be a source of confusion for some children—those who have had no claim to equipment or space in their prior experience and those who come from small families in large homes where almost all the territory is theirs most of the time. In terms of tricycles, parents teach children to use their own and to keep

[3] Ibid.

it in their yard, so the common usage of tricycles at nursery school is undoubtedly confusing.

Territoriality also refers to how close you like to have others come to you in a social interaction. Variations have been observed in adults and in different cultures. Even for young children territoriality could be a factor in their behavior—and certainly makes for differences between adult caregivers and teachers.

Pastalan suggests that *scale*, the number of people and their size who use the space, is related to the individual's feelings of mastery. As sensory acuities develop, individuals can cope with larger numbers of people and larger spaces. He particularly warns against density and overcrowding as producing negative effects on behavior.

Considering this idea with regard to nurseries and nursery schools helps us understand one reason that babies and small children cope better in small groups. It may explain, in part, why most parents don't think their preschooler is ready to shop alone in a store even for one or two items. That is, parents feel that there are too many people, too much space, too many competing stimuli for the child to cope with in our urban stores on his own.

These observations also support our experience that young children in small groups of up to twenty have a more satisfactory nursery school experience than when organized in larger groups. To divide even the twenty children into smaller groups improves personal relationships and learning within the group. It should make us pause in some laboratory schools and count the number of observers, researchers, student teachers, and the like present in the children's life space.

Social psychologists have long maintained, on the basis of experiments with adults, that participation in groups of three or four is fairly evenly distributed, but as the group size increases to eight participation is concentrated in fewer persons. It is anticipated that if this study were done with children the results would be even more striking; that is, participation would decrease even more with increase in group size.

Social psychologists also indicate that group unity

decreases as the size of a group increases. They find that when there is high "goal achievement" in a group, the group is stronger and more unified. In their studies, they have found that control can be maintained over only five adults without resorting to authoritarian means.

Studies of this nature with children might help support the experience of most nursery school professionals that an organization of small groups produces the most effective guidance and learning in young children.

Child-sized equipment and low latches on doors facilitate mastery. Child-height lavatories, toilets, and drinking fountains help children gain control of their own personal care sooner. Low chairs and tables, child-height bulletin boards and easels, and equipment stored on open shelves that are readily accessible to the child invite him to get things out for himself and to put them away when finished.

Mastery in the gross motor skills is the particular contribution of the playground environment of the school. Outdoor equipment must also be suited to children's sizes. There must be sufficient spaces for the number of children using the space. The ease with which equipment is stored contributes to its use and to its care and maintenance. Protected play areas that allow for fresh air and exercise even in inclement weather should be a serious consideration of all planners.

A principle applied in the Montessori schools is that each toy or learning device has its own special space for use. The child is taught where to use a toy, and he is also taught to return the toy to its rightful space on the shelf when finished.

Space that is easily kept clean contributes to the child's mastery and eliminates numerous problem areas where children might be admonished to "be careful" or be reprimanded if they spilled something. Carpeting has contributed to tension in this regard in some centers. Either teachers do not believe that carpeting is as washable as some companies now advertise it to be, or the center does not boast a professional janitorial service that will really keep it clean. For these reasons, carpeting may well be eliminated where food and paints are used.

ORGANIZED SPACE AS ORIENTATION

A space that has only one purpose and use helps people predict appropriate behavior, according to Pastalan. He would not favor multipurpose rooms but rather those with a more specifically defined use. He suggests that attention be given to three types of space: personal, social, and public. Rooms can be color-coded and decorated to signal the functionally different space uses. The purpose is to make each space stimulating to the several senses, especially sight, touch, and sound, in a distinctive manner. This will help children recognize use and behavior appropriate for each area. For example, children will recognize personal space as clearly private, social space as clearly for the use of the whole group, and public space as clearly for the use of others outside the group.

In applying these ideas in the nursery school, we can signal private space by painting lockers and cots a different color from other furniture and repeating that color in name tags and individual labels. Certain colors can be used in rooms or alcoves designed for small groups, other colors for quiet and loud areas, and a different color for walls or dividers in the social space where all gather. Then still another color can be used for the public entryway, office, and parking lot, designating public space.

Given boundaries and clues such as these, children could more readily learn the appropriate behavior for each space. With this much attention given to the space utilization, even the staff would be more consistent regarding what behavior is appropriate for what space. In some schools the phrase "walk, don't run" might not be needed.

ORGANIZED SPACE AS STIMULUS

The stimulus dimension of space involves the principle of getting the message across largely through sensory stimulation. Messages that we want children to respond to and to learn must be repeated by numerous kinds of sensory stimuli—sight, sound, smell, taste, and touch. According to Pastalan, the environment becomes a meaningful language to people and appropriate responses are feasible. He uses winter as an example of how many sensory clues we get to conceptualize our environment; that is, we see the

Orderly arrangement of blocks encourages children to learn to classify according to size and shape. (Michigan State University Laboratory Preschool, Connie Lisiecki, Photographer.)

snow on the ground and ice on the pond, we feel that the air is cold, we hear the wind, and so on.

The open school concept, which allows children free movement among learning centers, permits them to respond to stimuli perceived through any sensory mode. It might be the sound of their best friend laughing in the block corner, the sight of a piñata being constructed in the art area, or the smell of cookies baking in the kitchen. As the child responds to a stimulus and moves in any one of these directions, he uses prior experience to guide his response or behavior. If he needs help in learning a new behavior, the adults advise him through application of guidance techniques.

Space can be beautiful and orderly. It can be clean. These are particular qualities that can impress young children. Pastalan suggests that attention be given to lighting, textures, acoustic balance, and density. An orchestration of these various dimensions can produce a supportive environment for a special population.

CONCLUSION

Pastalan's research has been done with regard to another highly vulnerable group—the aged—but the principles of analyzing the human environment are applicable to any age group. Pastalan's work seems particularly helpful when planning for children's new "life space" or home-away-from-home. We can use these dimensions to help us analyze both the homes and the schools where young children are growing up.

APPLICATIONS

1. Observe a child playing at home or at school. Does the child have well-defined play areas? Can he tell what activity he is free to do in a given area? Answer with an example and explanation.
2. Observe a young child at home or at school. Can you determine whether the child is claiming any given space as his own? What does he say or do? Explain.
3. Observe a child in a school or home play space and identify the stimulus dimension of the space. Explain how you saw a child respond to the environment.
4. Report the life space of your case-study child. Give examples of both home and school if feasible and applicable.

FOR FURTHER READING

Cohen, Monroe. *Learning Centers: Children on Their Own.* Washington, D.C.: Association for Childhood Education International, 1970.

Hess, Robert D., and Doreen J. Croft. *Teachers of Young Children.* New York: Houghton Mifflin Company, 1972.

Hirsh, Elizabeth S. "What Are Good Responsive Environments for Young Children?" *Young Children,* Vol. 28, No. 2 (Dec. 1972), 75–80.

Kritchevsky, Sybil, Elizabeth Prescott, and Lee Walling. *Planning Environments for Young Children: Physical Space.* Washington, D.C.: National Association for the Education of Young Children, 1969.

Lueck, Phyllis. "Planning an Outdoor Learning Environment." *Theory into Practice,* Vol. 12, No. 2. (Apr. 1973), 121–127.

Marion, Marian C. "Create a Parent-Space—A Place to Stop, Look and Read." *Young Children,* Vol. 28, No. 4 (Apr. 1973), 221–224.

Osmon, Fred Linn. *Patterns for Designing Children's Centers.* New York: Educational Facilities Laboratories, Inc., 1972.

Pastalan, Leon A. "How the Elderly Negotiate Their Environment." Paper prepared for *Environment for the Aged: A Working Conference on Behav-*

ioral Research, Utilization and Environmental Policy. San Juan, P.R., Dec. 17–20, 1971. Mimeo.

PASTALAN, LEON A. "The Simulation of Age Related Sensory Losses: A New Approach to the Study of Environmental Barriers." Mimeo.

PIERCE, CHESTER M. "Becoming a Planetary Citizen: A Quest for Meaning." *Childhood Education,* Vol. 49, No. 2 (Nov. 1972), 58–63.

Scheduling Activities to Meet Children's Needs

Jan entered the four-year-olds' nursery school, hung her coat in her locker, and proceeded to the housekeeping corner to play. In another group three-year-old Jeffrey said goodbye to his mother at the gate where his teacher waited. He ran to climb the jungle gym with other children.

JAN AND JEFFREY were showing they knew the schedule of activities of their respective schools. They knew what behavior was appropriate because the schedule was substantially the same every day. Children find security from a routine sequence of events and so do the adults who work with them.

SCHEDULING DECISIONS

There are a vast number of decisions that each individual has to make each day, and it helps considerably if some of the decisions can become habits. Habits develop out of having satisfactorily made a decision enough times that it has become routine and, therefore, requires less time and energy to make. If we had to deliberate long over all the choices we make every day, we'd make little progress.

A routine schedule or sequence of events in the nursery and child care center gives both children and teachers security. It helps us have confidence in the other people when we are all operating on the same schedule. The schedule is an indirect guide to appropriate behavior. In the opening anecdote, Jan knew that she would eventually play outdoors, so even though she walked right past the jungle gym enroute indoors she was not tempted to stop to play. For her, playing indoors came first. Quite the oppo-

126

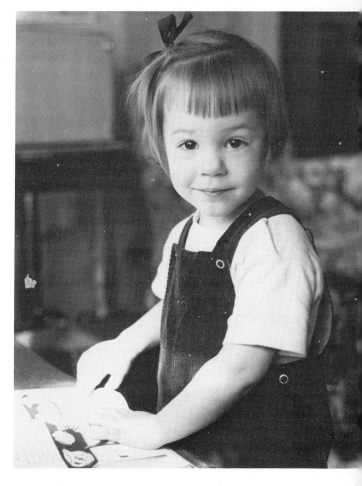

A good schedule or sequence of events leaves time for a child to "read" books during the day. (James Page, Photographer.)

site, Jeffrey, all dressed for outdoor play, didn't run to see what was going on indcors because he knew that after he had played a while outdoors he would have ample time indoors.

Young children do not tell time by the clock, but they learn early to interpret routines and to know what comes after what. Knowing the routines helps them carry on independently without adults telling them what to do.

Many factors go into making up the schedule for a group of children. They are

1. The objectives of the school.

2. The time children come to school and leave.

3. The amount of time they stay at school.

Opportunity for vigorous activity has an important place in every preschool schedule. (University of Idaho Laboratory School, Ed Breidenbach, Photographer.)

4. The number and ages of the children.
5. The number of adults on the staff and their schedules.
6. The flexibility of the facility.
7. A balance of active and quiet activity.
8. The time of year and weather.

The Objectives of the School

Schedules differ between short-day nursery school groups and all-day child care groups. In child care centers there must be time for all the routines of eating and resting that need not be allowed for in short-day groups. In some schools where the objectives are concentrated on intellectual development, schedules would allow a larger share of time for such activities and less time perhaps for outdoor play. In schools serving children who have few playmates at home and microscopic backyards, the schedule may allow lots of outdoor playtime with less time spent on some other aspect. If an objective is also to serve needs of parents or students, then their schedules must be considered when planning children's schedules.

The Time Children Come to School and Leave

If the teacher makes the suggested home visits and opens real avenues of communication with parents, she will begin to know the underlying reasons for the schedule the family lives by. From this information, plus knowledge of how children grow and develop, and from observing children in the group, an appropriate school schedule can be developed with activities paced to suit the needs of the children.

Schools have many times that children may be entering the school. In day care centers arrival of children may begin as early as 6:00 A.M., and continue into the afternoon, depending on the requirements of families for care of their child. In short-day groups there is typically less of a range of arrival times, with children arriving within about a half hour span. The sequence of activities must be flexible enough to allow children to enter

Naptime must be a part of every long-day schedule. (Michigan State University Spartan Day Care Center, Connie Lisiecki, Photographer.)

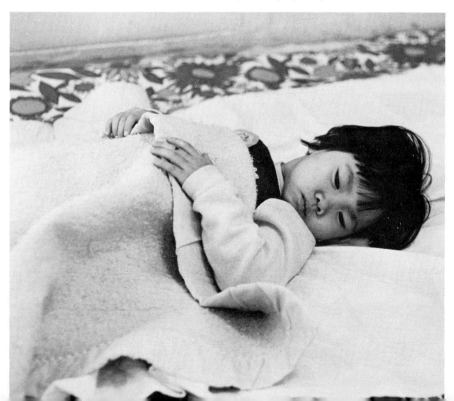

comfortably and pick up the thread of activity without feeling strange or left out.

The first activities planned will need to take into account what children have been doing just before they come to school. If they have been hurriedly routed out of bed, then their breakfast needs must be considered as well as their physiological habits relative to bowel movements and urination.

Children may sleep late when enrolled in short-day groups. In these groups it makes little sense to plan a "rest" time for children around 10:00 A.M.; they may only be fully awake by then. Afternoon groups may arrive shortly after lunch, whereas others may take their naps at home and then arrive at school between 2:00 and 3:00 P.M. For young children not taking naps, the afternoon program must be paced slower to avoid overfatigue. We also take into consideration what children have typically done during the morning to avoid exhausting them before going-home time. That is, if they play actively outdoors all morning, then more restful activities will be necessary in the afternoon.

The Amount of Time They Stay at School

The length of the child's school day must be considered along with the general objectives of the program. In short-day programs the choice of learning projects and field trips must be made in light of the time available. Full-day programs allow larger blocks of time and a more leisurely pace. However, there is the difficulty of having more routines to include and the fact that preparation for eating, sleeping, and frequent dressing takes considerable time.

If centers are accepting part-time or drop-in children, they may wish to group these children apart from full-time regular attenders to meet their needs more adequately. Because they may attend infrequently and never really get acquainted with each other or with the staff, special attention must be given to making these children feel comfortable in the continuously strange setting.

The less regular the attenders the more competent the teacher needs to be. A person who is sensitive and experienced in interpreting children's needs should be the teacher for a part-time group. Scheduling of short-range or quick-to-complete learning projects, instead of long-range multifaceted projects, helps children feel closure (project completion) even when they attend on irregular bases.

The Number and Ages of the Children

Children's ages give us some clues to appropriate scheduling. The older children are able to pursue more activities in a given length of time without becoming exhausted. The younger children will need more individual help and, therefore, require longer to go through routines. In mixed age groups there is sometimes difficulty with this fact, and the older children have to be allowed to move ahead of the younger ones to avoid being impatient or bored.

A small group of children can usually be accommodated in a flexible schedule. However, to accommodate large numbers of children where the sharing of equipment and space is required, tighter scheduling is inevitable. Care must be exercised in large groups to avoid forcing children into schedules that fail to meet their needs. Rigid rotation of groups of children among rooms and onto the playground often disregards children's needs and interests. For example, children should not be kept on the playground until another group is finished with an indoor activity if the children outdoors are getting cold and are ready to come indoors.

The Number of Adults on the Staff and Their Schedules

The teacher-child ratio influences the schedule. The larger the number of children each teacher must help, the less time teachers will have for each child and the less time there will be for additional learning activities. For example, if there are several helpers, then clean-up time goes quickly, or boots get put on in short order. If clean-up time goes quickly, perhaps the teacher has time for an interesting story and singing time, but if there is limited help then this vital part of the program may be curtailed. The number of adults will determine whether activities can be scheduled simultaneously in separate parts of a building, both indoors and out, or in small groups rather than in a large group.

The long days and sometimes evenings in child care centers require shifts of workers in order to get the work done. Coordinating incoming staff and assuring continuity is a constant task for all.

Communication and cooperation between shifts must be facilitated and encouraged. For example, late-afternoon staff and children can set up the room for the next morning's early arrivals. In addition to teachers' and caregivers' schedules, those of custodians, cooks, bus drivers, and nurses must be considered.

The Flexibility of the Facility

When space is used for many purposes, for example, for both eating and sleeping, then some difficulties in scheduling may arise because these activities overlap.

Some facilities are arranged so that some children can be scheduled indoors and others can be outdoors at the same time, whereas other buildings and climates do not permit children free movement back and forth.

Centers, especially those where children stay all day, must arrange space and schedules to get children out in the sunshine and fresh air to use their muscles in vigorous play even during cold and hot seasons. Some protected outdoor play areas are a must if all children's needs are to be met day in and day out throughout the year.

A Balance of Active and Quiet Activity

Within each group of activities a child should be free to select the type of activity his physical, physiological, social, and emotional clock is calling for. The teachers should be alert to each child's needs and, when necessary, guide a particular child into some activities that would be particularly helpful to him.

The Time of Year and Weather

Good schedules can change with the season. For example, using the outdoors early in the morning in spring may not be feasible because of spring rains. It may also be unfeasible for morning groups in winter because early morning may be the coldest and darkest part of the day. However, using the outdoors first for afternoon groups in winter gives children exercise they may miss from being at home all morning. This schedule enables mothers to dress children for outdoor play when they are getting them ready for school.

No matter what the season, each school needs a backup schedule for stormy days. All staff members need to know what the routine will be on days children cannot go outdoors. They can then quickly make the decisions that help keep children from getting confused and overstimulated. If staff members have prior agreement on the stormy-day routine, then they will proceed to guide children with calmness and confidence even if a rain comes up suddenly.

It should be emphasized that once a schedule is learned by the children any changes can cause mass confusion unless teachers take pains to guide children confidently. They can tell children several times during the morning, "Remember, we are having a backwards day today" or "Today we are playing outside first, then we are all going to hear a lady play a harp." More verbal guidance will be necessary when routines are interrupted. Children may get in the wrong places at the wrong times, and teachers should realize that this confusion is part of having the regular world jumbled up. However, as soon as the schedule stabilizes, children will again fit into whatever routine the teacher sets up, if it fairly accurately fits their needs for rest and action.

FLEXIBLE PLANNING

If all the foregoing factors that tend to influence scheduling are taken seriously, then the best plan is a flexible one. Using a *time block plan* enables the teacher to achieve objectives and still allows for the necessary flexibility. Large time blocks can be shortened or lengthened without disturbing children's sequence-of-events orientation. A time block plan readily accommodates to children's needs to the various activities, and to the surprises that each day brings.

Time Block Plan

In a short-day group in either morning or afternoon, there are usually three blocks of activities. They are (1) self-selected activity indoors, (2) teacher-instigated activity, and (3) self-selected activity outdoors. Though times on the outlines in Tables 1, 2, and 3 are designated, teachers feel free to vary them as their situations demand. For example, if during indoor self-selected activity period an especially intricate block structure is constructed that is completed at about 10:00 A.M. (the end of

Time Block I), the teacher may see a need for allowing children some additional time to play in their structure. This helps children feel that there is real reason to build something, for they actually get to play in it. Of course, it is always helpful that teachers make a habit of advising children when it is nearing

Table 1. *Sample Short-Day Schedule*

TIME BLOCK I—SELF-SELECTED ACTIVITY INDOORS

9:00–10:00   Greet children individually as they arrive. Each child puts his personal items in his locker and selects an activity from

Art	Blocks	Dramatic play
Science	Books	Small wheeled objects
Table games	Music	Language arts

TIME BLOCK II—TEACHER-INSTIGATED ACTIVITY

10:00–10:15   Clean up the room: each child helps with his area and then goes to the bathroom to use the toilet if needed and to wash his hands.

10:15–10:25   Snack: a low-keyed period of rest and refreshment. The children clear their own place and move quietly to the story area.

10:25–10:45   A combination of conversation, music, and story. The group may be divided into several small groups.

10:45–10:50   Toileting as needed. Dress for outdoor play.

TIME BLOCK III—SELF-SELECTED ACTIVITY OUTDOORS

10:45–11:35   Children dress for outdoors and move in small groups to the playground for self-selected activity:

| Large muscle equipment | Wheel toys | Sandbox | Science |

11:35–11:45   Clean-up time.

11:45   All children depart.

Table 2. *Sample Schedule for All-Day Groups*

TIME BLOCK I—SELF-SELECTED ACTIVITY INDOORS

6:00–8:00   Arrival of children.
Children put personal articles in lockers.
Breakfast for those who have not eaten.
Toileting as needed.
Self-selected activity (use of activity requiring minimum supervision because this is a period of low staff numbers).

8:00–9:30   Additional activities added to those previously available:

Art	Blocks	Dramatic play
Science	Books	Small wheeled objects
Table games	Music	Language arts

Table 2. (*cont.*)

TIME BLOCK II—TEACHER-INSTIGATED ACTIVITY

9:30–9:45   Clean-up time. Children assist in putting away materials in their correct place.
Toileting.   Hand washing.

9:45–10:00   Snack: a low-keyed period of rest and refreshment. The children clear their own place and move to designated areas for story, music, and conversation.

10:00–10:20   Story, music, and conversation in small groups.

TIME BLOCK III—SELF-SELECTED ACTIVITY OUTDOORS

10:20–10:30   Children dress for outdoors and move individually and in small groups to the play yard.

10:30–11:15   Children use large motor equipment, wheel toys, sandbox, science materials, etc.

11:15–11:25   Clean-up time.
Return to building.

TIME BLOCK IV—PREPARATION FOR AND EATING LUNCH

11:25–11:40   Removing outdoor wraps and placing in lockers.
Toileting and washing.

11:40–11:50   Quiet rest period, singing, story.

11:50–12:20   Lunch.

TIME BLOCK V—NAPTIME

12:20–1:15   When finished eating, each child goes to the bathroom to toilet and wash, then goes to nap room that has been prepared and darkened.

1:15–2:30   Sleep.

2:30–3:00   Awakening.
Toileting.
Dressing.
Quiet individual conversation or game.
Putting on outdoor wraps.

TIME BLOCK VI—SELF-SELECTED ACTIVITY

3:00–4:00   Outdoor play.

4:00–4:10   Clean-up play yard.

4:10–4:25   Snack time.
Toileting and washing as needed.

4:25–6:00   Quiet time indoors or in yard.
Story, singing, or records.
Dressing and dismissing children as parents arrive.

6:00   All children gone!

clean-up time. Children can then bring their play to some satisfactory conclusion. In some groups children have the opportunity to leave a block structure up for several days, adding to it and using it on ensuing days. This is feasible when only one group

Table 3. *Sample Daily Plan Sheet*
      Date _____

TIME BLOCK I—SELF-SELECTED ACTIVITY INDOORS

Time	Class of Activity	Specific Activity	Staff
9:00–10:00	Art	Fingerpaint	1. *Bob
	Science	Scrambled eggs	2. Mary
	Table games	Farm lotto	Mary
	Blocks	With telephones	Mary
	Small wheeled objects		Mary
	Books	On breakfast foods	3. Janice
	Language arts		Janice
	Music	Record player	Janice
	Dramatic play	Housekeeping	Janice
	Other		Janice

TIME BLOCK II—TEACHER-INSTIGATED ACTIVITY

10:00–10:15	Clean-up		1. *Bob
	Bathroom		2. Janice
10:15–10:25	Snack	Scrambled eggs, milk	1. *Mary
			2. Janice
			3. Bob
10:25–10:45	Story, music, and talk in small groups	Group 1. *Who's Got Farmer's Hat?*	Janice
		Group 2. *Farmer Small*	Mary
		Group 3. *A Visit to Grandpa's Farm*	Bob
		Songs: "Farmer in the Dell" and "Old McDonald"	
10:45–10:50	Toileting as needed		Bob
	Dress for outdoor play		Mary

TIME BLOCK III—SELF-SELECTED ACTIVITY OUTDOORS

10:45–11:45	Outdoors	Balance beam	1. *Janice
		Birds and leaves	2. Mary
11:40	Clean-up		3. Bob
11:45	Departure of children		

* No. 1 sets up activity, gets out equipment, completes clean-up.

uses the room and the space is not needed for something else, such as the placing of cots for sleeping.

A daily plan sheet, such as Table 3, is worked out in a regular planning session. The staff agrees on the goals they wish to achieve, and the main items are placed on the planning sheet. In some groups a large blackboard that is clearly visible to the staff is used to make a copy of the daily plan. This has the advantage that it can be checked from a distance. Seeing that Mary is on Snack, for example, the others would not worry about preparing and setting up Snack because they know Mary will take care of it. It helps to know which person will be first to go outside with the children, get out wheel toys, and set up new arrangements of equipment. In groups where assignment of duties is not agreed on in advance, shirking of responsibilities may occur—especially assisting outdoors when it is cold or helping at clean-up time. For good staff relations, a balanced, rotated schedule is most helpful.

A posted schedule of events and responsibilities helps everyone, children and staff alike, to know what comes after what and who is responsible for seeing that events happen. Also, parents coming into the center can see what is happening at a glance. A written plan aids in later evaluation.

When rain pours or an unexpected learning opportunity arises, changes can be made within the time blocks, thereby confusing the children as little as possible. For example, on a rainy day Time Block I can be extended a half hour and Time Block III shortened a half hour. Children may play some active games, do calisthenics indoors, or take a walk with umbrellas during the last half hour to give them vigorous exercise within the limits imposed by the total picture. If a special guest offers an unexpected learning opportunity, the teachers might agree to shelve the plan for the stories and listen to the visitor during the minutes usually devoted to stories.

When planning a field trip, if most of the sequence of events can be preserved—even though abbreviated—the children will have fewer questions about "What do we do now?" and "Where do we go?"

CONCLUSION

Scheduling is the structure that gives freedom to the preschool. The minutes on the clock are used only as approximations. Each group usually evolves a rather unique schedule, giving the preschool a flexible, easy-going feeling that makes it clear that the schedule is not a straitjacket. It takes careful thought to make the schedule meet the needs of everyone concerned.

APPLICATIONS

1. Copy down the posted schedule of a preschool. Observe to see how closely the teacher follows the schedule. Make notes where she deviates. Do you know why she made the changes? If appropriate, discuss the schedule with her. Summarize your findings.
2. Discuss the home routines a mother follows with a young child. Make a time block plan for the child's day.
3. Assist with a child in a home or a school for several hours. Can you observe that the child understands the schedule? Explain.
4. Describe the schedule that your case-study child seems to find comfortable. Note any rough spots as observed or reported by teacher or parent.

FOR FURTHER READING

AUERBACH, AARON G. "The Bisociative or Creative Act in the Nursery School." *Young Children*, Vol. 28, No. 1 (Oct. 1972), 27–31.

HILDEBRAND, VERNA. *Introduction to Early Childhood Education.* New York: Macmillan Publishing Co., Inc., 1971.

HILDEBRAND, VERNA. "Learning Tasks in the Preschool Years." *What's New in Home Economics*, Vol. 37, No. 1 (Jan. 1973), 27–30.

READ, KATHERINE. *The Nursery School.* Philadelphia: W. B. Saunders Company, 1971.

TODD, VIVIAN E. *The Aide in Early Childhood Education.* New York: Macmillan Publishing Co., Inc., 1973.

TODD, VIVIAN E., and HELEN HEFFERNAN. *The Years Before School.* New York: Macmillan Publishing Co., Inc., 1970.

Guiding Children's Toileting Routine

Remember
When you were a wee little tot,
When they took you out of your warm warm cot,
And told you to wee-wee whether you could or not?

T H U S goes a limerick that tickles the funny bones of the school-aged set. But there is more truth than fiction in the lines. The toileting routine has consumed much of parents' and teachers' time over the years. With more infants in public nurseries and more children entering nursery schools and day care centers, teachers' concern for the toileting routine remains.

"I think Mark is well enough trained that he can go to the nursery school now," says Mark's mother. Betty's mother wants to go to work, and Jackie's mother has to go to work. Their children are recent graduates to training pants. How will the teachers and their assistants help these children complete their toilet training? How can we help them become self-directing in the matter of elimination and maintain their happy personalities in the process?

INFANTS AND TODDLERS

Now with younger and younger children enrolling in nurseries and child care centers we may be getting over the unbending rule calling for toilet training before entering school. It would eliminate mothers' tongue-in-cheek statements and a lot of pressure on some children.

Babies and toddlers in diapers do take more time to attend than toilet-trained youngsters. That's one reason the adult-child ratio must be higher for these

139

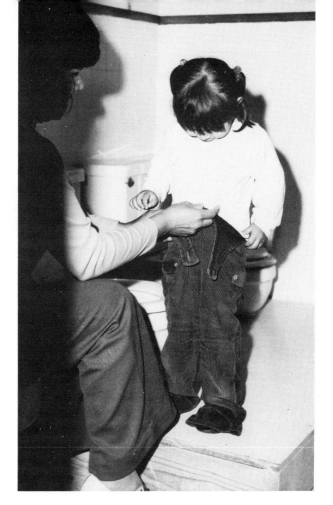

Caregivers find it convenient to sit while helping children with their dressing and with many other tasks. (University of Houston, Rebecca Hines, Photographer.)

children. The routines and attitudes developed by caregivers are highly important to the child's feelings about this important function of eliminating body wastes. Dr. James Hymes, Jr., said some years ago, "everyone of us accepts the fact that babies wet. We don't let wetting throw us off our stride. We plan for it and arrange our lives accordingly. What do we do with babies? We let them wet."[1] It is an attitude that is worth adopting.

In the high-quality infant care center, care is taken to change the baby when needed, to use clean supplies, and to dispose of soiled diapers in a sanitary manner. It is important to follow the prescribed

[1] James L. Hymes, Jr., *Behavior and Misbehavior* (Englewood Cliffs, N.J.: Prentice-Hall, 1955), p. 30.

procedures. Also important is for a caregiver to talk to the baby during changes to let him know that she loves him and enjoys making him comfortable.

Any unusual bowel movements should be reported to the health supervisor, because these may signal some health change or problem with a food. Diarrhea is a serious ailment for babies, and caregivers should recognize it and report it immediately. Babies should never be spoken to harshly because they need a change. They are simply not mature enough to do things any differently. Harsh treatment can cause babies to become fearful and therefore may actually delay their eventual training. Acceptance of the baby and love during the training period are essential. Babies simply need to be changed as their diapers become wet or soiled.

At about eighteen months the child usually matures sufficiently for adults to consider toilet training. The child may fuss immediately after he wets or soils his diaper, indicating that he doesn't like it. When changed immediately, he gets the feeling of improvement related to being dry. A caregiver or mother may begin to note that the child urinates or defecates immediately after eating or waking up. These habits indicate that these may be good times to try him on the toilet. The toilets should be low and small to help the child feel safe and secure. A potty can be used for training. The toddler may be in the bathroom when others use the bathroom. The child can be allowed to see the results of using the toilet—the urine in the potty. Or he may hear the urine running into the toilet water. He will feel pleasure and new comfort in having eliminated into the toilet. You can simply say, "A good job" or "You DID it!" The child likes to please parents and caregivers.

If the child cannot use the toilet after a short stay, then reattach his diapers and plastic pants and wait for more positive signs. If he shows resistance to being placed on the toilet seat, then forget it until a later date.

Sometimes a change to training pants helps training, because the child can see and feel the urine coming out. This might be feasible when the child is going to be out in the yard on a warm day.

Even among the Marks, Bettys, and Jackies whose mothers think they are trained, the teacher must be constantly vigilant. Experienced teachers learn the signs of need, such as holding the genital area or dancing around. Some children get unusually quiet when they are having a bowel movement, some even hide.

Each child will be different, but it helps the child and saves the teacher time and trouble if she can read the signs before the "accident" occurs. She will try to teach the child to tell her when he needs to go or to go on his own to the bathroom. Don't tarry when the child tells you he needs to go, because the time between when he recognizes the signal and when he starts urinating may be only a split second. The teacher should check with each mother for her child's word for toileting, because there are some unusual ones used whose meaning might not be guessed until it was too late. Mothers may need guidance regarding the type of clothing that is most helpful to training. Play pants with elastic waistbands seem to be the quickest and offer the child the best chance for self-help.

A routine of toileting reminders is customary in most nursery schools. As noted on the sample schedules in Chapter 9, toileting is scheduled after breakfast, after playtime, after outdoor play, just before lunch, after lunch, after nap, and after being outdoors in the afternoon. These are times when the teacher methodically checks each child to see if he needs to eliminate. Both indirect guidance and direct guidance—verbal, physical, and affective—are useful in guiding children in toileting routines. These techniques can be reviewed in Chapters 4 and 5.

Because nursery school aged children are in the "negative" stage, it is well to learn to avoid asking them directly if they need to go to the bathroom, for they will surely say, "No." Say instead, "Time to go to the bathroom." You can just accept it if a child volunteers, "I don't need to go," but you can still invite him to "wash your hands." The presence of the toilet and other children using it may be suggestion enough if he needs to go.

It is important to allow children to grow in their

ability to hold the urine and not contribute to their urinary frequency. Therefore, if a child can go all morning without using the toilet, then fine. Some mothers indicate the child uses the toilet the minute he gets home. If a child is afraid of the school toilet he may need to stay at school for only an hour or so each day until he becomes comfortable at school.

There are wide individual differences among children as to when conscious control of bowels and urination is a fact. Boys are trained more slowly and at an older age than girls, according to studies that have been made, and teachers and mothers of boys should keep this in mind. It is simply not fair to expect them to be trained as quickly as girls, and lots of little boys would be happier more relaxed people today if their parents and caregivers had known this. Pressure to be trained before the muscles are mature enough does not help training and can have detrimental effects on a child's personality.

Some children are actually fearful of the flushing noise of the toilet, so teachers may need to trip the lever themselves after the child leaves the bathroom.

Tooth brushing is a hard skill to learn. It deserves emphasis by both parents and teachers, for long hours without brushing may hasten tooth decay. (Southern University, Baton Rouge, Louisiana, Eddie Hildreth, Photographer.)

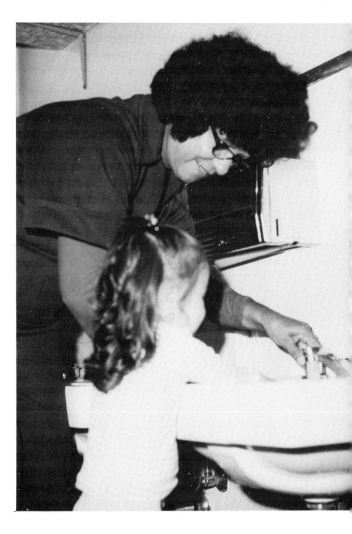

Washing hands is the nicest part of getting ready for lunch. Children may enjoy a few moments of water play as they wash up. (University of Houston, Rebecca Hines, Photographer.)

Actually, another child will often oblige, having no hesitancy about the noise himself. Flushing is not a necessary part of training; therefore, teachers are well advised to keep the emphasis on the important part, the use of the toilet.

Little boys can sit to urinate, and some girls can stand! The convention will eventually be learned, so you need not worry. Because boys have poor aim, they will get the toilet seat wet unless they lift it before urinating. Raising the seat, like flushing, is part of the routine you can help with if it seems too complicated for a given child. Occasionally little boys have erections when they start to urinate, which makes it difficult to aim accurately. They may urinate on the floor, quite by accident. Cleaning around the toilet with a disinfectant is essential if the bathroom is to remain a pleasant place. This is a standard practice of good custodial service. Aerosol spray helps with the odor but should be kept out of the reach of children.

Both boys and girls toilet together during nursery school and kindergarten. They learn valuable facts about sex differences in this casual way. Their questions can be answered matter-of-factly and without embarrassment. Teachers and caregivers should take children's curiosity as a matter of learning, not premature sex deviance.

Helping in the bathroom means lots of buttoning and bending. When there is room, you will be more comfortable if you sit on a low chair near the door. Your presence and counsel may be all that is necessary. The child doesn't need a tall observer looming over him.

The child having a bowel movement needs to wipe and may require some advice about folding the tissue. Sometimes adults may need to help with wiping.

Accidents will happen, so accept them cheerfully and move to remedy the situation as quickly as possible. Children usually keep a set of dry clothes at school for this and other types of accidents. Each helper should know where the child's clothes are kept, for the child will be much happier wearing his own clothes rather than those the school might keep on hand for emergencies. The child who wets should be encouraged to use the toilet—he may not be finished! The child who defecates may practically need a sponge bath.

When possible, it helps avoid embarrassment for the child to take him to a bathroom where you can clean him up in private. Otherwise you just have to explain to his curious friends that "He had an accident like some of us do sometimes. I'm helping him get fixed up." Some children make critical comments to the child. Even parents and the child's siblings may not be sympathetic. The teacher may offer them guidance as to a more helpful reaction.

Once the child is dry, the soiled clothes must be

wrapped and put in a paper sack, labeled with the child's name, and placed in his locker to be sent home.

Kindergarteners will be very embarrassed if they have an accident. These usually happen because they do not want to interrupt an activity to take care of toileting. Teachers may simply note the signs and quietly advise them to go before they have an accident.

The average child is not dry at night until he is three. This statistic means that half are older than three before they are dry at night. The same patience is required in caring for wet sleeping children as for awake ones. They should be loved in spite of wetting. They should be taken to the toilet just prior to going to bed and immediately upon awaking. If a child awakens wet, have him try to use the toilet, for he may not be through urinating and would likely wet the diaper before you got him back in bed.

It is better to place double diapers and plastic pants on a child than to bother him once he is asleep, unless awakening him actually keeps him dry. Very likely the less pressure that is placed on the child the sooner he will be trained. His muscles simply must mature, and usually he does want to be trained. The pediatrician should advise parents when other measures should be taken.

Children usually enjoy washing with soap and water. They may actually prolong the process, liking the feel of the soap and water. If children repeatedly tarry at the lavatory, some arrangements for water play during self-selected activity period might be indicated. The crucial time to wash is before eating, others may not be worth making an issue of.

In some schools tooth brushing and hair combing are taught as routines. Little holders for each child's toothbrush and comb are made and carefully labeled for him. Baths also may be in order for children who do not have such care at home. Caregivers are, of course, cautioned never to leave the child alone in his bath, for a small amount is enough water for drowning.

Some children handle their genitals more than others. This is called *masturbation*. It gives children a pleasurable sensation and is sometimes comforting. Masturbation is itself a harmless habit, but the punishing or admonishing attitudes of adults may actually make it into a problem for the child.

Handling of genitals may be a symptom of need to urinate. Some children seem to be literally holding it back, sometimes because they want to finish a game or something they've started. If you promise to "save" their place, they may be willing to go take care of their need. Occasionally a child has a rash in the genital area that he is merely rubbing. Teachers should be alert to advise parents or the nurse that the child may need medication. Underwear that is too tight or improperly cut can contribute to the child's pulling at it, which may be interpreted by some as masturbation. This, too, is a problem that is far more easily remedied than tension produced over masturbation.

Toilet training, like everything else the child learns, is not all learned at school. The child is at home more than he is at school. Communication is essential with each child's mother so that successes, failures, and techniques of training may be shared. Because a change in toilet habits may signal some illness, you should report these to parents. Any emotional crisis—a move to a new house, a new baby at home, or a parent being away on a trip—may be emotionally upsetting to a child and interfere with training. Parents should advise teachers about any unusual events that might influence behavior at school, especially toileting, eating, or sleeping.

CONCLUSION

Guiding children's toilet-training habits should be done in a helpful, happy way. A supporting teacher and parent who have patience enough to work with and not against the natural maturation of the child will be most successful. Pressure results only in resistance, negativism, unhappiness, and often damage to the child's personality. Children can get the upper hand as they exercise their autonomy, so it is wise to relax when you see indications of resistance. Both the indirect and direct techniques of guidance will be useful in guiding children's toileting.

147 *Conclusion*

APPLICATIONS

1. Assist with at least two children in the toilet room either at home or at school. Did they go to the toilet on their own initiative? Were they able to attend to their clothing independently? Were they comfortable and free from anxiety in the situation? Explain your answers. What were the differences between the children?
2. Discuss toilet training with a mother or a teacher. Find out what she thinks is the best time for initiating toilet training. Find out what procedures she recommends to others. Write a report of your conclusions.
3. Discuss among your friends the various names that have been given the toileting experience. Write them down to share with the class.
4. Report the toilet-training history of your case-study child. Confer with parent or teacher or both.

FOR FURTHER READING

BRECKENRIDGE, MARIAN E., and MARGARET NESBITT MURPHY. *Growth and Development of the Young Child.* Philadelphia: W. B. Saunders Company, 1969.

HILDEBRAND, VERNA. *Introduction to Early Childhood Education.* New York: Macmillan Publishing Co., Inc., 1971.

LANDRETH, CATHERINE. *Early Childhood: Behavior and Learning.* New York: Alfred A. Knopf, Inc., 1967.

SMART, MOLLIE S., and RUSSELL C. SMART. *Children: Development and Relationships.* New York: Macmillan Publishing Co., Inc., 1972.

SPOCK, BENJAMIN C. *Baby and Child Care.* New York: Pocket Books, Simon & Schuster, Inc., 1968.

STONE, L. JOSEPH, and JOSEPH CHURCH. *Childhood & Adolescence.* New York: Random House, Inc., 1973.

TODD, VIVIAN E. *The Aide in Early Childhood Education.* New York: Macmillan Publishing Co., Inc., 1973.

TODD, VIVIAN E., and HELEN HEFFERNAN. *The Years Before School.* New York: Macmillan Publishing Co., Inc., 1970.

Guiding Children's Eating Behavior

Annette, age three, handled her spoon with ease at the lunch table. She liked the tomato and apple wedges that she ate with her fingers. She poured herself three small glasses of milk. She talked very little during the meal.

ANNETTE was considered a good eater in the child care center's lunchroom. Her meal was small by adult standards, but she was growing and was full of energy for the many activities that kept her busy. Annette's present good eating habits are an outgrowth of the attention that good nutrition and feeding were given during her mother's pregnancy and since her birth. Some of these early feeding concerns are discussed in the following section because infant caregivers today may care for some babies only a few months old and will need an understanding of infant feeding practices beginning with birth.

FEEDING INFANTS

During pregnancy the mother's health and nutrition significantly affect the baby developing within her. Regular checks of her diet are made. In addition, she plans with her doctor what type of feeding she expects to give her new baby. If she is going to breast feed the baby she will begin to prepare her breasts, toughening them a bit through massage so they won't feel sore when the infant nurses.

She will begin nursing the first day after birth. The child will get colostrum, a thin yellow liquid, and not milk. The colostrum contains antibodies that help prevent illnesses during the early months

149

Considerable skill is needed to get spoon, mouth, and food coordinated. The first efforts at self-feeding are about like this whether the child starts helping himself age fourteen months or age three. (Frances Kertesz, Photographer.)

of an infant's life. This colostrum is one of the decided advantages that breast-fed infants have over bottle-fed ones, because a substitute for it has not been found to supplement formula.

A baby who is going to be bottle fed will be given some water and eventually some formula in the hospital nursery. Babies have an instinctive sucking reflex that permits them to feed during their first days even though they have never had to feed before. They also have a rooting reflex whereby they actively seek the nipple when touched on the lips or cheek.

Self-demand Schedule A self-demand schedule is advisable for babies. This means that they are fed when they appear to need it and are not made to wait until some magic time on the clock. This type of schedule allows for the wide differences that exist among babies. At first, one may need to be fed every two hours whereas the baby next to him in the nursery may not need to nurse for four hours.

If the mother is planning to bottle feed her baby, she is given a hormone drug that keeps her milk supply from coming in. For breast-fed babies the mother's milk supply comes in about the fourth to fifth day, stimulated by the several days of sucking of colostrum and rooting by the baby. When hospitals have a "rooming-in" plan allowing mothers to have babies in their hospital rooms much of the day, they help them gain knowledge about baby care and the special needs of their own babies.

Usually the mothers do not bring their babies to infant care centers for at least three months after birth. Many take a year's maternity leave in order to spend the first year at home with the baby. Increasingly, employers are making such allowances in their contracts with women—some indicating that childbirth is just as valid a reason for "sick leave" as an appendectomy or a male's hernia operation.

The first months are the most critical for the infant's feeding. By three months most problems with formula are corrected, and routines have been established. Usually the child's diet will be supplemented by solid foods by then.

If the child is bottle fed, he should be cuddled closely just as he is when he is breast fed. This close relationship with the mother at feeding time is of greatest importance to the development of security and trust in the child. This close relationship during feeding should be carried over into the nursery by the caregivers in charge. They should learn from the mother as much as possible about the usual habits of the baby. Propping the bottle is not a recommended feeding procedure at home or in a nursery.

Solid Food and Weaning   The doctor will determine when the baby will be given his first "solids"—actually *strained foods* such as cereals, mashed banana, and applesauce. The baby is held in a semi-sitting position for feeding. The little plastic baby carrier makes a good feeding seat for an infant about four months old, for in it his head is elevated enough to avoid choking. The mother or caregiver uses a small spoon and talks to the baby as she feeds him. Most of us find that we open our own mouths and move our lips much as we expect the baby to as he eats.

In a month or two the baby will begin *self-help*. He will reach for the spoon while he is being fed. He is beginning to learn to imitate feeding movements. He may enjoy being able to munch on a graham cracker. Even though toothless, he has strong gums that break off bits of cracker, and as it mixes with his saliva he actually begins feeding himself. The food must be placed far back on the baby's tongue. When placed on the tip of the tongue, the baby simply pushes it out of his mouth. It takes months of practice before a baby can load a spoon and move it to his mouth without spilling.

"Solids" with their new flavors and consistency may seem strange to the baby, so it is wise to try only a select few at first. This enables you to determine which ones the child likes and to use them for a time before branching out. When a child seems to dislike a food, then it should be omitted for a time. There are so many good foods available that there is no use making an issue over a specific food.

Chopped foods gradually replace strained foods in the diet. Even though the teeth are of minimum chewing help during the first year, the gums are strong and the child can handle and enjoy firm foods such as banana, cooked green beans, beets, and potatoes. By nine months most infants can sit with the family occasionally during one of their three meals. Midmorning and afternoon fruit juice and milk may be given in the bottle at naptime.

Weaning from the breast or bottle usually comes during the last three months of the first year. The baby can adapt to a cup gradually as sips of orange juice, water, or milk are offered. He learns gradually how to manage the cup and to avoid the spilling that is a part of learning. When gradually done, weaning is a comfortable process of growth.

Whether infants are cared for by parents or caregivers, eating habits are established during the early

A midmorning snack provides rest and helps restore energy needed for play. A dietitian may check on quantities children like. (Howard University, Flemmie Kittrell Project, Scurlock Photographers.)

months that make a difference in the baby's later growth and development. Feeding must be individualized, carried out with warmth and with attention to details of sanitation and nutrition. The goals of feeding during these early months are

1. To establish an eating pattern that will provide the baby adequate nutrition for optimum growth.

2. To acquaint the baby with a variety of foods of high nutritional quality that he will learn to enjoy eating.

153 *Feeding Infants*

3. To develop food habits that will make future feeding easy.

4. To encourage the baby's growth toward self-feeding.

FEEDING PRESCHOOLERS

Food needs of preschool children are less and appetites diminished compared to infancy levels because the rate of growth is not now so fast as it is during infancy. A child who may have once been a "good eater" may disturb his parents or teachers with this change. At this time he also presses for more decision-making and may say "No" and close his mouth to previously relished foods.

Feeding times in nursery schools and in day care centers vary according to the length of the time children stay in the center. Breakfasts for children arriving early are usually served. Some nursery schools serve only a midmorning snack, whereas others also serve a lunch. Afternoon children may arrive just in time for lunch, then have midafternoon snack.

Guiding preschoolers' mealtimes is an important aspect of helping them toward self-direction. Satisfying food needs contributes to the child's physiological needs, which in turn influences his social and emotional behavior. For example, studies indicate a much greater number of anger outbursts when a child is hungry. Angry outbursts will make it more difficult for him to get along well with other children.

Breakfast

Breakfast is an important meal because during the night the body has its longest period without food. The fuel supply simply must be replenished just as an empty gas tank needs a supply of gasoline so the car can move. There are many delicious and interesting foods to entice children to eat breakfast.

There are differences among children as to when they prefer breakfast. Some like it immediately upon awakening, whereas others like to play a while and then eat. In child care centers we must accommodate to each type of child.

Mothers find that children eat a better breakfast if the mother sits with them, engaging in social conversation rather than going busily about household chores. Duties such as picking up and washing dishes, telephoning, and so on may distract the child and may communicate the message that the mother is in a hurry and the child's breakfast is in the way.

In day care centers caregivers should also sit with children, giving them guidance and personal attention during this crucial mealtime. The breakfast menus should vary just as luncheon menus vary. In one center it was sad to see small children with sleep still in their eyes eating their bowls of dry cereal at a lonely and uninterestingly arranged table. They sat all by themselves while caregivers hovered together at a distance gossiping over their coffee.

Breakfasting children usually arrive a few at a time. Some may want to play or even rest a while before eating. Breakfasting children should be served at a small table by an adult who can talk to them and encourage their eating. The adult might eat her own breakfast there or drink a cup of coffee in a sociable manner. Children not eating well may be ready for a substantial snack by midmorning.

It is highly probable that the child's bowel movement will occur shortly after breakfast or after a short period of activity that follows breakfast. Therefore, adults should be alert to guiding children toward the bathroom at this time to aid in regularizing elimination habits.

Lunch   Serving lunch is usually done on a more total group basis than breakfast, because children will be together and the time will be set to complement the other activities of the day. After a busy morning including outdoor play, it helps to gather the children in quiet groups after they have toileted and are washed up for lunch to have them rest before eating. Rested children will eat better and more independently than tired children. The group can listen to a story, sing quiet songs, and stretch out on a carpet if they desire. This quiet time can be more informal than a regular naptime. Calling it "quiet time" or "singing time" may remove the curse that rest time often has for some children.

If children are keyed up from active outdoor play

Meals of nutritious food are essential for healthy bodies. (Howard University, Flemmie Kittrell Project.)

or from other active events and are brought directly to the lunch tables, caregivers will soon discover they are inviting disorder during the lunch period. These children often will not relax in their chairs, but will want to be up moving about. If they are tired, they may also be argumentative or want to be fed by the caregiver.

Seating   Each child should have a designated spot for his eating space. Place cards will help designate the spot as his own personal space. It is helpful if the child eats with the same teacher or assistant every day, because she can provide security for the child at a time when he may be somewhat more susceptible to strain. If the same person helps at a child's table each day, she will learn his eating habits and be able to help him most effectively. The seating can be arranged so that compatible children eat together.

Occasionally children who you feel would be friends if they knew each other better may be seated together. Experienced good eaters may be seated with less experienced or finicky eaters to serve as models for them. Generally an adult can effectively help five or six children at most. She should be seated near the middle of a small table where she can reach each child. Volunteers should be enlisted if there are not enough helpers for this ratio.

Serving Family-style service is best. The prepared food is placed before the teacher in serving bowls. She serves each child the amount of each food she thinks he will eat. A few peas or only a teaspoonful of potatoes may be a serving for some children, whereas others may want much more. One teacher calls tiny servings that she hopes children will taste the "No thank you" portions. She asks them just to taste one bite. Of course, they frequently like it well enough to ask for more.

The teacher may serve seconds or allow the children to serve their own seconds. It is convenient to give the children a small dessert spoon when letting them serve seconds. Serving himself helps a child learn to gauge his needs.

The rule "Take what you'll eat and eat what you take" is helpful for children to learn. It usually is far better to serve an amount that the child calls "not enough" and let him have seconds than to serve him "too much." A clean plate is a worthy goal, but the servers must be careful to do their part in achieving that goal. Obesity is a growing childhood, as well as adulthood, problem that may result from rigid adherence to a clean plate rule.

Other problems may arise from giving children an overlarge portion. For example, on one occasion the teacher was distracted by a conversation with a child as she filled a plate. She put a "too large" serving of the main dish on the child's plate, but told the child that he didn't have to eat it all. It would have been better to have removed some of the food before handing it to this child. He was a very conscientious child who tried to follow the clean plate rule. He ate and ate until he was virtually in pain before he gave up.

Milk is best served in small glasses. Seconds can be poured by the child himself from a small pitcher that doesn't tip easily. Adults should pour into the small pitcher only the amount required by the glass, or the child is likely to run the glass over. Pouring his own milk increases the child's feeling of independence and his milk consumption.

Toast sticks, sandwiches, and vegetable pieces can serve as pushers as the child learns to maneuver his food onto the spoons and forks. Say, "Use your pusher to help keep your fingers out of food." Many finger foods are provided in nursery school to aid the child in being a self-feeder. Carrot sticks, orange or apple slices, green pepper, cabbage or tomato wedges are examples. Even some meats can be served this way. Others can be cooked soft enough to be easily cut by the side of the fork. Knives are quite hard for nursery school children to manage.

Dessert should be planned to add to the nutritional quality of the meal and should, therefore, be given to all children and never used as a reward for eating all of the main meal. It is customary in many groups for the child to carry his first-course plate to the serving cart to receive his dessert. This movement gives the child a little chance to exercise, which some children need. After eating his dessert he then takes the remaining dishes and silverware to the cart before proceeding to the bathroom to wash.

Bibs are important for the younger children who are learning to feed themselves. Napkins will suffice for the older ones. They may need advice about spreading them out on their laps for maximum protection.

Regardless of the care given to toileting prior to lunch, children may realize a need just at mealtime. There is no alternative but to allow the child to go to the bathroom. Hopefully, a lunchroom helper is available to attend to such a child so the teacher at the table does not have to leave her group.

When children expect to be fed by an adult, prior training is likely at fault. However, the child might be tired, and an earlier lunchtime or more attention to rest during the morning may be called for. Also, the child might not really be hungry, so he can be encouraged to feed himself and the amount he eats accepted.

Atmosphere The atmosphere of mealtime should be quiet and as relaxing as possible. Mealtime should be set (or the amount and timing of the midmorning snack adjusted) so that children are hungry but not starving. Attention should be focused on the eating tasks and less on conversation. Young children have a hard time attending to both at once. Conversation between tables should be highly discouraged, for it has to be loud to be heard and raises the tension within the room. Adults should be attending to children's needs and conversation and not conversing among themselves.

Mealtime is a time a child may be lonesome for home. The foods offered may be so like what he eats at home or so different that they make him homesick. Tiredness may contribute to this problem, also. A new child may need several weeks to become accustomed to the type of foods and manner of serving it in nursery school.

Sufficient time should be allowed for children to eat without rushing. If they show indications of merely dawdling or playing with their food, they should be encouraged without admonition to take their plate to the cart, get their dessert, and complete their meal.

Some children may not be accustomed to sitting down for any sustained period during mealtime. Explaining to them that "We get up when we are ready for dessert" may be an appropriate reminder. Then if a child gets up, tell him "If you are finished take your plate to the lady at the cart." If he is indeed not finished but must give up his food, he'll likely remember it on the next day and stay in his place. A helper in the lunchroom should firmly direct children who get up too soon back to their table. This help will avoid the distraction for the teacher at the table.

A helper should be available in the bathroom to receive children who are through with lunch and need to wash. This allows the teacher to remain at the table until the last child finishes. Children usually need to urinate and may need to have a bowel movement after lunch.

Menus Preschool children can learn to enjoy a wide variety of new foods. However, new foods should be introduced in small quantities along with familiar, well-liked food. Children like their food "apart," as one child called it. Therefore, separate vegetables are preferred to a mixed salad, and a meat is preferred to stew.

Children prefer foods of a lukewarm temperature —neither very hot nor very cold. You should allow the soup to cool before serving. Children like ice cream, but you often see them stir it or allow it to sit for a while before eating.

Crisp toast and sticks of vegetables make good chewing for children's teeth and are good "pushers" that help them get foods onto the spoon.

Foods high in roughage or highly seasoned are not considered best for young children because they irritate the lining of their immature digestive tracts.

Color, flavor, and textures are important in young children's menus as they are in adults'. If you wish to experiment to see how children notice color, as one teacher does, try having everything a single color one day. She even colors the milk green!

Children's menus usually have a meat or meat substitute, a cooked vegetable, a raw vegetable or fruit, a dessert, and milk. Excessive sweets are avoided in drinks and desserts. Some children tend to fill up on anything sweet and thus miss needed nutrients.

Foods especially enjoyed by various ethnic groups should be worked into the menus. Sometimes these can be main dishes, at other times they can be tasting experiences. Parents can be helpful in suggesting favorite foods from their ethnic group. These foods offer a learning experience for children and staff outside the ethnic group as well as provide a touch of familiarity to the children from the group.

The land-grant colleges in most states have nutrition advisers who can work with nursery school and day care center lunch programs. They give help with menu planning and with securing and using surplus commodities.

Accidents   Spilling and even breakage may occur. A helper should have a dustpan, broom, and sponge handy to make quick work of any accident. The child should not be scolded for the accident. With some assessment of the situation, preventive measures might help avoid accidents. For example, in one group the addition of a small side tray made the children's table less crowded, and fewer spills occurred.

Attitudes   Adults' attitudes may interfere with good mealtime guidance. Good food costs money and takes time to prepare and should be appreciated, they think. Thus it is very hard for some adults to see a child refuse food that they like. They feel it is wasteful, too, because they know the food will be thrown away. We have our own food attitudes, which may be very different from those of our coteachers and the children. If we can accept the differences among the adults, then we should be able to accept them between ourselves and the children.

We wouldn't tell our coteacher that she should eat sweet potatoes because we like them. We wouldn't tell her to eat more mashed potatoes or squash, or that she'd had enough milk, so we shouldn't tell children that. The amount required and the kind of foods liked are very personal tastes.

The family's culture, life style, education, income, and values will make the meal situation in each home different. As teachers, we must learn to respect these differences, as they are bound to affect the children in our groups.

As adults serving children's food needs, we should be open to trying new foods and never display food aversions to the children. If there is something you can't eat, don't talk about it—just don't serve yourself any.

Children will especially enjoy food they have helped make. With a little careful planning and coordination of functions, children can help prepare an item for their lunch. Perhaps it will be a soup that takes two days to make, or a Jello dessert. Whatever it will be, they will surely pronounce it "good."

Midmorning or Midafternoon Snack A refreshment break helps the child in several ways. He gets a little fuel for his furnace, he rests a bit, and he has good fellowship in the process. He may be introduced to important concepts through foods such as classification of foods as vegetables, fruits, meat, and so on.

Snacks may be simple or elaborate depending on children's needs, other meals at the school, finances, and the snack planner's creativity. There are numerous opportunities within the curriculum of the school to plan experiences with food that can be used as the snack for the groups. Food experiences offer some children a personal involvement that they may not find in other curriculum materials. They like to work with food—and to eat it!

There is no need for snacks to be humdrum and ordinary. The list of possible food and cooking projects gets longer and longer as creative teachers set their minds to the task. From instant puddings to pancakes, banana bread, applesauce, deviled eggs, or self-squeezed orange juice, the projects that are most successful are those to which the child can contribute by cutting a fruit "all by himself," by squeezing, by stirring, or by adding an ingredient. Following a good learning experience, with a delicious aroma filling the air, and all his friends trying it, what child could resist the food even if it was one he'd declared to his mother he "hated" numerous times?

Beverage for snack is important for children. They do get thirsty with so much talking and running. Water might well be served more frequently during the day than it is in many groups. An accessible, easy-to-work fountain is a "must" for children's centers both indoors and out. Milk is such an important food in children's diets that it often is a preference for snack times. Even children who claim they don't like milk may change when they see their friends and teachers enjoying it.

Service of snacks can be more social and laced with learning experiences than may be possible with meals. Snacks are merely refreshments, so children can consider a few other things while eating them. A casual arrangement with perhaps only a paper cup and a napkin is needed. Place cards are useful to guide children to appropriate seats and to challenge their reading skills in addition to defining "personal space." Name tags can be color coded to match place cards at the table. After a child is finished, he should be able to take his cup and napkin to a designated tray or wastebasket. Some children may enjoy taking turns being on a committee responsible for setting up the snack, cleaning up after the snack, and helping plan the menus.

To avoid spilled beverage glasses, help children form a habit of setting their glasses toward the center of the table. You can say, "Mary, put your glass at the top of your plate." A child's inclination is to set the glass near the edge of the table nearest the hand he uses most in eating, thus making it easy to knock over the glass when not looking.

Guiding Table Behavior   Guiding children during meals and at snack time calls for adults to apply the basic guidance principles discussed earlier. Much of this chapter has dealt with setting the stage for children to become self-directed eaters, that is, through indirect guidance. Clearly, many instances of direct verbal, physical, and affective guidance are called for. Positive statements such as "Chew and swallow your food, Cammie, then you may talk" are often helpful. Giving the child a choice when one is feasible such as "Would you like more milk?" often comes in handy. Physical modeling of behavior that you want the child to learn such as "Cut your meat, like this," accompanied by a quick demonstration, may be helpful. Using short sentences and giving only one direction at a time such as "Feet under the table, Bob" usually bring results.

Guidance techniques are needed to help children learn the eating rules or "manners." These rules or manners help people know the acceptable behavior within a group. Teachers will think of table manners in a broad context. They can decide on some fundamental rules or "manners" that they feel the children are capable of learning and that will make their living together more pleasant. In their decision they will consider the age level of the children and the type of experiences they have had prior to coming to school.

Table manners vary among families. Teachers must be careful not to evaluate the manners that the families have as "good" or "bad."

In a group it will help the service if each child waits his turn while the teacher serves the food. This is a school rule or "manner" to be learned. Passing a plate of carrot sticks with each child taking "one" may be a new "manner" for some children.

Chewing with the mouth closed and learning to chew food and swallow before talking are other "manners." Wiping the lips with a napkin, holding the napkin on the lap, and wiping the hands on it are also "manners." Holding a glass without spilling and drinking milk without blowing bubbles are "manners." Swallowing food before drinking may be difficult for some children whose parents may have encouraged them to wash down their food. Talking quietly at the table and waiting while others finish are "manners."

Holding tools correctly is a convention that must also be learned, as well as using the appropriate tool for a particular food. Keeping food on the plate instead of laying it around the plate as is allowed on the highchair tray may be a new "manner" to learn.

"Please" and "thank you" will come as children imitate adults who use these phrases. As you see, our manners are the rules we use at mealtime to make the occasion more pleasant for all concerned.

TEACHERS' MEALTIMES

Teachers' food needs usually must all be met as they deal with the children in the meal situation. They too need food in order to have energy to work and emotional stability to keep them on an even keel with their colleagues and the children. A systematic arrangement of the mealtime allows teachers more of a chance to relax, eat well, and still guide children effectively. A seating plan should be posted periodically and should divide among the adults the difficult children who need closer attention. This will minimize arguments among children and avoid many last-minute changes that are apt to be disruptive. Advance planning can assure more equity for both children and teachers. A teacher feels more effective when no more children are assigned than she can relate to comfortably.

Children's food tends to be too bland for most adult tastes. Consequently, salt and pepper should be available. It may be desirable to have coffee available, also. Adults should be sure to eat sufficient food even on those difficult days when frequent interruptions occur.

New teachers and substitutes should be briefed regarding children's eating habits to enable them to carry on as effectively as possible with the plan being followed for each child.

CONCLUSION

From the moment of conception, nutrition plays an important role in the child's development. After birth, infant feeding is regarded as a very serious matter that is critical to life itself. Caregivers who assume the care of an infant will expect to build on the foundations of diet and procedures established by the mother in the early months. The goal is to provide sufficient nourishing foods to fulfill energy and growth needs.

Preschool children's appetites appear to decrease as their growth rate decreases. Parents and caregivers are cautioned against pressuring children to eat. Children should be allowed to decide when they have had enough. The "clean plate" rule may contribute to obesity.

In child care centers the primary goal of mealtime and snack time is to provide nutritional foods required for energy and growth needs; however, these periods also afford opportunities for rest, for socialization, and for learning facts about foods. Teachers and parents alike must use suitable guidance for establishing good food habits and mealtime behavior.

1. Remember the goal is for children to eat sufficient nourishing food to provide for energy needs and growth, not to eat any particular food.

2. Remember that the preschooler's food needs are less than when he was younger because he isn't growing as fast.

3. Give the child a rest period just before mealtime.

4. Serve meals before the child gets overly hungry or tired.

5. Serve foods in small servings, making it possible for the child to serve himself seconds.

6. Serve new foods in small amounts with known and liked foods.

7. Accept the fact that children like lukewarm foods.

8. Allow children to feed themselves finger foods.

9. Avoid excessive sweets in drinks, desserts, and snacks that would interfere with the child's eating nutritious foods.

10. Prepare foods with contrasting colors, flavors, and textures.

APPLICATIONS

1. Assist with one or more children eating a meal. What hand is used? What tools are used? What foods are served? What foods are liked? What size are the servings? Does the child take seconds? Use descriptive phrases indicating the temperature of the food when eaten.
2. Assist with children during snack time. What hand is used? What tools are used? What foods are served? How much does the child eat? Can the child eat and talk? Explain your answers.
3. Assist with children helping prepare a food. Explain how they participate, what they say, and how they seem to be understanding what is taking place.
4. Report the eating history of your case-study child. Confer with both parents and teacher if feasible.

SUGGESTED FILM

Jenny Is a Good Thing   Color   20 minutes
Available in Spanish as well as in English. A film about Head Start
children with a focus on food and nutrition. Shows warm feeling among
staff and children. Modern Talking Pictures, 1212 Avenue of the Americas, New York, N.Y. 10036. Free from any Head Start office.

FOR FURTHER READING

BRECKENRIDGE, MARIAN E., and MARGARET NESBITT MURPHY. *Growth and
Development of the Young Child.* Philadelphia: W. B. Saunders Com-
pany, 1969.
FOSTER, FLORENCE. "Nutrition and Educational Experience: Interrelated
Variables in Children's Learning." *Young Children,* Vol. 27, No. 5 (June
1972), 285–288.
HILDEBRAND, VERNA. *Introduction to Early Childhood Education.* New
York: Macmillan Publishing Co., Inc., 1971.
LANDRETH, CATHERINE. *Preschool Learning and Teaching.* New York: Har-
per & Row, Publishers, 1972.
RAND, HELENE. "Experiential Learning Reevaluated." *Young Children,* Vol.
25, No. 6 (Sept. 1970), 363–366.
SMART, MOLLIE S., and RUSSELL C. SMART. *Children: Development and
Relationships.* New York: Macmillan Publishing Co., Inc., 1972.
SPOCK, BENJAMIN C. *Baby and Child Care.* New York: Pocket Books,
Simon & Schuster, Inc., 1968.
STONE, L. JOSEPH, and JOSEPH CHURCH. *Childhood & Adolescence.* New
York: Random House, Inc., 1973.
TODD, VIVIAN E., and HELEN HEFFERNAN. *The Years Before School.* New
York: Macmillan Publishing Co., Inc., 1970.

Guiding Children's Sleeping Behavior

"Has your baby begun sleeping all night?" "Is the baby still taking two naps a day?" "My baby has given up his daytime naps but he goes to bed early." "What do you do to get your baby to go to bed so early?"

THESE ARE COMMENTS you might hear if you spent an afternoon listening to casual conversation among mothers. A baby's sleep is another of the routines that concern mothers and caregivers. They work hard to get the sleep routine on an even keel.

INFANTS

There are individual differences in sleep patterns, as indicated by the mothers' questions just quoted. One baby is a regular sleeper from the beginning. Perhaps he took a couple short naps during the morning as a tiny baby, then one in the afternoon, and slept all night starting at his third month. He does this regularly every day. Another baby may seem to have a different pattern every day, perhaps sleeping a lot one day and little the next, making it hard to predict his sleep pattern.

In infancy and throughout the preschool years, the sleeping routine will require the special attention of caregivers, especially when the child is in the center for more than a few hours. The sleeping routine must be handled with loving care whether at home or school. Sleep is indeed "nature's tonic." It restores the body after the physical and psychological activity that the young child typically participates in. Periods of rest and sleep are essential to the individual's well-being.

168

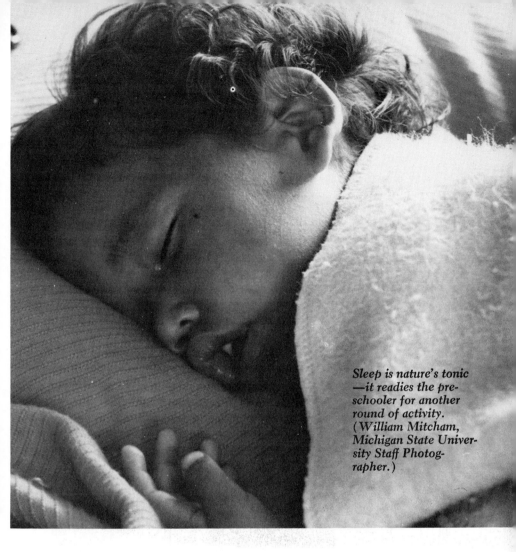

Sleep is nature's tonic —it readies the pre-schooler for another round of activity. (William Mitcham, Michigan State University Staff Photographer.)

Schedules   Individualized schedules often help caregivers meet the needs of several infants. Fortunately, in a center babies are seldom all awake and demanding food and changing at the same time. Some sleep while others are awake. Some sleep longer at a given time than others. This is another routine in which we feel the child should be allowed some "self-demand." However, it like other routines requires caregivers who know the child's needs and who can set the stage for the sleep and rest a child's body requires. Infants need more rest at shorter intervals than toddlers and preschoolers. Toddlers need more than preschoolers.

169 *Infants*

All schedules for infants and preschoolers, whether at home or in a center, need to be balanced between active and quiet activities. If there are both types of activities available, then the child can choose the one he needs. Fatigue develops without sufficient rest and sleep; it interferes with growth and disturbs the child's social relations. The child may become hyperactive and easily disturbed —crying and overreacting to situations and disturbing other children and adults.

Overstimulation is frequently a problem in group care situations. Continued contact with other babies or children, the continued presence of equipment for vigorous activity, the number of people in the

Safe in the crib, this toddler is sociable after a nap. (Joe Kertesz, Photographer.)

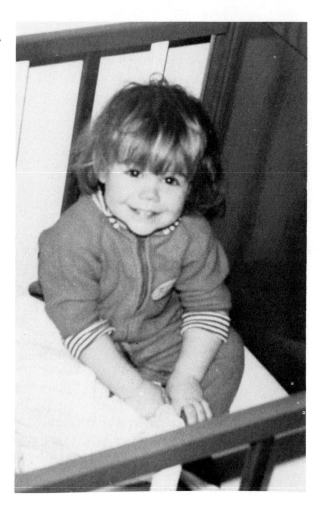

setting and their voices and actions combine to make group care highly stimulating and therefore likely to be overtiring for children. New children may need a period to adjust to so much bombardment of stimuli.

All centers that keep children all day should expect infants and children through the third year to sleep during the day. For four-year-olds and older children, some rest arrangement should be provided but allowances made for those who do not feel like sleeping.

There is general agreement that infants should sleep. Cribs are major equipment in nurseries—and costly in terms of dollar outlay and space usage. Most infants will not fight sleep but find comfort in a routine of eating, sleeping, changing, playing, eating, sleeping, changing, playing, and so on.

Considerable loving, cuddling, conversation, even singing, should go into making going down for a nap a pleasant and happily anticipated event. The crib must never become a punishing spot but a place to enjoy, "Your nice little bed." Therefore, when a child is having difficulty, is fussy or hungry, his nonsleep needs should first be alleviated before he is placed in his crib.

Even young babies do quite a bit of moving during sleep. That's one reason for padded crib sides, and the reason for never leaving babies unattended on a big bed or table from which they might fall.

Babies like to lie in their cribs and play with their mobiles, rattles, or toes even when they are not sleeping. They often practice their vocalizations during this time. As an infant caregiver you can respond to the verbalizing babies with returned bits of conversation, smiles, and momentary games.

Babies also like to be turned over until they are able to perform this feat themselves—it gives them something new to look at, as well as easing the pressure on certain muscles. A change to a playpen may also be in order to give the child new toys, new things to look at. Babies should not be placed with other infants for long periods of time, because it can be too stimulating and tiring.

Mothers of infants will want caregivers to report how their child slept during the day. It will help a mother plan for her child during the rest of the day and evening.

Some working parents whose infants are in day care develop a family pattern of keeping the baby up quite late in the evening when they are home to enjoy playing with him. This probably presents little problem while the baby is still not very active. However, in the toddler years such a pattern is often unfortunate, because most centers offer stimulating morning programs that do not always allow for morning naps. Also, the toddler may begin playing with his active peers. If he is too tired from a late bedtime the previous night, he can be both frustrating and easily frustrated. Caregivers need to watch for this kind of problem and communicate with parents to work out a happy solution in the interest of all parties.

PRESCHOOLERS

Space Arrangement

The sleeping room for both infants and preschoolers should be located so children can be easily moved out in case of fire. Exits must not be blocked with cribs or other furniture. Fire extinguishers must be readily available, and every nap room supervisor needs to know how to work them. Fire regulations should be known, and all workers should see that they are adhered to. Sufficient staff must be on duty to remove children in case of emergency.

If children are adequately separated at naptime, disturbances will be minimized and caregivers will be able to move rapidly among the resting children as needed for emergencies and for normal care.

Each child should have his own napping space. Each cot should be labeled with a child's name and placed in a regular place each day to help the child feel he has "personal space," which will give him a sense of security. Some licensing regulations do not require cots for napping. If waterproof pads are used, they should be protected with a covering—perhaps like a pillowcase—that can be laundered regularly. Each child should have his own pad or mat.

The teacher should plan the sleeping room cot or mat arrangement to facilitate guidance. Two children who are developing a strong friendship may

Going to sleep may take as long as thirty minutes for some children. (Michigan State University Spartan Day Care Center, Connie Lisiecki, Photographer.)

want to talk and may therefore disrupt others and not go to sleep. They may be widely separated. Dividers in front of toys and between cots or mats may be helpful to reduce stimulation. Dimming the lights and drawing the curtains help set the stage for the resting behavior desired. Distracting entries of either adults or children should be eliminated. The temperature of the room needs to be adjusted to the amount of cover the children have. Drafts must be avoided.

Guidance   Several indirect guidance techniques are helpful at naptime. The organization of the space has been mentioned. By establishing a regular sequence of events or schedule, the teacher helps children know when naptime is approaching. Usually it follows lunch, with only toileting, hand washing, removal of shoes, and perhaps removal of play clothes intervening between lunch and nap. The nap room is prepared while children eat and is ready and waiting for them. A quiet period of low-keyed voices and nonhurrying routines helps children get in the mood for resting. A busy morning filled with many interesting activities and including plenty of fresh air and exercise outdoors will cause most children to welcome the opportunity to rest.

Some children seem to go right to sleep once they are in bed, but others may take as long as thirty or forty minutes to relax and go to sleep. Following are a number of direct guidance techniques that teachers find useful in helping children at naptime.

A child may be comfortably tucked in only to announce that he has to go to the toilet. There seems to be no alternative except to allow him to go, for one would not want to be responsible for an "accident." Some children's bowels move shortly after eating. Careful attention to post-lunch toileting may help alleviate this problem. If a child learns that such an announcement is a sure route to delaying bedtime, then teachers may encourage that particular child to use the toilet before entering the nap room. Children should be encouraged to use the toilet immediately upon waking up. This is a time when most will need to urinate; however, no pressure should be applied if they do not.

To help children relax you may want to sit on the floor by a child's cot to massage his back or talk quietly to him. You may sing to children in a quiet voice. Little songs that mention each child's name may be useful in helping them quiet down and relax. Some children relax better if they turn face down. It helps them avoid being distracted by movement in the room. Children will not relax if afraid. Avoidance of any threat is imperative.

Naptime may be a time when visions of mother and home may be strongest, making the child homesick—even one who has been happy all morning. A toy or blanket from home may be helpful to such a child. Some may suck their thumbs or twist their hair. This is not a time to mention these habits. Adults should understand that these habits serve comforting functions and should be patient with the child. It helps sometimes to mention post-nap activity or that they will see mother after snack or after outdoor play—whichever is factual. You may want to remind a child that you will take good care of him while he is asleep.

Four-year-olds and fives may be outgrowing their afternoon naps, especially if they are getting a good night's sleep at home and sufficient opportunities to do restful activity during the day. It seems important for teachers to avoid making an issue over actual sleeping. Children who appear not to need to sleep may be allowed to read on their cots or to relax on a carpet in another part of the building away from sleeping children. Calling the period "rest" instead of "sleep" takes the curse off it for many children. Reassuring them that "You only have to stretch out, you don't need to sleep" may help some. Because these older children typically enjoy visiting with each other, it usually helps to separate them widely.

The amount of daytime sleep to encourage in preschool children depends on their needs and the needs of the families. In some homes that are crowded and disruptive the child has a hard time getting sufficient sleep, so long nap periods in the day care center are called for. In others, the mother much prefers to have the child take a short nap at the day care center so he will be ready for a reasonably early bedtime in the evening. Working mothers

This position helps some children go to sleep quickly. They see less to distract them. (Michigan State University Spartan Day Care Center, Connie Lisiecki, Photographer.)

Sometimes you are tired and just want to sit without playing.

You rub your eyes.

have many other responsibilities in their evening hours, yet these are really the only hours they see their children except perhaps during the weekend. The school may be able to help the evening bedtime by allowing the child to be awakened after one and a half to two hours. This is usually not too difficult if the lights are turned up and the curtains opened.

Rest Time in Short-Day Groups Do we really need "rest time" in short-day groups of nursery school and kindergarten children? This is a question that has bothered teachers, parents, and even children. It has been a custom until recently to require the children to stretch out prone for a given length of time to "rest." Observation showed that these times were quite mislabeled, for in many

You even close your eyes.

Then you hold your head. "When will it be rest time?" you wonder. (William Mitcham, Michigan State University Staff Photographer.)

groups they were anything but "restful." Because of the rest requirements, children have been known to virtually refuse to attend school or to "hate" the rugs that they have to take to school for resting. Teachers have found the rest period was one they did not look forward to. These problems have caused teachers to rethink rest time.

In many groups that meet for only two and a half to three hours, the rest time is a quiet period for snacks, singing, and stories. These organized and interesting periods, which do have other important objectives to fulfill, also provide time for the child's body to become rested and refreshed. Many children will actually lie on the floor to hear a lullaby or two, or to do a quiet finger exercise, or to move their

177 *Preschoolers*

eyes from side to side. They enjoy these times even though they tend to dislike rest.

In short-day groups the children come later in the morning than in day care groups. Therefore, they usually are able to complete their cycle of sleeping at home. Some children actually arise about 8:30 A.M., eat breakfast, and arrive at nursery school by 9:00. If they have had a good night's sleep— eight, ten, even twelve hours for some—they surely aren't in need of much rest by 10:00 or 10:30 A.M. Many will go home to a good afternoon of napping if they need it. Afternoon groups often need a more slowly paced program if the children arrive at school without napping.

The point here is for teachers to take a good look at the amount of sleep children are getting at home and to balance the quiet and vigorous activities they are offering at school, then decide if there is a real need for formal resting. Teachers should remember that such activities as sand play, listening to records, painting, or playing with puzzles can be restful. Children can be guided into these activities if they show signs of fatigue.

CONCLUSION

The sleep and resting routines of the nursery school and day care center are among the most important points of the day. Children must have ways to alleviate fatigue. Fatigue interferes with growth and with good social relations. Communication with parents about nap and rest time can help them coordinate their plans with those of the school. The following ten guides are suggested for teachers who may be asked by parents for help with planning their children's sleep at home.

TEN GUIDES TO HAPPY BEDTIMES

1. Put the child to bed when he is sleepy and tired. Rubbing eyes, crying, irritability, hyperactivity are indications of fatigue. Adults must take the responsibility for putting a child to bed when he is sleepy or tired.

2. Consider the kinds of activity and the amount of sleep the child has at school in determining appropriate bedtime. The longer the nap the later the bedtime. An interesting day including fresh air and outdoor play will help the child's body really need sleep.

3. Establish a regular sequence of events that helps the child know when bedtime is approaching. This helps him know what behavior the parent is expecting. For example, each night after supper the child perhaps plays with his parents, has a bath, hears a story or song or both, goes to the bathroom, and gets a drink, then retires to his bed—all in that order. The babysitter can follow the same routine.

4. Plan for the least stimulating of activities during the pre-bedtime period. If the child is overstimulated by rough-housing, he very likely will have difficulty going to sleep. He will be having such a good time that he will want the events prolonged.

5. Allow the child to choose a light, a night light, or total darkness as he prefers. If a child is feeling scared in any way, a light may be most helpful, for he will be able to see all the corners of his room.

6. Accept comforting habits such as thumb sucking, hair twisting, and blanket or toy caressing that help the child relax.

7. Accept the idea that the child may take a half hour or more to go to sleep.

8. Rather than permit the child who seems to be having difficulty going to sleep to return to the family group, sit near the bed and sing to the child until he relaxes.

9. Avoid admonitions regarding toilet training and keeping dry. Reduce liquids and take the child to the toilet just before tucking him in bed. Put double diapers and plastic pants on him until he stays dry all night without being taken to the toilet in the night.

10. Reduce environmental noises as much as possible during the child's going-to-sleep phase. Especially turn off the TV or keep it low; keep voices and especially laughter low.

APPLICATIONS

1. Discuss with a mother the sleep habits of her child. Ask about how long he sleeps, where he sleeps, what routines precede bedtime, whether he sleeps dry, and his usual behavior when waking up. Write a report of your findings.
2. Discuss resting and sleeping with a nursery school teacher. Report whether all children sleep, how long they sleep, where they sleep, where the teachers stay while children sleep, and what techniques teachers find work best for this routine.
3. Assist with a child at rest or sleep time. How is he behaving? Does he appear tired? How can you tell? What does the adult do to help him? Summarize how you think the situation seems to the child.
4. Report the sleeping patterns of your case-study child. Confer with teachers and parents if feasible.

FOR FURTHER READING

BRECKENRIDGE, MARIAN E., and MARGARET NESBITT MURPHY. *Growth and Development of the Young Child*. Philadelphia: W. B. Saunders Company, 1969.

SMART, MOLLIE S., and RUSSELL C. SMART. *Children: Development and Relationships*. New York: Macmillan Publishing Co., Inc., 1972.

SPOCK, BENJAMIN C. *Baby and Child Care*. New York: Pocket Books, Simon & Schuster, Inc., 1968.

STONE, L. JOSEPH, and JOSEPH CHURCH. *Childhood & Adolescence*. New York: Random House, Inc., 1973.

Guiding Children's Dressing and Undressing

Patrick sat in front of the teacher. He pulled on his boots. He laid his opened ski jacket in front of him on the floor with the collar at his feet. He bent over and slipped his arms into the sleeves. He raised the jacket over his head and it slipped into place. "I did it!" he exclaimed with joy.

PATRICK was learning to be independent in his dressing. The teacher was nearby to offer physical and verbal guidance if he needed it. She too felt happy when Patrick was able to get his coat on "with no help at all."

Dressing and undressing children in the nursery and nursery school can require a great deal of the teachers' and caregivers' time and energy. In cold climates the numbers of garments and complication of the dressing tasks must be experienced to be believed. Dressing in winter especially can be very frustrating and time consuming for children and adults alike.

INFANTS AND TODDLERS

Infant clothing usually comes with adequate zippers to aid the caregiver. It is common knowledge that babies dislike things pulled over their heads. In group care for infants there is still a need to get babies outside for fresh air and perhaps a "walk" in a carriage or stroller; therefore, dressing babies is one of the common tasks of caregivers.

Babies are quite easily distracted, and if you talk to them while dressing them they will protest less. As they get older and understand the meaning of

181

"I'd like to try lacing my shoe."

words and signs, if the caregiver puts on her outdoor hat first and says, "Outside," the infant may then allow his outdoor clothing to be put on without so much protest. Infants, like everyone else, get over-heated quickly, so someone should be ready to go outdoors with a child when he is finally dressed and not make him wait until others are ready.

Toddlers can help with dressing by handing items to the caregiver. "Bring me your socks" or "Bring me your shoes" helps children learn the names of garments and helps keep their minds on the task, too.

"Now, I wonder which way it goes?"

"Maybe it will be easier from this position." (James Page, Photographer.)

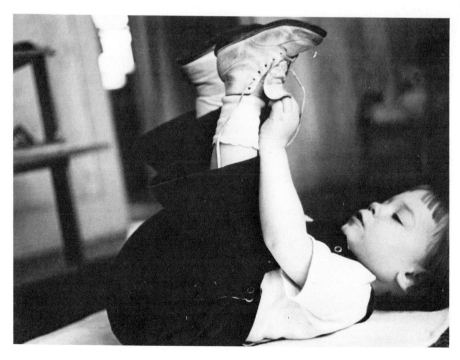

Getting your coat from your locker is the first step in dressing for outdoor play. (Michigan State University Laboratory Preschool, Connie Lisiecki, Photographer.)

PRESCHOOLERS

Probably one of the reasons teachers dread the outdoor play period is that dressing the children seems like such a hassle. Following are a few hints that may be useful to help simplify the process as much as possible.

Each child's clothing should be kept in his locker and should be marked with name labels. This will enable him and you to find his clothing quickly. Extra clothing should be kept in the lockers for children who may have a toilet accident or an accident during play with water, mud, or paint. In some schools a pair of boots is regularly kept in the locker because the grass is wet most mornings when children are ready to go outdoors. A clothespin labeled with the child's name is used to clip boots together.

Before dressing children in their snow suits, it is helpful to remind them to use the bathroom, because even they soon recognize the inconvenience of undoing the outdoor garb. When a child must use the toilet after he is fully dressed, it usually requires the help of a teacher and one should be assigned to care for children who express that need.

When children need considerable help with boots and zippers, dressing is easier to manage if the teacher sits on a low chair with a group of children around her. (They bring their snow suits and boots from their lockers to sit in the circle.) She can see all the children at once and can give a boot a tug here, a mitten a push there. She can remind children to put snow pants on before boots. She can give children advice and encouragement that helps them become more independent and she can follow through with a demonstration as a child needs it.

For example, you can guide even small children in the "tricky" way to put a coat on. Place the opened coat front side up with collar at the child's feet. He bends down, places an arm in each sleeve, and throws the coat over his head. As he does so, the coat or jacket slides onto his arms, and "hocus pocus" it's on! Another method is to lay the opened coat out on the table and have the child back up to the table and slip his arms into the sleeves. Either way the next step is the fasteners. It may take a start of the zipper or at least verbal advice about getting the fastener far down into place. Buttons might be started, too, just to give the child a feeling of completing the act.

Boots can create many difficulties. Sometimes they aren't the right size, for children outgrow them quickly or wear hand-me-downs that aren't exactly right. If you assure the parents that children will go outdoors daily, they might feel that the expense of new boots is worth it. A small plastic bag pulled over the shoe before trying the difficult boot will help the boot slip over the shoe. The small size bag avoids bunching around the ankles and will not fit over heads. (Of course, don't allow children to play with plastic bags, because they are dangerous.) Most schools keep a good collection of used boots on hand so that children who do not have their own boots or "forget" them can go outdoors. If your school doesn't have any extra boots, perhaps someone should visit rummage and garage sales to get a supply.

Removing wraps also has its problems, especially with winter clothing. If the children are snow covered, it is wise to have a small broom at the door to sweep it off before they enter. In the entryway keep several cotton rugs to collect the snow and drips from melting snow. These can be shaken outdoors and hung to dry after all children have entered.

Arrange small chairs near the entryway and have children take off snowy clothing there, thus avoiding tracking melting snow across the building where lockers may be. If children enter from the play yard a few at a time, one adult can help four or five children with the undressing process while seated on a small chair. Children then can carry their clothing to their lockers for storage—or to a drying area if that is preferred. Boots may need drying out with a towel to be ready for the next time.

Sitting while helping children with their clothing not only encourages independence, it also saves the teacher's back, which is particularly crucial when she spends long hours at the job. Sitting at the child's level rather than standing over him also makes guidance more effective because you are at his eye level, can get his attention more effectively, and can see that each child is carrying out your guidance. Many dressing hints can be demonstrated while sitting, such as putting fingers in gloves and mittens, tying shoes, pulling on boots, putting zippers together, snapping hat straps, and buttoning. Words and smiles of encouragement can be communicated more easily.

Children become very impatient when they are anxious to go outdoors. They may demand more help than they usually need. Organizing the process of dressing will move it along with the greatest ease.

As indicated in Chapter 9, some schools utilize the mother's help in dressing as much as possible. She can be encouraged to help the child remove wraps in the mornings and can put on wraps at the end of the day in some schedules. In an afternoon group, the mother can bring the child fully clothed for outdoor play when this is scheduled to be first. This has the added advantage that mothers realize you really will take children outside. Mothers who dress their children also realize some of the difficulty

Having the teacher help with those last buttons is surely appreciated. (Michigan State University Laboratory Preschool, Connie Lisiecki, Photographer.)

children have with poorly fitting boots or mittens and might better understand the need for new ones.

A common need is to remove wraps when children are active outdoors and seem to be getting uncomfortably warm. This is a hard point for adults to understand who stand around without being active and feel that a child with only a light wrap must be freezing. Actually we should let children have much more to say about how much clothing they wear than we usually do.

Tying shoes is another problem spot. After naps and frequently after outdoor play, the shoes get untied. Sometimes you will want shoes off for music and rhythm experiences. In most preschool groups the teacher simply must retie the shoes. This is a motor skill that most children will not be able to learn until kindergarten or first grade.

A five-year-old whose coordination is advanced will learn to tie his shoes quickly—he even enjoys practicing. If the adult sits with the child on her lap or in some way that allows her the same vantage point as the child, she can demonstrate the tying operation. Some people make a loop of each string and then tie the loops into a double knot, and this is satisfactory for some children. One way that has been successful is to label the loops "bunny ears" and demonstrate the tying operation, then encourage the child as he begins to understand the process.

Tying shoes, apron strings, and the like is difficult, and to expect it of the younger preschool children is futile and frustrating. Children do not seem to mind having their shoestrings dangle, much to their elders' dismay. For example, a teacher said to a five-year-old, "Dean, your shoe is not tied." He said, "So?" The teacher said, "Can you tie it or shall I?" He quickly said, "I can do it," and proceeded to show his skill. In one sense the adult was interfering with Dean's train of thought, for he was busy with something and quite uncaring of the shoestrings.

As mentioned, parents frequently need guidance regarding the type of clothing that will make it easy for their child to become independent in dressing. Occasionally a garment simply jeopardizes the child's success in toileting, and parents should be so informed. A one-piece jumpsuit that buttoned on the shoulders was such a garment. A competent four-year-old came in one of these and cried when she didn't get it unbuttoned in time. On advice of the teacher, the child quit wearing that garment to school.

The child's locker is his "personal space" where

his clothing belongs while he is at school. Learning to hang up his own clothing is a step toward independence for the young child.

The teacher's guidance during dressing should be supporting. The child should be helped with tasks he can't perform, aided with those he can almost perform, and allowed to do the tasks he is capable of. Praise for accomplishments is one of the best guidance techniques. It is ridiculous to see a five-year-old with an easily handled fat zipper being zipped by a hovering adult. An observant teacher can see when frustration is about to set in and offer a little help or a word of advice and demonstration. Sometimes children do not know an easy way to do a task. It is well to divide the group into small groups of children that an adult can effectively help rather than to assign her greater numbers and have the growth in independence actually hindered for many children.

CONCLUSION

Independence in dressing is a task a child seems to want to achieve and the adults in his life are happy for him to learn. We should set the stage for his learning by purchasing clothing that is easy to manage and by guiding his learning until he does become independent. We reward his independence in dressing when we let him go outside immediately after he dresses.

APPLICATIONS

1. Assist a child with putting on some pieces of clothing in either a home or a school. What is the child old enough to do? What help does he ask for? Does he feel independent? How can you tell that he feels independent? Summarize.
2. Discuss with a mother or a teacher tips for buying clothing for children that helps them become independent. Summarize your findings.
3. Browse in a children's clothing department and eavesdrop on conversations between mothers and clerks. What qualities are mothers looking for in children's clothing? If children are present, what part do they play in clothing selections? Write a brief report.
4. Observe your case-study child in the dressing routine for nap, toilet, and locker room. Summarize your observations.

FOR FURTHER READING

HILDEBRAND, VERNA. *Introduction to Early Childhood Education.* New York: Macmillan Publishing Co., Inc., 1971.

LANDRETH, CATHERINE. *Preschool Learning and Teaching.* New York: Harper & Row, Publishers, 1972.

Guiding Children on the Playground

What shall we do when we all go out?
All go out, All go out;
What shall we do when we all go out?
When we all go out to play?

We shall climb on the jungle gym,
Jungle gym, Jungle gym,
We shall climb on the jungle gym,
When we all go out to play.

WHEN THE TEACHER began this song, it sig-
naled to the children that singing time was over and
that they could proceed to their lockers for their
wraps. They chimed in on the words as they rose
and moved with haste to get their clothing. Going
outdoors was indeed a joyous occasion for these
children, as it is for most preschoolers.

Play in the out of doors appears to hold a never-
ending attraction. Children need this period in the
day whether at home or at school. Adults who work
with children can use the period to teach many
worthwhile concepts relating to every aspect of the
child's development. Outdoor play gives you many
opportunities to use all of the guidance techniques
and to make a significant contribution to the child's
learning.

TEACHING VS. SUPERVISING

You can be a far more important person to the
children on the playground than a mere supervisor.
Usually supervisors just stand around, waiting until
something unpleasant happens, then try to do something about it. Teachers, on the other hand, interact

191

with children, stay close to them, listen to what they say, what they ask, what they need. Teachers are quick to give the appropriate guidance that encourages children to grow in knowledge, in independence, in skill, and in personal relationships. Being alert and involved, teachers adjust the situation to avoid having unproductive situations take place.

Beginning assistants are frequently given lots of time on outdoor duty. For example, one student said, "Somehow I always get out there with the children. I wonder if the other teachers are afraid they might get cold." The student went on to relate how she had had a marvelous time with the children in the snowy yard. She had helped them examine snowflakes under the magnifying glass, knocked snow from branches, and made snow angels "just like Peter in *The Snowy Day*." Those "other teachers" may have thought that playground duty was being done by the "low man on the totem pole," but this intelligent young woman hadn't allowed herself to treat the children as though it were. Directors and head teachers should set an example by demonstrating their appreciation for and utilization of this outdoor learning environment by participating outdoors.

Actually, teachers often find vigorous outdoor activity as enjoyable and tension-releasing for them as it is for the children. Playing follow the leader, walking in the "giant's tracks," flying like a bird or an airplane, or playing some version of shadow tag can be as much fun for the teacher as for the children. Teachers serve as models for children, and enjoying the outdoors helps children develop an appreciation for nature and for body skills that can help them throughout life. Some children need to be taught how to relate to the out of doors. It is unfortunate for children to have teachers who find excuses to keep children indoors—ignoring the resources of the playground and of nature. Male teachers should protest if they are always expected to be the "outdoors teacher," allowing the women to toast their toes by the fire. Both should share all aspects of the school programs.

"Mr. Snowman, I've never seen you before. I like being outdoors, do you?" (Mary Gray, Photographer.)

DRESSED FOR THE JOB

One important key to teachers' enjoying the out of doors is to dress for it. Warm enough in the winter and cool enough in the summer is the key in outdoor dress. Nursery school teachers, including those who are oldest and largest, should be among the most grateful of the professionals who enjoy the new fashion of wearing pant suits and slacks to work. Nothing else is as practical for nursery school teachers, so gone are the days when we freeze on the playground to please "dame fashion." Comfortable shoes are musts, and fashion has smiled on this garment, too, as far as nursery school teachers are concerned, for those wide-toed and -heeled shoes give you firm footing on walks, in the yard, on stairs, and when carrying equipment and children. Warm scarves, mittens, boots, and a coat that can take the rugged use it will get are important in winter climates. Attached hoods on coats help teachers always to have their hats handy.

Summer and warmer climates should leave you just as free to dress in shorts or slacks with cool blouses as you may prefer. Teachers will meet the outdoor period with the same enthusiasm as the children, if they are properly dressed and if they also use the time to get refreshed.

Children should be comfortably and adequately clothed for the weather. Details regarding dressing were given in Chapter 13.

Your guidance on the playground will serve to enhance the child's development. It should promote physical-motor development, intellectual development, social development, emotional development, and creative development. You can utilize both indirect and direct methods of guidance, as indicated in Chapters 4 and 5.

OBJECTIVES

In the following discussion you will learn some of the broad objectives that can be achieved during the time when children play out of doors. You can also learn how your guidance can be directed toward achievement of these objectives.

Physical-Motor Objectives

To provide fresh air, sunlight, and exercise, which promote good health.

Nature provides vitamin D through sunlight's activation of a substance on the skin. Vitamin D is essential for the growth of strong bones and teeth. Because infants and young children have important growth to achieve in bones and teeth, they need regular doses of vitamin D. Merely by providing some time outdoors in the sunshine each day, the child can receive this health-giving vitamin.

Oxygen, which is of course found in fresh air, is essential for life. Oxygen is essential for the brain to function, and deficiency of oxygen will cause brain injury. Young children use much more oxygen for a given volume of brain tissue than adults.

Exercise is essential to aid all the body's inner systems to grow, develop, and function as they should. Respiratory, circulatory, digestive, and elimination systems all function more fully when the child has adequate exercise. Fortunately, children are happiest when they are allowed to move and be active; exercise comes quite naturally to most children. Parents and caregivers must understand how

Tricycle-operating skills are usually learned by age three. A trike hike through the park is a pleasant change. (William Mitcham, Michigan State University Staff Photographer.)

essential exercise is so they will encourage and plan for it rather than try to quiet the child down to keep him from becoming so active. Exercise and fresh air will create the need for eating, and good nutrition is essential in overall good health.

To provide a setting and equipment that motivate the child to practice motor skills and develop independence.

Skills in using the body and holding the body erect are promoted during the outdoor play. The gross or large motor skills develop first in the child's repertoire of skills. They are such skills as walking, running, climbing, pedaling, pushing, and pulling. The child with the best-developed motor skills is frequently a leader in the group.

Two physical education researchers, John Haubenstricker and Vern Seefeldt, are learning from studies of children carried on for a number of years that when a child's large motor skills are poorly developed at age five he may never really become skilled, even with remedial help. For this reason they are advocating that teachers of young children help children learn and practice certain motor skills.

These researchers studied three types of skills: (1) body management skills, (2) locomotor skills, and (3) projection and reception skills. Body management skills include such things as bouncing on a trampoline, jumping board, or mattress. Hopping exercises with eyes opened and closed and walking a balance beam forward and backward are body management skills. Climbing and descending various ladders and stairs and hanging from climbing structures are helpful exercises. Stunts, such as pretending to be snakes, frogs, kangaroos, or ducks, give experience handling the body. Sitting and rolling forward, backward, and around are interesting to children and useful for body control.

Locomotor skills include walking backward and forward, running toward a goal, running with a stop-and-go signal, or running on tiptoes. Jumping, galloping, and hopping can be encouraged through various games either indoors or out. A bamboo pole, placed with one end on the ground and the other

Ball throwing is a skill to begin practicing early. (James Page, Photographer.)

end propped up on a sawhorse, encourages practice in hurdle jumping, with each child selecting the appropriate height for him.

Projection and reception skills are those of throwing and receiving a ball or kicking a ball. Big balls and beanbags are useful for beginning games with large targets such as wastebaskets to receive the balls. Observing how skilled players follow through with the total body makes one realize how much a preschooler has to develop to become skilled. It is important that the child be encouraged to practice these large motor skills.

Free, open space is important for many of these skills. Room to move quickly without interfering with other children is essential. Another requirement is a sufficient number of play spaces and pieces of equipment that allow the child a choice in exercising muscles and developing skills of particular interest at the moment.

As the small toddler begins using the play yard independently, the adult will stay close by to lend

197 *Objectives*

a supporting hand when necessary. Some tumbles that might discourage further adventures can be prevented. The adult can also prevent one child from inadvertently interfering with another. That is, one toddler may tumble or push, causing another child to fall unless an alert adult guides the play, foresees points where interference might occur, and diverts the movement of the child. Young toddlers have a low center af gravity, but may tumble easily. They are also well padded, so the falls are usually not hurtful, and the adult need not say much more than "You're all right. Hop up," and the child will be on his way again.

Wheel toys need to be sized appropriately for the children using the yard. Toddlers can't feel successful trying to reach the pedals of the four-year-old's tricycle and the four-year-old won't be able to enjoy the toddler's toy either. Each yard should afford some equipment that offers a challenge to the children in the group. Swings that two children can push and pull to make themselves swing are a challenge to the pumping skills of threes and fours.

Independence in swinging on a traditional swing can be promoted by building a ramp under the swing. This can be either a permanent construction or a temporary inclined plane built with a board and a sawhorse. The child holds tight to the swing chains and with the swing behind him walks backward up the inclined plane. He walks as far as the swing reaches and sits down in the swing. Gravity carries him forward, and his body achieves the posture required to keep the swing moving. The child feels a new-found independence as he makes the swing go "all by myself!"

The urge for independence and achievement can be a highly motivating drive for a child. When the child challenges himself, he usually will go only as high as he feels safe. Wise teachers stay close by when one child is encouraging another child to go beyond where he feels safe, because this is a situation that often creates fear, and the child may let go if he is scared. Adults should avoid motivating one child to achieve heights or speed just because another has. If a child is prone to show off to other

When climbing skills are developing the child will usually venture only as high as he feels safe. (Southern University, Baton Rouge, Louisiana, Mary Odell, Photographer.)

children or to adults, this, too, is a situation of danger. Once a child learns a skill he can be told about a new feat that is now appropriate for his skills. "Since you can climb this ladder, Jim, you might try the tree house tomorrow" encourages a child to continue developing his climbing skills.

The guidance of the teacher should be very personal—given directly to the child in quiet, reassuring tones. Shouts across the play yard are usually totally ineffective. Children don't know that you mean the shouts for them, and they may actually not hear what is said.

*To provide an opportunity for a child to imitate
his peers and to compare his motor skills with
theirs on an informal basis.*

Sharon watched Pam climb a tree and decided to
try it herself. She tried several times and finally succeeded in getting into the tree. When she had firm,
secure footing she smiled, then laughed, then yelled,
"Look at me! I'm up here!" She took time deciding
to jump down; when she did, she laughed, skipped
around, and climbed into the tree again. Sharon
was a quiet child who knew when she was ready.
Watching Pam had helped her decide.

Children learn many things from watching their
friends. If something looks like fun, they will want
to try it and they won't need adults to press them
to do it. The adults can help by having several pieces
of equipment so that one child does not have to
give up his place to allow a novice to try. For example, at the carpentry bench an experienced ham-
merer can show the newcomer some tricks of the
trade. With tricycles, the skillful driver may lead
the less skillful, teaching them his skills in the process. The child who dangles from his knees on the
jungle gym usually encourages his friends to try his
"trick."

The adult may need to protect the less skillful
from the ridicule of the more skillful by comments
such as "After he practices a while he'll be able to
do it like you" or "Don't you remember only a short
time ago when you were learning?" "Yes, he's taking
longer, but that's all right. He's learning." This
helps the beginner to know that his friend was once
a beginner too.

As mentioned earlier, it is poor procedure to motivate children by comparing them to their friends.
Avoid statements like "Jimmy climbed up here, you
try it" or "See if you can beat Jimmy to the top of
the climber." The child might be secretly admiring
Jimmy, but this puts them in open competition,
which may leave both children quite uncomfortable.

Children may want to wrestle, and a good rule
is that "wrestling is for outdoors." Then allow only
two children at a time and have the understanding

that the goal is "to have fun." They should also agree to stop if one partner says "Up."

Intellectual Objectives *To provide opportunities for the child to develop concepts of the order and beauty of nature.*

Children have to learn that spring follows winter and summer follows spring. In their short life spans they will not know this from experience. By having it drawn to their attention, they will begin to have some appreciation of the order of nature. They will also learn to see as beautiful the wonders of nature that unfold around them each season, if adults will look for, show, and talk about these natural wonders. Children will need names of all the things in their small world, because these, too, are new to them.

Beautiful! The cold outdoors offers many interesting things to investigate. (James Page, Photographer.)

Names should be accurate. Adults should develop curiosity and interest in nature and learn correct facts to relate to the small children in their care. From the puddle that freezes over on the first cold night of fall to the bloom on the crocus in spring, the teacher has untold opportunities to teach children about nature.

To provide an environmental laboratory for learning about nature, weather, plants, animals, and insects and about such concepts as number, speed, gravity, height, weight, and balance.

A laboratory is a place where you try things out. It is action packed, not quiet like a library. The play yard can be full of experimental situations.

In guiding children in their experiments, the teacher needs a curiosity of her own and should happily encourage children's curiosity. "What would happen if we . . .?" can be a question she often asks children. "How did you make it do that?" is another. "Tell me what happened. What do you think the (worm, bird, squirrel, and so on) is trying to do?" can encourage children to relate what they have observed. The important thing is that the teacher be alert to the child's activity. She comments on something a child sees, what he picks up, even what he fears, and uses that as a learning situation. Sometimes the episode is only for one child, sometimes it can be developed or repeated so that the total group benefits from it. Teachers should feel that stimulation of one child's sense of inquiry is significant and probably of far more worth to him personally than numerous group experiences she might plan. This type of experience is usually spontaneous, growing out of the child's own interest.

Children make a number experience out of a delightful time on the large wooden rocking boat. They chant

Teeter totter, Full—
Teeter totter, Full—
Teeter totter, One More, (*One child rolled off.*)
Teeter totter, Two More, (*Another rolled off.*)

Teeter totter, Three More. (*Another rolled off, then they climbed on and began the chant over.*)

Science experiments should be planned frequently for the outdoors to supplement the experiments that may be going on indoors with somewhat different equipment. Observations done indoors can be checked outdoors and vice versa. Gravity, the properties of inclined planes and teeter boards, and balance are examples. Labeling these concepts indoors and again outdoors helps children learn that knowledge carries over and is applicable to other situations. Planting seeds and bulbs in a garden or flowerbed makes a challenging learning experience. Children realize the time lag between planting and sprouting and the "long time" to wait before blooming or harvesting.

To learn how to use and care for the outdoor environment, property, and equipment.

Rules related to safe usage of equipment must be repeated numerous times before they become effective in children's actions. Memory is required, and the rules must be recalled at the right time. "Both hands on the jungle gym," "Drive the tricycle this way around the circle," and "Play inside the fence" are samples of rules you may be stating to children to help them remain safe and sound on the playground. Rules stated in positive form, in short direct sentences, help the child know the behavior that you want from him. Because the children might not understand all the words you say—"inside," "behind," "around"—you will also lead or gesture to give them further clues about what you'd like them to do.

Rules will also be made to protect the learning environment, equipment, and other children. These rules are important to facilitate individual learning, to preserve what you have for tomorrow and for future classes. Tricycles won't last long if they are abused by running them together. Wooden blocks will split if dropped from heights. Paint will chip off wood fences if hammered. The carpentry bench

is the place for hammering rather than a fence or
a part of the building.

Guidance, rules, and reasons for all rules can be
short and factual, given in a positive tone that anti-
cipates that the child will follow your guidance.
Even young children must learn that there are limits
to their behavior, so you needn't apologize for setting limits or for refusing to allow a child to do
something.

The point is to use guidance in a fair manner
with a suggestion for an acceptable alternative that
fits in with the mood or need of the child. The child
who wants to drop something from the top of the
treehouse can make paper airplanes and fly them
from there. The child who wants to paint the building can paint with water. The child who wants to
climb high must do it on the jungle gym instead of
on the storage shed. Children will follow a confident
teacher who has an honest explanation and a helping hand and thus be moved into the right course.

| Social-Emotional Objectives | *To grow from an egocentric infant to a cooperative kindergartener.* |

When infants go outdoors, they enjoy the change
of scene as much as others. They are self-centered,
playing in their own places with their own toys
without much regard for others unless their familiar
caregiver gets out of sight—then they may be unhappy. We call this the *solitary stage* of play.

During the late toddler and early nursery school
period, the children are in a *parallel play stage* where
they enjoy the presence of other children. They like
to be near them but still do their own thing. Interactions, when they occur, may be rather rough—
perhaps one grabs a shovel or pushes another child
—almost as a way of getting attention. The kiddie
car, the little wagon, the swing are popular toys at
this age. As language develops, interaction becomes
more friendly.

Four-year-olds become able to express their needs
and ideas through words. They plan their play—or,
perhaps more accurately, they evolve a theme as
they play. Their play lasts for longer periods of time

A wagon encourages cooperative play among pre-schoolers. (Southern University, Baton Rouge, Louisiana, Eddie Hildreth, Photographer.)

than it did during earlier stages. Their group is larger. This is the *cooperative play stage.*

Five-year-old boys enjoy large groups of boys. Girls start having "best friends" and may exclude a child from their circle in a rude manner that can be disrupting to the social harmony in a group. Five-year-olds may play alone, too, because they now have a sustained interest in some project—not because they lack social skills.

These stages should be kept in mind as you guide children's play. Adults often are anxious when a child plays alone, although he may be playing very normally for his age.

A new child may play alone until he gets the "lay of the land," so to speak. It is wise to allow him time to decide for himself where he wants to join in.

To learn and practice social skills that enable children to get along with adults and with their peers.

Social objectives are of equal importance to other objectives. Children simply must learn to get along with others. Living in harmony with other human beings may be one of the outstanding challenges for the whole human race. Infants are very self-centered or egocentric, concerned with their own interests and needs.

Sharing is a social skill that is fostered in outdoor play, as in numerous other segments of the nursery school program. Sharing is an attribute that parents and teachers alike wish that children would learn early. Sharing is a spontaneous act of generosity with play materials, play space, and the like. If adults force children to divide up, it is really not sharing. Sharing must contain the generous feeling to be genuine sharing. Geri shares in the following example.

Sherry joined the children at the sand pile after the sand shovels had been divided by the three children present. Sherry said nothing for a while, just watched as the three children scooped and filled their containers. Geri looked at her and said, "Oh, you don't have a shovel. You can have one of mine." Ben said, "She can't have none of mine." Mary, the third child, said nothing. Sherry played happily with the shovel Geri gave her.

Such examples of generous behavior will be noted frequently as you observe. If an adult had said, "Geri, it was nice that you shared your shovel," she would have helped the children learn the concept of sharing by labeling the behavior. Her praise would indicate to the children that sharing is desirable, and they might conclude that if the act were repeated it would be further praised.

Ben and Mary probably had their reasons for not feeling generous. All of us have to feel we've had "enough" of something before we feel like sharing some of what we have. "Enough" is very individually defined. Empathy and sympathy are not common traits in young children.

Spontaneous generosity is the desired behavior, although dividing up may be called for at times. The often-heard phrase "You gotta share" is quite ineffective in promoting the desired behavior and accompanying feeling, because forced sharing only makes a child feel that adults are on the other child's side. Children who have difficulty sharing should be helped to have long, sustained experiences with equipment and supplies that no one forces them to relinquish, so they can finally feel that they have "enough."

Sharing need not be related to material goods. It can be verbal, like sharing a joke, a song, or a story. The following conversation was heard as two children played in the improvised housekeeping area in the play yard.

Doug: I am going to iron.
Mary: I'm the mother around this house. Doug, you're the father.
Doug: No, I'm the maid.
Mary: Oh, let's eat breakfast. (*She laughed as though she had a hidden secret.*) Did you see *Sesame Street?* It was so funny.
Doug: No. Did you see *The Wizard of Oz?*
Mary: (*giggling and waving her hand in a sophisticated manner*) Yes, that silly ole lion.
(*Both of the children laughed.*)

Taking turns is another type of sharing that is a behavior we'd like children to be born with but unfortunately must be learned. It comes more easily in fours and fives, who have language to express their needs and who can respond to verbal guidance, as the following example indicates.

The teacher brought water to the yard in a pitcher. Pam grabbed a cup and held it to the teacher, pushing in front of Diane who was already there. "Pam, Diane was here first. First come first served, you know," said the teacher, helping children learn a rule for taking turns the next time.

Leadership, another social behavior, develops as the child matures and learns language to communicate his ideas. Children must take turns leading and being led in the group situation. In mixed age groups the leadership almost always goes to the older children. The cooperative play of four- and five-year-olds is extremely interesting to observe from the point of view of leadership—who, and how, and in what situation a child leads is interesting to note.

The concepts of sharing, taking turns, being leader, and being led can all be interlaced with rules of safety and rules of fair play. Learning to get along with others is fostered in the free activity of the outdoor play yard.

The teacher stays near by, offering indirect and direct verbal, physical, and affective guidance as needed. Her presence seems to help remind children to follow the rules that they know.

To learn to handle their feelings of joy and satisfaction, or of anger and hostility.

Happiness, smiles, satisfactions, if life could be all of these some would not complain. We do indeed work to achieve more of these pleasant feelings and try to avoid unpleasant ones. We help children express their feelings through various media. In the out of doors we sense a feeling of freedom that often does not exist indoors. Perhaps it is the chance to be alone more, to test oneself instead of always being part of a group, that is refreshing about the outdoor period.

Inevitably there will be moments of frustration, anger, and hostility that adults and children must learn to cope with. The child should not be blamed for these feelings or admonished. He should be helped so that this form of reacting to a situation does not become a habit. The teacher can simply say, "I know you feel angry, but I can't let you hit Jimmy." When a child complains that something is too hard, you can say, "It is hard, but I think you can do it."

To allow children to express their feelings, to let off steam, to shout, to run vigorously, or to rest as desired.

A cooped-up feeling must often possess children. When they flock out of a schoolhouse or car into a play yard, they exhibit a happy abandon. They need to be free to shout and run. In guiding their behavior we should keep these needs in mind. The rules we state and the behavior we stop must be important. The life outdoors should be simpler and less confining than indoors. There are usually few reasons for limiting children's noise—compared to usual city noises, these are quiet sounds. The outdoor period should not be organized so tightly that children have no time to do what they want, or resistance will surely arise. If a child does not want to socialize, let him play alone. If he prefers climbing to carpentry, then allow him to decide. There should, however, be quiet places outdoors. The swing can be this—a place to escape. The sandbox can be a restful area. An autoharp under a tree or storybooks to look at and to read should meet the needs of children who like things less active or who are tired from vigorous activity.

Creative Objectives
To use ingenuity and creativity in devising new ways to use his body, the equipment, and space, and in creating games and dramatic play of his own choosing.

These objectives in a sense combine all the others. However, creativity is important to emphasize, and it occurs every moment on the playground. Teachers should be open to learning new ways that children play, for each group will surely teach you something new.

You can note the integration of all of the areas of development in the following instance of dramatic play.

The large wooden packing boxes in the yard were lined up somewhat like a train, but in the middle there was a blank space. Only two boxes were not already in the line, a very large green box and a smaller blue one. David and Mark tried to put the green box into the space. It was too heavy. David said, "Hey teacher, get these hooked up better and turn it over, upside down." The teacher went over to the boxes and David said, "Turn it upside down and put that—you're doing a good job!" The teacher stopped because it wouldn't fit, and David said, "Hot dog, help me! Hook this one on—Hook it on, teacher! Get that end and put it up there." The teacher said, "Both ends of the box won't fit. Do you want to use the blue one here?" The boys were disappointed and wandered off, seeming to abandon their idea. Then Mark came back, stood the big green box on end at one outside edge of the open space and the blue box at the other side. David put a ladder down into the enclosure they had made, and Mark shouted, "Come see the monkey house!" The boys with a little of the teacher's help had spent almost the entire play period making their "monkey house." On Monday when they returned they had it built in less than five minutes and played inside it the entire period.

The teacher was supporting but never overdirected the boys. They had their idea, and she allowed them to pursue it. They used language and gross motor skills. They applied what they knew about monkey cages—ladder and all. They were accepting of each other's ideas, and they worked together in a harmonious, mature manner. The children used themselves, the space, equipment, and time in a creative manner.

PLANNING

Outdoor play should be given attention during the regular planning sessions each week. The indoor activities and the outdoor activities should be varied and challenging. They should never offer a "Ho-hum, I've done this all before" appearance. New arrangements should be made with equipment to challenge the children's motivation to use equipment.

In planning, each child's motor needs should be considered and equipment arranged to challenge and test his skills. Many scientific concepts can be learned in the outdoors. These should be planned on a regular basis. Spontaneous interests may supersede the plan, but plans must be made or a program will surely stagnate.

The amount, type, storage, and maintenance of outdoor equipment should have top priority with the planning team. If children are having an unusual number of disagreements on the playground, then the number of play spaces may not be sufficient—perhaps there are fifteen places and twenty-five children are using the yard. Or perhaps there is the wrong kind of equipment. If the sandbox is overcrowded, perhaps the group needs two. If the swings have too many customers, perhaps the group needs more swings or needs the type where two children can work one swing. Tricycles may need a trailer to enable two children to cooperate, and so on.

Storage of outdoor equipment must be arranged to protect the equipment from the elements and from damage from stacking. Inadequate storage

Older children can help younger children investigate nature. Include them in field trips when possible. (William Mitcham, Michigan State University Staff Photographer.)

for equipment can also be a factor if teachers dislike the outdoor period. Storage should be arranged so that getting equipment in and out is easy. Children should be able to help put nearly everything away. If teachers must lift items into inconvenient storage, then it is natural for them to dislike the task. Maintenance of outdoor equipment is of utmost importance. Nothing creates frustration in a child like having a tricycle or other toy that doesn't work. Wheel toys should be oiled regularly. Broken parts should be fixed. These kinds of costly items are worth maintaining well. Nonworking toys should be removed from the playground until repaired. The teacher should watch for such items and call them to the maintenance person's attention. A teacher can learn to use pliers to make minor repairs.

One teacher should take the responsibility for setting up the outdoor learning environment each day. She may also be the one to go out with the first children to get dressed for their outdoor period. Nothing rewards fast dressing like a chance to be first at the equipment.

Understanding must be arrived at among staff as to who will put equipment away—many harmonious relationships can be disrupted if staff members slip away just when this hard part of the day arrives.

The beauty of the playground should be given some attention in planning. Keeping litter off the grounds and equipment placed in an orderly arrangement will help children to learn about aesthetics and to care for their own living space.

In some climates and in fall and spring in others, virtually the whole program can be moved outdoors. Children enjoy having art, music, and literature outdoors. These activities allow the child quiet interludes that keep him from becoming overfatigued. A balance of quiet and active activities should be planned.

EMERGENCIES

A plan for emergencies should be made in policy-making sessions prior to the admission of children. Names of parents and their telephone numbers at home and at work should be kept at each telephone of the school and in the teacher's purse for use on field trips. The child's doctor's name and phone number should also be on the list. Written permissions are needed on file for the school to contact emergency medical service if parents cannot be reached. The staff should know general procedures to use in case of emergency and the reporting procedures required.

Emergencies can occur both indoors and outdoors. Serious emergencies should be few if you have sufficient adults for the number and ages of the children and if adults are spaced well throughout the classroom and play yard so they are indeed interacting with children as discussed here. Safety will remain a prime concern of all adults.

Adults will never leave children unattended. If someone feels an activity is dangerous, then it should be stopped until the staff can decide whether it should be permitted. Of course, children should not be smothered by adults to keep them safe, but being on the safe side is the best rule.

Occasionally a new teacher wonders if the children are customarily permitted to do something she sees starting. The best procedure is for her to take the child by the hand and say, "Let's ask Miss X if it is all right for you to do this." This way she fits her standards in with ongoing rules.

If a child falls or appears hurt, a teacher's calm behavior is a first requirement. If you get hysterical, the child—and probably the whole group—will get hysterical, too. Have the child stay quiet, do not jerk him to standing or into your arms. Reassure the hurt child. Advise helpers how they can help. Perhaps they can call the parent or doctor or both. Tell them what to say and do. The person whom the child knows best should stay with him to comfort and reassure him until the parent arrives. This is a period for the utmost professional behavior of adults. You must remain calm, or you will disturb all around you.

Someone must be delegated to continue with the rest of the group of children, and they will likely need a calm explanation of what has happened and how the child is feeling. A quiet time for talking about the times when they have been hurt may be called for. The experience will be meaningful, as they have known such accidents previously. They may be extremely fearful and need reassurance.

CONCLUSION

To meet the objectives for outdoor play, each teacher should give special thought to the opportunity and responsibility she has in guiding children's activity there each day. She should use all of the guidance principles discussed in Chapters 4 and 5 and apply each one in a creative way with each child. Children are individuals with differences in development, as discussed under each objective. The teacher's challenge is to determine where each child is on his developmental ladder and to help him reach a higher rung each day.

TWELVE GUIDES TO OUTDOOR PLAY ACTIVITIES

1. Plan at least one outdoor activity period for all children everyday.

2. Vary the outdoor activities and arrange to challenge and test motor skills.

3. Seek natural environments to give children an opportunity to know nature and help them learn to protect the environment.

4. Participate actively in children's learning and in their vigorous activity as a teacher, not just as a supervisor.

5. Be sure that you, as well as the children, are dressed appropriately for enjoying and participating in the outdoors in every season.

6. Encourage independence, creativity, and socialization in children's outdoor activity.

7. Introduce games that will build children's body management, locomotor, projection, and reception skills.

8. Motivate a child by identifying the next skill in the sequence that he appears ready to learn.

9. Avoid motivating children through competition with others.

10. Encourage the tension-releasing behavior and appreciate the generous sharing behavior exhibited by children.

11. Encourage investigating, questioning, and generalizing of information observed out of doors.

12. Follow and teach rules of safety for protection of individuals and property.

APPLICATIONS

1. Assist children playing on a playground. What are they doing? Are they playing in groups or alone? Would their play be classified as active or quiet? How much help do they need? How are conflicts settled? Summarize your findings.
2. Note two instances of physical guidance used on an outdoor playground. Note two instances of verbal guidance used. Were these instances effective in getting the child to do the desired thing? Explain.
3. Count the number of play spaces available on the playground. How many are there? Evaluate the number in terms of the number of children using the yard at any one time. Is there enough equipment? Summarize.
4. Spend some time with your case-study child on the playground. Report his activity.

SUGGESTED FILM

Outdoor Play . . . A Motivating Force for Learning   Color   30 minutes
Focuses on the unique physical and intellectual development provided by outdoor play activities and presents the extensive use of improvised materials. Campus Film Distributors Corporation, 20 East 46th Street, New York, N.Y. 10017.

FOR FURTHER READING

BAKER, KATHERINE READ. *Let's Play Outdoors.* Washington, D.C.: National Association for the Education of Young Children, 1966.
HILDEBRAND, VERNA. *Introduction to Early Childhood Education.* New York: Macmillan Publishing Co., Inc., 1971.
HILDEBRAND, VERNA. "Learning Tasks in the Preschool Years." *What's New in Home Economics,* Vol. 37, No. 1 (Jan. 1973), 27–30.

KLUGE, JEAN. "What the World Needs Now: Environmental Education for Young Children." *Young Children,* Vol. 26, No. 5 (May 1971), 260–263.

KRITCHEVSKY, SYBIL, and ELIZABETH PRESCOTT. *Planning Environments for Young Children.* Washington, D.C.: National Association for the Education of Young Children, 1969.

LUECK, PHYLLIS. "Planning an Outdoor Learning Environment." *Theory into Practice,* Vol. 12, No. 2 (Apr. 1973), 121–127.

McCORD, IVALEE H. "A Creative Playground." *Young Children,* Vol. 26, No. 3 (Aug. 1971), 342–347.

ROBISON, HELEN F. "The Decline of Play in Urban Kindergartens." *Young Children,* Vol. 26, No. 3 (Aug. 1971), 333–341.

STONE, JEANNETTE G. *Play and Play Grounds.* Washington, D.C.: National Association for the Education of Young Children, 1970.

Guiding Children's Art Experiences

Clair was painting at the easel. She drew her lines and splashed paint in the square shape. Libby asked, "What are you painting?" Clair answered, "I don't know." Using orange and green, she painted in the squares she had outlined. The colors mixed, "Look, it's brown!" she exclaimed. Libby said, "Well, I'm going to make a rainbow with every color."

THE GUIDANCE for Clair and Libby was indirect, because the easels had been set up side by side with large, clean sheets of paper, long-handled brushes, and glasses of paints. Libby and Clair were free to go to the easel during their self-selected activity period. These two four-year-olds were having in this one activity an experience that was meeting objectives for motor coordination, intellectual development, social exchange, and creative and emotional expression.

OBJECTIVES

Art activities, like many nursery school experiences, offer opportunities to fulfill many objectives related to children's growth and development. *Doing* the activity or the *process* is the important aspect of the art activity, *not* the product. The guidance of the adults is important at the time the child is engaged in his creation. Guidance must be based on objectives the teacher has for the individual child that can be achieved through the art media. Skills practiced in art activities carry over into other areas of learning.[1]

[1] For experiences of an art educator see Elaine Pear Cohen, "Does Art Matter in the Education of the Black Ghetto Child?" *Young Children*, Vol. 29, No. 3 (Mar. 1974), 170–181.

217

Eye-hand coordination is an important outcome of experiences with art materials. Thus art activities offer the children many pre-writing and pre-reading experiences. The children are developing skill with writing tools—crayons, brushes, and chalk. They are training the small muscles of the hand and the eyes as they paint and draw, cut and paste, or pinch and mold their many materials. The drawing of squares and circles and differentiating between them helps in later reading, where children must note the differences among squiggles on a page.

Older children enjoy a cooperative project at the easels. Notice the easily pulled down easel paper. (University of Idaho Laboratory School, Ed Breidenbach, Photographer.)

The toddler welcomes a chance to draw. (Joe Kertesz, Photographer.)

The teacher will label the child's products with his name using manuscript printing with upper and lower case letters. This is the first writing that the kindergarten or first grade teacher will teach, so it is less confusing if manuscript printing is used on products and when a child writes his own name.

The teacher should start names in the upper left-hand corner to help the child learn that writing and reading are done from left to right. She encourages him to start at the left, too, when he wants to write his name. If the child starts near the right-hand side to write his name, he is likely to run out of space. Then he will often place his last few letters in front of the first ones, creating what may look to his parents like the beginnings of "mirror writing." They may get worried and tell him how wrong it is, and thus discourage him. Both the teacher's writing and his own give the child further pre-writing and pre-reading experiences.

Most art projects are social in nature in that children share materials around a common table and take turns with various items of equipment. They frequently have delightful conversational exchanges such as Libby and Clair had in the anecdote that opened this chapter. Therefore, language development is enhanced.

The opportunity to be creative, to do something original, is one of the most important objectives. The child can independently decide what type of art activity he wants, what designs to use, how long he wants to stay, what he wants to do with the product when finished, and so on. He can be very independent and self-directed if adults will allow him to be. The materials are his to use and control.

Intellectual concepts are learned during every project. For example, in the opening anecdote Clair and Libby were learning the names of colors— "Look, it's brown!"—the concept that orange and green make brown, and the concept that "every color" can be used to make up a rainbow. Clair and Libby are moving into the preschematic stage where they attempt to represent things they are observing and to paint from memory objects they have seen previously.

Art activities offer emotional release. Watch children pound the mud clay or playdough. See how they draw figures in their fingerpaint, then with one swoosh erase them. Observe how they laugh when they draw something that pleases them. Many very personal feelings will be expressed that only the most sensitive observer who knows the child well will be able to interpret.

STAGES

The toddlers who first enter a group will use a crayon to make random, uncontrolled marks in what Lowenfeld and Brittain[2] call the *scribble stage*. Later the child enters the *named scribble* stage. He may

[2] Viktor Lowenfeld and W. Lambert Brittain, *Creative and Mental Growth* (New York: Macmillan, 1970), Chapters 4 and 5.

Representational drawings usually begin with a head. The human body receives less detail in the child's drawings for many months after he can draw a head. (Michigan State University Laboratory Preschool, Connie Lisiecki, Photographer.)

say it's a "dog." Even five-year-olds might be in the scribble stage if they have had only a few art experiences.

At about three years of age, the child makes his scribbles go in whatever direction he desires, such as diagonally or in a circle. These are *controlled scribbles.*

The *preschematic stage* occurs between four and seven years, and the child makes his first representation of an object he sees. Usually he makes a head first by joining up his circular scribbles. He tries putting in the eyes, nose, and mouth. Don't be surprised if these are not where you would put them.

He also makes rectangles and fills them in. The next stage observed in five-year-olds is the *schematic stage* where the child focuses on drawing the human figure—usually himself or someone in his family.

Teachers can make use of these stages by not expecting too much of the young children they teach and by helping parents understand that their child is "normal" when he only makes scribbles on his paintings and drawings. The same stages also are useful when looking at clay products.

PLANNING

Good guidance begins with planning. The art activities should be planned during the regular planning sessions, with the needs, interests, and skills of the children in mind. There should be an interesting variety of projects offered to the children.

Easel painting, drawing paper, and crayons are usually available daily. Materials such as stapler, masking tape, glue, and scissors are openly available to encourage children to make props for their dramatic play. For example, they might make tickets or paper money for a plane ride.

Other projects are rotated on a regular basis, with interesting variations added to encourage children to experiment with the materials. The teacher who wishes detailed explanations of suitable art materials and interesting variations is referred to Chapter 7 of the author's textbook, *Introduction to Early Childhood Education*, which is listed at the end of this chapter.

Only nonstructured materials that leave the child wide latitude for using them are appropriate for preschoolers. Coloring books and the related dittoed pictures that are sometimes prepared for children to "color" fail on all counts to meet the objectives for creative nursery school art activities. These emphasize a product—a very stilted and unimaginative one at that. Any observer will quickly note that children fill in the spaces they draw, too, such as Clair did with the orange and green paint in the opening example. Thus Clair was learning not just to fill in spaces as provided in a coloring book, but was actually making the spaces in a planful way, as well.

Materials must be prepared for the activities of

For variation it is nice to use white chalk on black paper. (Michigan State University Laboratory Preschool, Connie Lisiecki, Photographer.)

the day. These may be prepared in the afternoon for the following day's classes in order to have them ready when the children arrive in the morning. Good guidance of art projects begins by having materials out when children begin arriving.

In planning, you must think through the entire project to foresee possible problems. Do the children need aprons? Do they need a place to wash after the project? Do you need a sponge at the art table? Do you need a place to dry the products? Will newspapers on the tables make clean-up easier? How many children can one adult comfortably interact with? This planning is the now familiar indirect guidance.

Group Size   A group of five preschoolers is the largest that one adult should try to interact with at a time during arts and crafts projects. In this size group or smaller, the adult can help the children as needed. In small groups the intimate conversation and answering of questions can take place that is so important to the child's satisfaction and learning. A small table with only five chairs (or fewer) helps children know that only five can do the project and that if the chairs are filled they can have their turn later. When there is big demand for the activity, it can be repeated on ensuing days until all children are satisfied.

TEACHER'S GUIDANCE   The teacher will stress to each child that he can decide what he wants to do and how he wants to do it. It is the child's ideas that are important, not some preconceived notion of the teacher. "Let me see what colors you like" or "You can decide. Do you like long strips or shiny pieces?" she might ask. Each child will use materials differently and come up with different products.

Children may wait for the teacher to give them ideas. Adults without a creative orientation usually tell children what to make or draw. However, you be different. Do not shower them with your ideas, but respond as a professional by encouraging them to explore the materials and see what they come up with. Praise their effort by saying, "You worked hard to choose which materials to use, didn't you?" or "You did a good job in deciding on your colors."

Because the process within the child is important, you won't care how the product (painting, drawing, or clay object) looks. You will never make a model for the child to copy, because it is the child's ideas you want to bring out.

Actually, adults who are tempted to make models for the children should work with the materials in a staff meeting and take turns telling other adults how to make their product. You will quickly understand why making models hurts motivation and hinders creative expression.

Avoid praising the children's products—to be consistent with the principle that the product is unimportant. Some teachers "ooh!" and "ah!" over

A coloring book holds the child's attention, develops some coordination, but fails to stimulate as much creativity as a less costly plain sheet of paper. (William Mitcham, Michigan State University Staff Photographer.)

products until the children realize that adults really care after all, even though they say, "You do it your way." Praise such as "You did a good job" should be given to individual children in a quiet, personal way, too. Otherwise others will look at the complimented child and try to imitate him.

Many activities suitable for nursery school children are messy. In fact, that is one reason they are planned for the children. Children today are kept so clean that they don't know the joy of icky gushy messy material such as mud, clay, and fingerpaint. Try to be accepting of this material and learn to enjoy it as children will. Cover the tables with newspaper to make clean-up easy. Cover the children with wide aprons to make them easily cleaned up. Then watch them enjoy some of these messy activities. You'll see how much emotional release they receive. Watch them become relaxed. Listen to their conversation. If some child seems all up tight about getting messy, don't press him. You can sit with the

225 *Teacher's Guidance*

children and manipulate the material in the same way they might just to show that you like it and don't mind getting your hands messy. You need not talk much about what you're doing, just relax and they will learn from you.

Listen to what children say as they create. They often tell what they are making. Avoid asking them "What's this?" Since they are free to just experiment with materials, this question places too much emphasis on a recognizable product.

Give children plenty of time to do a project without rushing. A product that pleases the individual child often takes lots of time and thought and sometimes some rearranging. Try to plan enough play activities in the room so that children will have other things to do while they wait for a place at the art table or easel. This way the children who are

"We use pretty doilies for making pretty hats," explained the children to their parents after this project. (Nazarene Day Care Center, Lansing, Michigan, Gerald Seelhoff, Photographer.)

there can savor the experience and really learn from it.

Allow children to help with the art clean-up. They learn from cleaning up and they enjoy it. Washing paint brushes or sponging the easels will be a special privilege if you set it up right. Many like to be known as "helpers." In some groups clean-up jobs are rotated each week, and children go to their area and clean up regardless of whether they have used the material.

For example, four-year-old Pam was helping clean up the sink after cleaning the paint brushes. She said, "I want you to pour Comet in here to kill germs. Another child, Diana, poured in a liberal amount. Pam said, "Let's give it a quick rinse out. Where's the sponge? Where's the Comet?" She added some more Comet!

A suitable place for drying must be planned. Some projects may need to be kept overnight. Fingerpaints, for example, may require a great deal of drying time if children are allowed as much paint as *they* desire. Because children and teachers are primarily interested in the process, the use of a plastic tablecloth with fingerpainting done directly on the cloth may be desirable at times. Or serving trays can be used to paint on; then the paint can be washed off in the sink when the painting is finished. Children usually care very little about a painting when it is held over to another day to dry. They even forget which is theirs.

Children's art products can add nice color and design to the nursery school classroom. The displays can be artistically arranged with colorful mats behind drawings and paintings. They are more interesting to children if changed frequently. Every child's work must be displayed from time to time. The teacher customarily asks a child if she can display his product, for some feel strongly about taking the product home.

The guidance of parents and their reactions to the child's art is important. They often need help in understanding their child's level of representation. Some overemphasize a product until a child may dab a glob of paint on a paper just to have something to take home. A child who uses the blocks creatively may need some help in explaining to his parent why he does not have an art product to bring home. Siblings, too, can create problems. They may criticize a young child's painting or press him into competition with them. Parents may need help from teachers in alleviating this problem.

CONCLUSION

Art activities are an important part of the pre-school program. The opportunities for appropriate teacher guidance are many. From adequate indirect guidance through planning and placement of the materials to direct verbal and physical guidance as the children use the materials, the teacher has many opportunities to help the child fulfill objectives for growth and development that can be achieved through use of art materials. An understanding of the stages of artistic expression helps the teacher plan appropriate guidance for each child. By listening to each child personally, you will learn much about his inner thoughts and feelings.

TEN GUIDES TO CHILDREN'S ART ACTIVITIES

1. Place emphasis on the *process*, not the product, when presenting or commenting on children's art experiences.

2. Encourage the unique creative expression of each child by avoiding models for children to copy or coloring-book type drawings, both of which interfere with creativity.

3. Appreciate the various stages through which children progress in their ability to represent "reality."

4. Plan and prepare activities in detail to leave time to appreciate the individual responses of each child using a material.

5. Provide nonstructured materials to which the child can add his personal touch.

6. Avoid asking children "What are you making?" or guessing what they have made.

7. Use physical, verbal, and affective guidance as appropriate for the age and stage of the child.

8. Think of art activities as pre-writing and pre-reading experiences.

9. Teach intellectual concepts through art activities, such as colors, sizes, and shapes.

10. Interpret to parents the goals and procedures of creative art education for children.

APPLICATIONS

1. Assist a child using art materials at home or at school. Give an example of the adult's verbal guidance. Was the guidance understood? Did it help the child? Did it interfere with his work? Explain.
2. Assist a child using art materials at home or at school. Give an example of the adult's physical guidance. Was the guidance helpful? Explain.
3. Talk to a teacher or a parent about children's art projects. What types of projects do they provide? What objectives do they appear to be working toward? Explain.
4. Summarize your observations of your case-study child using art materials. Collect a sample of his work.

SUGGESTED FILMS

Early Expressionists   Color   15 minutes
A delightful film of two- to four-year-old children recording their spontaneous and rhythmic movements in art media. Filmed in the Golden Gate Nursery School in San Francisco. Modern Talking Pictures, 1212 Avenue of the Americas, New York, N.Y. 10036. Free from any Head Start office.

My Art Is Me   Color   25 minutes
A variety of art materials are used by nursery school children in an atmosphere that promotes discovery. The University of California (Berkeley) laboratory school is the scene. University of California, Extension Media Center, Berkeley, California 94720.

FOR FURTHER READING

HILDEBRAND, VERNA. *Introduction to Early Childhood Education.* New York: Macmillan Publishing Co., Inc., 1971.

LOWENFELD, VIKTOR, and W. LAMBERT BRITTAIN. *Creative and Mental Growth.* New York: Macmillan Publishing Co., Inc., 1970.

Seefeldt, Carol. "Boxes Are to Build—A Curriculum." *Young Children,* Vol. 28, No. 1 (Oct. 1972), 5–11.

Taylor, Barbara J. *A Child Goes Forth.* Provo, Utah: Brigham Young University, 1970.

Timberlake, Patricia. "Art—For the Child's Sake." *Young Children,* Vol. 26, No. 6 (Aug. 1971), 355–357.

Todd, Vivian E. *The Aide in Early Childhood Education.* New York: Macmillan Publishing Co., Inc., 1973.

Guiding Children's Science Activities

Kevin was sawing a piece of wood with much vigor. He pulled out the saw and touched it. He drew back his finger and exclaimed, "Ouch!" He asked the teacher, "Why is it so hot?" She explained, "You rubbed the saw and wood together when you were sawing so fast. You made a lot of friction. That made the saw hot."

FRICTION MAY NOT BE a scientific concept that is high on nursery school priority lists, but Kevin discovered it that morning at the carpentry bench. He perceived a stimulus through his sense of touch. He reacted, asked a question, and received a knowledgeable answer from his teacher. This is the most effective order for preschool children's scientific education to follow.

MENTAL DEVELOPMENT

Developing an understanding of the world around us is a lifetime process that begins at birth. The regularity and predictability of the universe is important knowledge to have. This knowledge is learned through mental processes and sensory perceptions. The ability to use all the sensory modes—seeing, hearing, touching, tasting, and smelling—is required for maximum development of the mental processes.

Good nursery schools have always held high priority for children's intellectual learning. Today the emphasis is greater than ever because new research is being reported that helps teachers better understand the mental or cognitive processes that are at work in the child.

231

"Now how do you suppose this thing works?" Learning begins with curiosity. (Frances Kertesz, Photographer.)

When you're two, it's easy to say "hello" to a pig.
(Mary Gray, Photographer.)

Jean Piaget,[1] the Swiss psychologist, is probably the most noted of the researchers who are shedding light on children's learning. He says that infants are in the *sensorimotor stage* of intellectual development. They make sense out of the world by interacting through reflexes and perceptual-motor activities. They are learning through tasting, grasping, and manipulating objects they come in contact with.

Toddlers and preschoolers are in what Piaget calls the *preoperational stage*, which lasts until about the seventh year. The two- to seven-year-old focuses on one variable at a time. He is confused, for example, if you try to teach him brown and round, but he can concentrate on color and shape as separate variables.

One of the important things that can be learned from Piaget is that the child learns as he interacts

[1] John L. Phillips, Jr., *The Origins of Intellect: Piaget's Theory* (San Francisco: W. H. Freeman, 1969), pp. 15–66.

with forces and things in his environment. His learning can not be imposed from the outside. The child must interact with his world. His learning follows a definite sequence that cannot be hurried by any adult.

The major way adults can influence the child's mental development is to set the stage so there are lots of stimulating things to do, time to experiment with the things, and someone to listen as the child reasons and questions. Catherine Landreth, a noted nursery school professional, said many years ago that young children tend to be laboratory not lecture students; that is, a child learns most through interacting with the things in his environment.

Give a child a real pumpkin to hold, lift, feel, and smell—and eventually to cut, look inside, and make into a jack-o-lantern. There is much more learning than would come from being told about a pumpkin or merely seeing a picture of one. (University of Houston, Rebecca Hines, Photographer.)

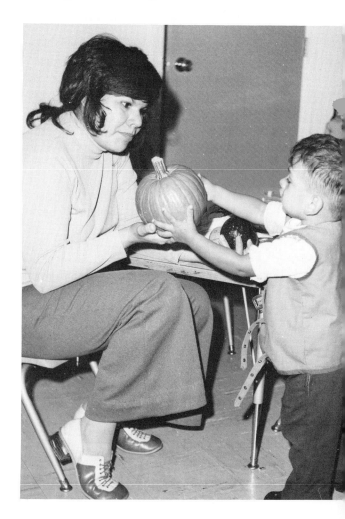

PLANNING

Careful planning must be done on a weekly and daily basis to assure a rich learning environment. Play can be learning, but it is not always as enlightening as it might be, unless the classroom and play yard have been planned to stimulate learning.

The first step in planning is to assess the level of the children who will be using the room and yard. For infants, the space should allow them room and equipment to practice the motor skills of grasping, reaching, pulling, mouthing, creeping, pulling to standing, cruising while holding on, and walking. The toys will be those the infant can grasp with big arm movements—a big teddy bear, a big cardboard block—or a toy to pull behind him as he lets go to walk on his own. Once he learns a skill, he practices continuously.

Preschoolers will be curious about most things that look new and interesting. Because young children are very self-centered, most of the science activities will have more meaning if they are related to the child in a personal way. The child learns many concepts simply through the normal routines that he follows every day. There are concepts about food, dressing, eliminating, sleeping, and family relationships. He learns the names of the various pieces of equipment and the names for his actions, if adults talk to him while they help him with the routine.

Table Games

Table games are commonly found in nursery schools. This label covers such toys as puzzles, parquetry, scribble sticks, lotto, construction sets of various kinds, beads to string, peg and shape sorting sets, stacking toys, matching cards, sequence boards, and peg boards.

Many of these toys can fulfill objectives for small motor development as well as test the child's intellectual abilities. Puzzles test the child's concept of spatial relationships at the same time that he learns the part-whole concepts. Beads and pegs can allow him to organize objects on the basis of color, shape, and size. Lotto and other games encourage matching, counting, or classification. Teachers should look at the games available and assess the scientific possibilities of each.

Toddlers enjoy peg board sets. At this age they have special interest in putting things in holes. (Michigan State University Laboratory Preschool, Connie Lisiecki, Photographer.)

The various table games should be rotated to keep the lot interesting and challenging. Some of the supplies should be stored out of sight so they will be new to add to the interest at a later time.

The teacher should store the games near the table where she expects them to be used. Children can be advised about proper care and usage. Children will first explore the item to see how it relates to something they already know. They may need help during the first use. The two- or three-year-old putting his first puzzle together needs one with fewer than six pieces. He may need advice about keeping the proper side up. When you tell him to "turn the piece," he may turn it over completely. (That shows how confusing our words must be at times.) You may even put your hand over his to guide the piece into place if he begins to be frustrated with the project and wants to quit. You might have a child who is having difficulty take out only one piece, look at it, feel it, turn it around and over, then put it back in place. You say, "That's the way to do it! Now try this piece," pointing to another piece. Completion will bring certain satisfaction and a return engagement within the moment, or tomorrow for sure. You, of course, will feel nearly as satisfied as the child when the puzzle is complete.

Because each child may be doing a different game, your guidance will of necessity be individually planned for each child. Watch to see what help the children need. Give only what help they need, not more.

An adult should be nearby to draw children's attention to particular points on each toy that will help them learn the concepts for which it is designed. The adult should be open to the child's discovering a new use for a toy. In the parquetry set, for example, the expectation is that children will match the wooden pieces to the geometric designs printed on paper in the bottom of the box. However, children may also learn by grouping the pieces by color and shape or by arranging them in some form, such as the "corral" one child made. Older children may organize the pieces on the table without benefit of drawings.

Some of the table toys have many similarities to

Plastic building blocks interlock to form interesting structures. (Michigan State University Laboratory Preschool, Connie Lisiecki, Photographer.)

those Dr. Maria Montessori designed for her children in "Casa Bambino" in Italy at the turn of the century. They have been adapted in new materials and colors, but the "self-correcting" nature of the materials is still one of their most important attributes. That is, the child can see when he's made a wrong move and can correct his performance himself without adults telling him.

One point in guidance is to avoid overcrowding of the table and to help children keep track of the pieces so they will not be lost. It is good teaching practice to check the puzzles and other games at the end of clean-up time. Occasionally a child absent-

Measuring beans and pouring them from one container to another are interesting learning activities. (Michigan State University Laboratory Preschool, Connie Lisiecki Photographer.)

mindedly puts a piece in his pocket. You can get children to look in their pockets by merely telling them, "We have lost one of our puzzle pieces. Everybody, look in your pockets to see if it happens to be there." Cooperation of custodians should be solicited to prevent loss of pieces under their brooms.

Experiments   Experiments have a definite place in the school program. These can be built around children's spontaneous interests, but they can also be planned to stimulate interests in materials and phenomena that might not arise spontaneously.

Studies of sound, air, gravity, temperature, tastes, small machines, heat, electricity, cold, melting, and so on are a few ideas for experiments that can be developed for children. The apparatus for experimenting should be arranged so that individuals and small groups can work with a teacher. Time should be allowed for the children to experiment—just to see what is happening before the teacher informs them about what she thinks they should know. Sometimes they already know what she expects to tell them, and that is interesting information for the teacher to learn. Sometimes they discover even more advanced concepts than she might have expected them to be able to comprehend.

Once the apparatus is organized, the teacher can keep it available to extend children's knowledge when instances come up spontaneously wherein they can relate an observation to an experiment. Experiments should have some bearing on the child's life, and efforts should be made to tie experiments to the child's here-and-now existence.

Some experiments and observations can be done with a single child who has a special interest. For example, when the teacher saw Ben leaning against a steam pipe she asked, "Ben, are you cold?" He said, "No, but this pipe is warm. Is it a gas pipe?" The teacher said, "No. It's a steam pipe. Would

you like to go downstairs and see where it comes into the building?" Ben was interested, and they made a quick tour of the building, tracing the source of heat for the classroom. Ben found his teacher a source of information that day and learned some facts that should help him grow in his understanding of heating.

Cooking Projects   Cooking projects and experiences with foods are full of important scientific concepts for children to learn. We must remember in planning such projects that children won't learn everything in the first few experiments. Projects with food are particularly popular because children will be allowed to eat the food and they may readily relate the project to home or other experiences they have had.

Small groups of children should be engaged at a time instead of rounding up the whole group and making them spectators. They will need to be involved to learn most. In planning, find ways to let each child stir a little, pour a little, or carry the pan. Teach the children to cut safely with a little knife on a cutting board. Try to allow them to eat the product the same day for maximum recall of the total project. Gelatin, for example, can be set with ice cubes to hurry the jelling process so children can eat it the same morning or afternoon it is made.

Clean hands should be required when working on food projects. Part of the teacher's planning and guidance goes into seeing that children wash before going to the cooking table. Because hot pans can be dangerous, special care should be taken to protect children without introducing unnecessary fear. A hotplate on a low table is better than having children try to see on the "too high" adult range. An electric skillet is a useful utensil for applesauce, scrambled eggs, pancakes, beef stew, and the like. The table for the skillet must be put near the electric outlet in a way that children are prevented from stepping across the cord.

While eating the product the children can discuss the sequence of its production. They can relate it to other concepts they have already learned. Vocabulary that relates to the project can be reviewed. With the aid of pictures, the project can be reported to parents through the bulletin board. This will also prompt recall for the children on future days.

A few food project ideas were mentioned in Chapter 11. Others are outlined in more detail in Chapter 14 of the author's textbook, *Introduction to Early Childhood Education,* which is listed at the end of this chapter. Refer to a good recipe book for details on specific foods. Experiment with the project at home before trying it with children.

Blocks Blocks offer opportunity to learn numerous scientific concepts, such as size, height, width, balance, weight, and classification. "We need all the round ones" or "Bring me the long ones" are statements indicating the children understand the concepts of classification. Blocks particularly prompt recall of family and community situations, which children incorporate into dramatic play.

Guidance for the block area includes helping arrange the space so children passing by do not interfere with the block builders. A carpet helps keep down the noise. Allow the children a long play period each day to encourage their building. They get discouraged if they work hard building something and seldom get to play in their structure. A child may need help in stabilizing a structure. He may not understand the concept of balance and would benefit from your helping him figure out why a structure is unstable. The block play is more interesting when you provide a number of props such as small cars or trucks, housekeeping equipment, puppets, or small plastic animals to be used in the play the children evolve around the blocks.

Some blocks are large enough to house the child as actor; in smaller sets he manipulates small figures as he plays. Some are small enough to be used on the table.

The teachers should plan to use words that help the child note various scientific principles. Words such as *behind, below, above, beside* can be learned as children play with blocks.

Carpentry Carpentry also helps children learn scientific concepts. Concepts are similar to those learned through

"The bit is what you use to make a hole," says the four-year-old, trying out a new tool. (Michigan State University Laboratory Preschool, Connie Lisiecki, Photographer.)

blocks plus the use of tools—hammer, saw, vise, and the like.

Rules related to safe use of the tools are important to learn. Overcrowding should be avoided at the carpenter's bench. If there are not enough spaces, then the project should be provided for a number of days to satisfy the children's interest. It should then be offered on a regular basis thereafter.

Good tools that really work will reduce the frustrations that children frequently express. Some children may enjoy using glue instead of hammering. Appropriate nail size helps reduce splitting of boards, so children may need help with nail selection.

Animals   Animals contribute important concepts for children's learning. In your guidance, help the child relate the animal's needs and appearance to his own. "How many legs does it have?" "What does it eat?" "Where does it sleep?" "How does it take care of its babies?" may be discussed with the children.

Animals must often be protected from children, for the children do not realize how hard they

"At the zoo we saw birds. Their wings went this way." (Southern University, Baton Rouge, Louisiana, Mary Odell, Photographer.)

squeeze. For example, the teacher can arrange a pen with large blocks for the bunny to play in while children watch him. She herself should hold the bunny while the children stroke its fur. Children can drop bits of lettuce into the improvised cage for the bunny. Animals are not toys and should not be carried around in doll carriages and the like.

Plants
Plants may be related to food, to house plants, or to the landscaping outdoors. Teachers can direct children's attention to new growth and involve them in care of the window box. Various projects can be offered in the proper season to help children appreciate the changes taking place in the outdoors. Many worthwhile experiences can be spontaneous events as the children play in the playground. The teachers should be alert to direct children's observations and to answer their questions.

Water Play
Water tables or other containers for water play provide opportunities for children to learn such concepts as volume, measuring, and pouring liquids. They see the effect of adding soap flakes to the water.

To aid in guidance, cotton rugs can be placed around the table to absorb the spills. Children should wear aprons. Overcrowding should be avoided. Children seem to relax when using the water table, so this is a good project for overactive children. Water play is popular outdoors when the weather is warm.

Mathematical Concepts
Mathematical concepts should be encouraged in many of the events of the nursery school. Adults should be alert to direct children's attention to numbers and to allow them to count. The number of children at the snack table, the number of eggs being put into the cake mix, the number of cups required for a bean-planting project, all offer opportunities for counting. It is important to have real objects for counting, to aid concept formation.

Field Trips
Important support for scientific concept formation comes from the field trips that are planned

either to stimulate children's interest and curiosity or to help children summarize information they have been learning in bits and pieces.

Field trips tend to offer some danger to children because the group is taken away from the familiar school, perhaps in some means of transportation. For this reason, special care must be taken in planning field trips to be sure they are safe and of true educational worth. Sufficient helpers must be available to insure safety of children. Each helper is responsible for not more than four children and keeps constantly alert to their whereabouts. Guiding their observations, she can point out important points that they seem to be missing. Questions are encouraged and answered factually.

In preparation for the field trip, the teacher will have visited the site and briefed all helping adults as to points of particular interest. Helpers often have the opportunity to interpret the words of

Bubble blowing stimulates interest and curiosity and is a new skill to learn, given a straw and a little detergent and water. (University of Houston, Rebecca Hines, Photographer.)

guides, who may not understand the level of understanding of young children.

When visiting animals such as in zoos or on farms, children must be kept a safe distance from fences or pens until you are sure the animals are harmless.

Riding in cars and buses presents some hazards. Children must remain seated and reasonably orderly to avoid disrupting the driver's train of thought. It is important to have two adults in the car.

More detail regarding field trip planning is found in Chapter 13 of the author's textbook, *Introduction to Early Childhood Education*.

CONCLUSION

Scientific education for young children fosters their mental or cognitive development. Specific plans need to be made on a regular basis to be sure that children are being stimulated intellectually to question and wonder about the world they live in. Teachers can set the stage for children to experiment and discover many of the concepts on their own. A rich environment, with interesting things to look at and to do, will motivate children to be curious. Answering children's questions and encouraging further questions are part of good guidance technique. Labeling the equipment, objects, and phenomena helps the children's scientific concept formation.

TEN WAYS TO FOSTER CHILDREN'S MENTAL GROWTH

1. Plan a wide variety of activities that challenge children's thinking, observing, and generalizing.

2. Remember that every activity of the home and school requires mental functioning and learning, and encourage this learning.

3. Give children experiences with real objects that they can handle and use for experimenting.

4. Develop projects around nature: animals, plants, seasons, and weather.

5. Plan cooking projects related to children's interests in eating.

6. Encourage the use of blocks as a medium for perceptual learning.

7. Encourage water play to teach concepts of volume and measuring.

8. Utilize every opportunity to count objects and use numbers.

9. Plan field trips to stimulate concept learning and integration of knowledge.

10. Encourage questions and never laugh at children's lack of knowledge.

APPLICATIONS

1. Assist children in a home or a nursery school. List the various equipment and toys available that you would classify as related to science. Write a summary of what children are doing with the equipment.
2. Write two guidance episodes related to scientific learning. Explain what happened. Explain which guidance techniques were being used.
3. Plan a science presentation for children and carry it out. Report to the class what you believe the children learned from the project.
4. Report on your case-study child's interest in learning. Record his questions and other indications of inquisitiveness.

SUGGESTED FILM

Blocks: A Medium of Perceptual Learning   Color   17 minutes
The accompanying narrative focuses on the perceptual learnings that are inherent in block building. The way the young child looks at the blocks and the space in which he builds are early learning experiences relevant to intellectual development and academic learning. Campus Film Distributors Corporation, 20 East 46th Street, New York, N.Y. 10017.

FOR FURTHER READING

ALTHOUSE, ROSEMARY, and CECIL MAIN. "The Science Learning Center: Hub of Science Activities," *Childhood Education*, Vol. 50, No. 4 (Feb. 1974), 222–226.

CARTWRIGHT, SALLY. "Blocks and Learning," *Young Children,* Vol. 29, No. 3 (Mar. 1974), 141–146.

DUCKWORTH, ELEANOR. "An Educator Looks at Sesame Street." *EDC News,* Issue No. 2 (Spring 1973), 5–6.

DYRLI, ODVARD EGIL. "Piaget Takes a Teacher's Look," *Learning,* Vol. 2, No. 2 (Oct. 1973), 22–27.

ELDER, CONNIE ZEHR. "Miniature Sand Environments: A New Way to See and Feel and Explore." *Young Children,* Vol. 28, No. 5 (June 1973), 283–286.

HAMMERMAN, ANN, and SUSAN MORSE. "Open Teaching: Piaget in the Classroom." *Young Children,* Vol. 28, No. 1 (Oct. 1972), 41–44.

HILDEBRAND, VERNA. "Trips for Preschoolers." *Childhood Education* (May 1967), 524–527.

HILDEBRAND, VERNA. *Introduction to Early Childhood Education.* New York: Macmillan Publishing Co., Inc., 1971.

HILDEBRAND, VERNA. "Trips for Preschoolers." In Monroe Cohen (Ed.). *A Lap to Sit on and Much More.* Washington, D.C.: Association for Childhood Education International, 1971.

HILDEBRAND, VERNA. *Planning for Young Children's Science Education.* East Lansing, Mich.: Michigan State University. Project No. 320424. Contract No. OEC–0–9–320424–4042 (010). Office of Education, U.S. Department Health, Education, and Welfare.

LANDRETH, CATHERINE. *Preschool Learning and Teaching.* New York: Harper & Row, Publishers, 1972.

LUECK, PHYLLIS. "Planning an Outdoor Learning Environment." *Theory into Practice,* Vol. 12, No. 2 (Apr. 1973), 121–127.

PHILLIPS, JOHN L., JR. *The Origins of Intellect: Piaget's Theory.* San Francisco: W. H. Freeman & Co., Publishers, 1969.

RAND, HELENE. "Experiential Learning Reevaluated." *Young Children,* Vol. 25, No. 6 (Sept. 1970), 363–366.

SEEFELDT, CAROL. "Boxes Are to Build—A Curriculum." *Young Children,* Vol. 28, No. 1 (Oct. 1972), 5–11.

TAYLOR, BARBARA J. *A Child Goes Forth.* Provo, Utah: Brigham Young University, 1970.

WEISER, MARGARET. "Awareness—One Key to Reading Readiness." *Young Children,* Vol. 25, No. 6 (Sept. 1970), 340–344.

Guiding Children's Dramatic Play

Jill said, noting the addition of an old typewriter to the playroom, "Look! We can have an office!" She sat down to type, jamming the keys. She pulled them back and typed more slowly. Jason arrived. "I wanta type, too," he said. Jill said, "First I'm gonna finish this report." Jason went to the dress-up rack and selected a white coat. As he returned, he said to Melanie, who had arrived on the scene, "This is a doctor's office. Do you want me to 'xamin your throat?" Melanie said "Wait," and went to get a small blanket. She spread it on the floor and lay down for Jason to examine her. He pretended to give her a shot. Jill finished her report and said, "Now Jason, you can type your report." She became the "doctor" calling in the patients one at a time.

JILL, JASON, AND MELANIE were happily engaged in spontaneous role-playing called *dramatic play*. They chose their roles. They selected their props and directed the scene. Except for a quiet observer who noted their words and actions, the children were for the moment in their own world. They were re-enacting the "office" scene that they knew best. They expressed their feelings and knowledge as they played.

INDIRECT GUIDANCE FOR DRAMATIC PLAY

The guidance for the office scene began when the teacher discovered an aged typewriter in the basement of the apartment house where she lived. Receiving permission to use the typewriter at school, she placed it where the first arrivals would notice it.

251

This set the stage for them to decide what kind of office they wanted.

A few rustic props can suggest dramatic play that may be carried on for days at a time. A well-stocked dress-up closet and a full-length mirror contribute to good dramatic play. Children never tire of seeing themselves. Besides admiring their dress-up clothing, they dance in front of the mirror, compare heights, and enjoy making funny faces.

The guidance also began when the teacher planned the schedule allowing plenty of time for children to dress up and to play their dramatic roles. When it seemed warranted, additional time was allowed—if the teacher felt that by extending the period the children would gain additional satisfactions. The schedule was relaxed, the atmosphere of the room encouraged creative expression. The teacher was nearby to offer support when it was needed.

The dress-up clothing was organized in a neat array on shelves and hooks that helped children see what there was without digging around in some obscure cupboard for it. Upon arrival the children often found the housekeeping corner set up with the dolls dressed and the dishes and pans neatly organized. Of course, it didn't stay neat long after the children arrived, but by then they were putting the items to use in their play, the objective the teacher had when she set up the center.

There were ample garments for those who wanted to play male roles. The teacher had selected some cast-off sixth-grade boys' shirts and coats, finding that men's clothing was too large and cumbersome for the small children. The children did, however, like some men's shoes they found there, for their own shoes easily fitted in them. They did not have to remove their own shoes to play dress-up.

The teacher allowed the children to form their own groups, never assigning them any particular place or group to play with. Friendships are important to small children just as they are to older ones, and friendships often begin because of the mutual interest two children have in some particular type of play. Melanie and Connie, for example, were two children who met when they first attended the three-year-old group at nursery school. They each enjoyed the housekeeping corner and daily played out the roles of caring for their dolls. They formed a fast friendship that lasted into their elementary years, until one of them moved away.

Children should be free to move from one area to another and to combine toys from one area with those of another. For example, they can move the housekeeping equipment to furnish a house that they have built in the block corner. They can move the doll bed to the hospital they have constructed. They freely use paper supplies to supplement their dramatic play by making tickets, labels, signs, and airplanes.

Children can play out only roles they are familiar with; therefore, for young children, the housekeeping roles are popular. (University of Houston, Rebecca Hines, Photographer.)

A *"businessman" uses a cash register in a store game.*
(*University of Idaho Laboratory Preschool,*
Ed Breidenbach, Photographer).

Spontaneity is the important characteristic of
dramatic play. The teacher's guidance is primarily
directed toward maintaining harmony among the
children, interpreting feelings, and adding props that
appear to be needed to expand the play.

When children have immature social skills, they
sometimes need to learn how to become accepted
by a group. They may keep asking, "Can I play?"
which nearly always receives a "No." Jennifer was
a three-year-old who needed this type of help. She
was having difficulty being accepted in the housekeeping area. When the teacher saw her approach
again, she said quietly, "Jennifer, let's knock here
on the door and see if anyone is at home." The
teacher stood by Jennifer as the "mother" arrived
to answer the door. "Mrs. Susan, we have come for

a visit," the teacher said. The children admitted them, and the teacher helped interest the children in the suitcase that Jennifer was carrying. Then the teacher quietly slipped out of the scene. Another day Jennifer was observed knocking before she entered.

By bringing in a new piece of equipment, the teacher can help extend the play to a child who is being rejected by a group. For example, Ron and Brad were building a space ship out of the wooden blocks. Dean was also building a space ship from the same supply of blocks. Dean made several overtures to Ron and Brad, hoping to be included in their play, but they were in a "You can't play with us" mood. The teacher sensed how much Dean wanted to be included. She said, "Dean, would you like to help me get something from the storeroom?" Dean was curious and followed her. They returned with a steering wheel, which Dean placed in his space ship. Rod and Brad were now a little envious. Brad said, "Dean, could we hook our space ship on to yours?" Dean, now in the driver's seat, said, "Okay," and the three boys played for the remainder of the hour.

The teacher helps children who are grabbing or hitting to use words to get what they want. She says, "Tell John that you would like to use the truck" or "Ask Mary to move instead of hitting her. She doesn't know you were using the telephone."

The teacher may protect one group from intrusion from others. Two bigger boys were involved in a cooking project. Meanwhile, other children had set up the blocks, making a railroad for their train. The bigger boys started to enter the block area with the intention of taking over—it being their usual domain. The teacher put her arms around the two bigger boys and said, "You fellows might play in the housekeeping area, or you could paint, but right now these children are using the blocks." After a moment of discussion, the boys selected painting and left the scene.

The teacher may sometimes see children who spank the dolls and shout at others during the "dinner." Realizing that the children are playing a role that may have deep meaning for them personally, the teacher allows them to express these strong feelings unless they harm another child.

The teacher may help a child get his anger under control so he won't hurt someone. Jay and Delbert were building roads in the sandbox. They stood a four-foot cardboard tube in a large juice can and filled it with water at the hydrant. With one boy at each end they carried it precariously back to the sandbox. Jay's end slipped, and down fell the tube spilling water on his pants. He grabbed sand toys and started to throw them at Delbert, blaming him for the accident. The teacher stepped up quickly and put her hands on Jay's shoulders, "Jay, it was

Housekeeping and grocery store play may get combined as children use the groceries they "buy" in preparing the meal for the family. (Howard University, Flemmie Kittrell Project, Scurlock Photographers.)

your end that slipped. Your pants will dry, why don't you go ahead with your road?" Her calm manner and the fact that Delbert was already working in the sand helped Jay return to his digging.

Guiding dramatic play calls for unobtrusive observation until the moment assistance is called for. Through observation, the teacher can receive many clues that help her understand the inner thoughts and feelings of the child. She also gains insights into his level of concepts and his misconceptions. For instance, when Jim was building a space station, the teacher asked him if he knew how big a space ship was. Jim said, "No." The teacher said, "It is taller than the tallest buildings downtown." Jim said, "Oh, I bet they are bigger than God."

By listening to conversation during dramatic play, the teacher may get ideas of things children are interested in that would make worthwhile field trips or class experiences for the future. The teacher also learns something of the life situation for the child at home with his parents and siblings; from this may come clues as to how the child could be helped. If the child dominates at nursery school, he may be gaining strength to cope with his home situation, where he is the dominated one. Releasing negative feelings during dramatic play may help the child. He should never be told he is "naughty" for his strong feelings.

VARIETIES OF DRAMATIC PLAY

A wide variety of dramatic play is possible. From the art table, where children pat out "biscuits" and "clay rockets," to the playroom, sandbox, carpentry bench, and play yard, opportunities abound. The teacher can provide props for some of the following types of play in one or several of these locations. The suggestions listed are described in more detail in Chapter 11 of the author's textbook, *Introduction to Early Childhood Education:* housekeeping, shoe store, grocery store, pet store, office, school, post office, hospital, restaurant, church, beauty and barber shop, fire house, gas station, car wash, camping, fishing, cowboys, road building, airplane, boat, train, and space.

The teacher has many opportunities to contribute to children's total development as she plans and guides dramatic play, the spontaneous role playing so popular with children in the nursery school. She sets the stage through indirect guidance, having everything set up invitingly as the children arrive. She helps where needed, but values the time for observing the child-child interaction taking place. She gets to know children better through studying this interaction.

TEN WAYS TO FOSTER DRAMATIC PLAY

1. Provide props and dress-up clothing to stimulate spontaneous role playing of familiar persons.

2. Introduce children to new workers' roles and ideas that might suggest roles for dramatic play.

3. Provide a full-length mirror to enable children to see how they look in their clothing.

4. Allow sufficient time in the schedule for children to develop dramatic play roles and themes.

5. Guide children unobtrusively, allowing them to solve social problems as much as possible.

6. Suggest a relevant supporting role for a child who is having difficulty entering a dramatic play situation.

7. Listen to conversations to learn what children's interests, feelings, experiences, and concerns are.

8. Set up areas and provide equipment on the playground for dramatic play.

9. Encourage language development by supplying labels for equipment, roles, and ideas children are dramatizing.

10. Allow children to make props and to use them for dramatic play.

APPLICATIONS

1. Assist children at home or in a school as they carry on in spontaneous dramatic play. What roles are they playing? How authentic are the roles?

Where do you think they learned the roles? Was a child playing a role similar to or different from his usual role? Explain.
2. Assist in a nursery school in the dramatic play area. Note what guidance opportunities arise. What guidance did you use? Did you achieve your objective? Explain.
3. When you recall your own childhood, what imaginative roles did you play? What props did you use? Do you think the play served any purpose for you? Explain.
4. Record your case-study child's participation in dramatic play. Interpret the meaning of dramatic play for the child.

SUGGESTED FILM

Dramatic Play . . . An Integrative Process for Learning   Color   32 minutes
Focuses on the intellectual, social, and emotional learning in dramatic play and the strategies used by the children in dealing with individuals and materials. Campus Film Distributors Corporation, 20 East 46th Street, New York, N.Y. 10017.

FOR FURTHER READING

HILDEBRAND, VERNA. *Introduction to Early Childhood Education.* New York: Macmillan Publishing Co., Inc., 1971.
RILEY, SUE SPAYTH. "Some Reflections on the Value of Children's Play." *Young Children,* Vol. 28, No. 3 (Feb. 1973), 146–153.
ROBISON, HELEN F. "The Decline of Play in Urban Kindergartens." *Young Children,* Vol. 26, No. 3 (Aug. 1971), 333–341.
SMILANSKY, SARA. *The Effects of Sociodramatic Play on Disadvantaged Preschool Children.* New York: John Wiley & Sons, Inc., 1968.

Guiding Children's Literature, Language, and Music Activities

Deanna and Peggy were looking at one book. Steve and Mark were looking at another book next to Deanna. Steve laughed and pointed, "Look at the monkeys!" The others looked and laughed with him.

B o o k s are for reading. Books are for sharing. Books are for enjoying. Books are for communicating ideas. The children's teacher had these objectives in mind when she arranged for informal "reading" of books by the children before she began the official storytime.

Literature experiences in the nursery and nursery school offer the children important pre-reading experiences. When a child is given time to enjoy and savor good literature early in life, the problem of being a nonreader rarely occurs.

PLANNING LITERATURE EXPERIENCES

Careful planning went into the literature and language activities of Peggy's and Deanna's class. The teacher kept in touch with new books that were appropriate for the children's interests and level of understanding.

Selecting Appropriate Books

For the youngest toddler, books may be single items on a page for them to point out and name. "Ball," "Cup," "Shoe," says the child as you turn the pages of his heavy cardboard book and let him tell you what he sees. The next books are those with one idea on a page, like Eloise Wilkins' *Busy Timmy* who "puts on his outdoor clothes and walks down the steps with no help at all." Characteristic of this level of book is that it depicts action familiar to the

260

A good book, a lap to sit on, and a teacher who enjoys reading—what more could a young child want? (Michigan State University Laboratory Preschool, Connie Lisiecki, Photographer.)

child. He is not yet worldly enough to have many experiences to relate to his reading matter.

Through the third year the books should be short and personally oriented for the child. It is better to read several short books to three-year-olds than to try a longer one and realize in the middle that they are not understanding the book.

Four-year-olds will enjoy longer books if they have had solid earlier experiences. The subject matter still needs to be quite factual and true to life. Toward the end of their fourth year, children will begin to understand fanciful stories. They'll know that animals don't really talk and trains don't say, "I think I can."

It is extremely important that the books chosen

for reading to a group be at the appropriate level. Some books might be read to individual children that are not suitable for the group, because when reading to one child you can elaborate and allow the child to question and discuss in more detail than you usually are able to in a group situation. If you are having trouble keeping children's attention at storytime, be sure you are selecting appropriate books and, if anything, err on the side of selecting them too simple. Once you have established a pattern of attentiveness, you may then be able to move to more difficult books. Good storytime guidance begins with selecting the right books.

Organizing Story Groups   Story groups should contain no more than four or five preschool children, especially when children are first learning to function as a group. Young children come to school from an experience of one-to-one storytime. They sit on the parent's lap for their story. If they are from homes where there are no books and they have never been read to, then they need the same experience as a toddler for a time. That is, they need to have one adult share a book with them and allow them to react to the pictures they see. After this experience, they can graduate to listening with a few children.

The group can be divided so that compatible children are in a small group. Logically, they are the children with interests in the same type of stories. A regular teacher for each group will help maintain continuity for the children. She will be able to build a logical sequence of experiences for the group when she is familiar with them.

A literature experience with a group of fifteen or twenty children does not do justice to the interests and needs of individual children. One has only to observe storytime in a large group to note that children do not get involved with a story in the way they do when the story is read in a smaller group. Much of the time is usually spent keeping order. "Experience in a large group" is often the stated objective or rationalization for organizing one story group instead of several. Teachers who keep large groups should realize that when coercion is required to keep order, it detracts from the literature experience, which should be fun for the children.

Because nursery school groups typically have several teachers and volunteers may also be available, it is usually possible to organize small story groups. If the group must be kept together, then the assistants should sit among the children to help with problems that arise. Storytime guidance is helped by organizing the groups to facilitate good listening for each child.

Preparing for Storytime

The teacher who has an inspirational storytime and meets the objectives that can be achieved by a good storytime does so by design, not by chance. It is a great loss when the teacher grabs a stack of ragged books on her way to storytime and expects to muddle through the next few minutes without preparation. Storytime needs planning. The teacher must know the book well and have some idea of how it will affect the children. She often prepares some teaching aids to use with books to help the children understand better.

Part of her preparation includes some quieting techniques that help the children get ready for the listening behavior she expects. These may be fingerplays and little songs that interest the children and help get the fidgets out of their bodies. After a few of these transitional techniques, the teacher can open her book and read.

Of course, the teacher does different things with the story period, keeping it a surprise each day so that children will want to come to see what she may have thought of next. Variety will indeed make storytime more interesting.

Reading or Telling the Story

When you know the story well, you'll feel free to allow children to respond, for you'll have confidence that you can resume the story, maintain interest, and keep the group together. By seating children with their backs to the window, you can prevent glare from interfering with their seeing the pictures. You can use voice techniques for speaking for the various characters but should avoid making them too harsh or scary. Young children are not interested in the author of a picture book, so once your quieting efforts are successful, open the book and begin reading at once.

Your storytime groups should be situated away from distracting toys. A portable screen may come in handy to shield toys from view.

If there is a child who simply will not sit still for a group storytime even when given a special place by the teacher, a volunteer should be engaged to read to him individually. Let him select the books he wants to read. Sometimes a cook can help supervise such a child while he listens to a story on a record player.

Because literature experiences are so important for learning to read later, teachers should do everything in their power to make books interesting for children. Some work with individual children can take place during regular self-selected activity time where a storybook corner is set up for individual browsing. The flannel board may be used there, too.

A flannel board story attracts an audience of eager listeners. (University of Idaho Laboratory Preschool, Ed Breidenbach, Photographer.)

Children can have a turn at telling their own stories with the figures.

In one day care center, a "storylady" handles much of the storytime for the center. She maintains a little library with loungers, easy chairs, and rugs where the children can browse through books. She reads to small groups as they are interested. She thus relieves some of the other teachers at various points in the day, although they all keep a story corner in their classrooms and prepare a story of their own each day. The "storylady" acts as a book reviewer for new books, giving the director a list of books to buy from time to time. She also procures books from a local library to supplement the supply of the center.

PLANNING LANGUAGE ARTS EXPERIENCES

Many of the literature experiences are also language experiences. In fact, language is an important part of all nursery and nursery school experiences and should be placed in high priority. Language is learned through talking, listening, and responding to language. A room full of meaningful conversations is far better than a quiet room.

We, as teachers, must watch that we allow children to do some of the talking. Sometimes we simply do not know how we dominate the conversation, and children may be only saying "yes" or "no" or even shaking their heads. The television show *Sesame Street*, which purports to stimulate children's language development, has been found to have a very high percentage of adult conversation.[1]

With each planned experience—art, science, dramatic play, field trip, visitor, or the like—the teacher should note the new vocabulary that naturally flows from it. As experiences are repeated throughout the year, the words will gradually find their way into a child's usage.

The free self-selected activity organization that is common in most preschools encourages children to practice the language that they know and to learn to respond to the language of their peers and the

[1] Herbert A. Sprigle, "Who Wants to Live on Sesame Street?" *Young Children*, Vol. 28, No. 2 (Dec. 1972), 103.

teacher. Dramatic play and outdoor play offer high language stimulation. Through conscious efforts, teachers can raise the level of conversation in their groups.

The ease of interaction in a group will contribute to the confidence a child shows in using language to make his needs felt. If he is treated with respect, he will try to communicate. If he gets answers to his questions, he will ask further questions. If he finds

A favorite song sung with gusto is suggested by a small instrument and a willing audience. (Southern University, Baton Rouge, Louisiana, Mary Odell, Photographer.)

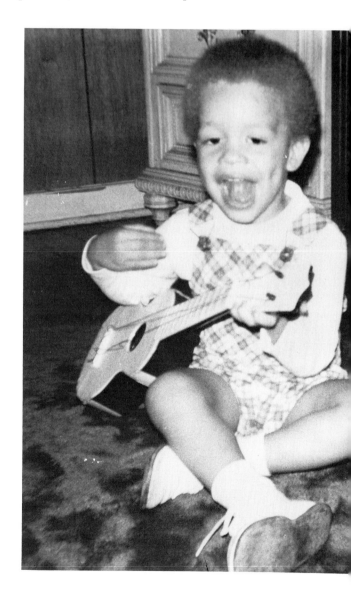

Children's Literature, Language, Music Activities

teachers who will listen, he'll tell stories of events important to him.

Children sometimes come from homes where the language is different from that of the teacher. They will have a difficult time for a while bridging this gap. The teacher's respect for them as persons will make it easier for them to learn her language. When there are helpers in the classroom from their language group, the child's needs may be more comfortably met. Teachers should consider the cultural shock they would feel in a foreign country and appreciate the feelings that a young child must have when he is first placed in a school where the language is different from that in his home.

Children may have some difficulty with language —with pronouncing certain consonants or with faltering speech. Such problems are not uncommon in young children, and most will be outgrown. It is important that a large group of adults does not add pressure to these children with language problems. It can only make problems worse if at every hand someone is making them repeat or asking what they said. A speech consultant should offer the school advice when a child has a problem. He may suggest a careful routine of therapy for the teachers to follow.

PLANNING MUSIC EXPERIENCES

Singing Time

Singing time easily dovetails with storytime. A period of singing can precede the story and help with quieting the group, as mentioned in the discussion of storytime. The teacher selects, prepares, and makes a list of a wide variety of songs and musical fingerplays in order to be able to choose those that are most appropriate on a given day.

Variety is important, for all children will not enjoy the same songs equally. They may tire of certain songs, and if asked specifically, "Do you want to sing . . .?" they may say, "No." It is usually better guidance if the teacher keeps singing time moving with new and known songs integrated in a way that keeps interest high. Giving children choices often slows down the event, and some children get bored waiting for their friends to come up with a choice, or they do not like the choice and the time is spent on that discussion. Therefore, it is usually best if the teacher knows the songs she wants children to learn and simply sings them through at a lively tempo, taking children's choices whenever they come up quickly and incidentally. Teachers may discuss choices of songs during snack time, having them ready to sing the next singing time.

Teachers of each of the small groups can be teaching the same songs, so that if the group meets as a whole or teachers are exchanged the children will be familiar with some of the same songs.

Singing can be encouraged out of doors or during any of the various nursery school activities. Guidance that is sung, such as, "Pickin' up toys, put them on the shelf," which is sung to the tune of *Paw-Paw Patch*, usually is quite effective.

Experimenting with the piano is an interesting musical experience. (James Page, Photographer.)

Creative Movement Creative movement is usually incorporated into the self-selected activity period. Small groups are easier to work with than large. Spontaneous response to music may be encouraged around the record player. Having rhythm instruments stored on convenient shelves nearby helps children feel free to use them with records. Long, flowing dresses that are part of the dress up wardrobe may also be incorporated into musical experiences as the children dress up to dance.

The key to guidance in movement and rhythm experience is to allow children lots of free expression. Preschoolers are not ready to do special steps to music, and such lessons usually leave them tense and unhappy with the experience. Children have some natural rhythms that are fun to recognize and encourage. When you see a child tapping out a rhythm, be it with his foot, his finger, or on the rocking boat, you might call it to his attention and even tap it out on a tambourine or drum.

CONCLUSION

Storytime and music time can be both spontaneous and organized events in the nursery school day. To keep a rich variety of material before the children, the teachers will be spending considerable time in planning. These are important periods during the day to stimulate the children's learning and to give children another opportunity for creative emotional expression. Language arts activities are really part of the total school day. Conscious efforts are also needed on the part of adults to be sure all children participate in conversations. The closeness the child feels to the adults will be an important factor in how comfortable he feels about expressing his ideas. See Chapters 9, 10, and 12 in *Introduction to Early Childhood Education* (listed at the end of this chapter) for more detailed suggestions concerning language arts, literature, and music activities.

FIVE GUIDES TO LITERATURE EXPERIENCES

1. Select books appropriate to the age and experience of the children.

2. Plan daily literature experiences for every child and, especially, an individual experience when a child seems unready for a group experience.

3. Use variety in literature and in storytelling techniques to attract children to this important pre-reading event.

4. Organize children in small groups, especially the youngest children, to make the literature experience most meaningful for the individual child.

5. Stimulate use of the library by young children and their parents.

FIVE WAYS TO FOSTER LANGUAGE SKILLS

1. Use every opportunity to increase children's vocabulary and to encourage practice in speaking and listening.

2. Plan a variety of games that encourage both speaking and listening.

3. Encourage spontaneous, vital conversations and interactions rather than quiet, submissive behavior.

4. Appreciate the handicap that a child with a different language background may be experiencing and aid that child to feel at ease and express himself.

5. Obtain advice from a speech therapist before attempting to correct children's speech.

FIVE GUIDES TO MUSIC EXPERIENCES

1. Plan a wide variety of musical experiences including many songs.

2. Teach songs using normal tempos, and, rather than rehearsing a new song, sing it for several days until children learn it.

3. Remember that the primary goal of music is enjoyment.

4. Keep any accompaniment to children's singing soft and as background.

5. Use music throughout the school day, indoors, outdoors, as guidance, as an expression of joy, to relieve tension, and to foster concept development.

APPLICATIONS

1. Assist children at home or at school as they use books. What books are they using? What roles do the adults play in the children's literature experience? Report your findings.
2. Assist in a nursery school with storytime by giving support to a teacher who is in charge or by telling a story that you have prepared. Report to the class what responses the children gave to the story.
3. Record three instances of children's conversation. How long are the sentences? What is the grammatical construction? Did the child achieve the desired goal through his verbal utterance? Explain.
4. Copy several poems or fingerplays on 3 x 5 cards. Recite them during appropriate moments with a few children. Report to the class on the outcome.
5. Visit the public library during preschool story hour. Volunteer to help the librarian. Give a report on your experience.
6. Report your case-study child's interest in and use of books. Record instances of his conversation and use of language. Report on his participation in music and movement.

SUGGESTED FILM

Creative Movement for the Developing Child   25 minutes
   A black and white film showing Clare Cherry's methods of involving children in simple, interesting, and creative movement experiences. CATEC Consultants, 2754 San Gabriel, San Bernadino, California 90069.

FOR FURTHER READING

BARRETT, KATE R. "Learning to Move—Moving to Learn: Discussion at the Crossroads." *Theory into Practice*, Vol. 12, No. 2 (Apr. 1973), 107–119.
CAZDON, COURTNEY B. (Ed.). *Language in Early Childhood*. Washington, D.C.: National Association for the Education of Young Children, 1972.
GERHARDT, LYDIA A. *Moving and Knowing*. Englewood Cliffs, N.J.: Prentice-Hall, Inc., 1973.

HILDEBRAND, VERNA. *Introduction to Early Childhood Education.* New York: Macmillan Publishing Co., Inc., 1971.

KERCKHOFF, RICHARD K., and SHERRY C. TRELLA. "Teaching Race Relations in the Nursery School." *Young Children,* Vol. 27, No. 4 (Apr. 1972), 240–248.

MATTICK, ILSE. "The Teacher's Role in Helping Young Children Develop Language Competence." *Young Children,* Vol. 17, No. 3 (Feb. 1972), 133–142.

MOORE, SHIRLEY G., and SALLY KILMER. *Contemporary Preschool Education: A Program for Young Children.* New York: John Wiley & Sons, Inc., 1973.

SMITH, GRACE. "On Listening to the Language of Children," *Young Children,* Vol. 29, No. 3 (Mar. 1974), 133–140.

SPRIGLE, HERBERT A. "Who Wants to Live on Sesame Street?" *Young Children,* Vol. 28, No. 2 (Dec. 1972), 91–109.

TAYLOR, BARBARA J. *A Child Goes Forth.* Provo, Utah: Brigham Young University, 1970.

Appreciating Positive Behavior

Rod, a new child, and Joan were playing in the sandpile. Sharon came into the yard and said, "I'm hollering at you, Rod. I'm hollering at 'cha." Rod smiled at her and kept playing with Joan. Sharon left and yelled, "Hey, Rod," several times. An adult said, "Seems like someone is calling you." He just glowed and said, "I know who it is."

ROD WAS FEELING the warmth of being accepted in a new group. Through this moment of child-child interaction, Rod's resources of self-confidence and security were enhanced. Acceptance by others contributed to Rod's sense of security.

**MEANINGFUL-
NESS OF
BEHAVIOR**

By becoming a careful observer of children's behavior, we can begin to learn how children are feeling and thinking. The positive or "good" behavior of children is sometimes overlooked by parents and teachers because we get so obsessed with correcting or eliminating their "bad" or negative behavior. By looking at strengths, we can often help children overcome weaknesses. For this reason, the emphasis in this chapter will be on positive behavior in the hope that negative behavior can be placed in a better perspective. Of course, there is no clear line between positive and negative behavior; this will be determined by each person's value system. The more positive the adult feels about himself, the more positive most behavior of children will seem to him, because warmth, understanding, and acceptance prevails.

273

Happiness is helping fold up the blankets after naptime is over. (Michigan State University Spartan Day Care Center, Connie Lisiecki, Photographer.)

Infants Babies will exhibit positive behavior if their needs are satisfied. Babies' behavior is the language by which they tell us what they need. When they are sleeping, quietly cooing, eating heartily, or kicking rhythmically, we assume they are having their needs met. They aren't hungry, or tired, or uncomfortable in any way.

Parents and caregivers receive positive feedback when the baby is being satisfied. Babies soon learn to gurgle and smile when their favorite person enters the room. They flail their arms and legs, shaking their mobiles or rattles, when someone stops by the crib or playpen to chat for a minute. Once they crawl, they go on all fours to meet a favorite person.

Babies thrive on attention. Giving them the

amount of attention they need does not have to be a constant job. They are better off with little bits of attention throughout the day. In an infant nursery there probably is not a worry in the world that the baby will get "too much" attention. Caregivers typically have too many charges for that to happen. It is just as important, though, for caregivers as for parents to be giving babies the attention they need. The kind words and conversation during diaper changes, the pointing out of things to look for, are part of giving babies the attention they need.

Happy babies are active. Once they are developmentally able, they roll over, they stand in their cribs, and they jump. It is pleasant to see them, for they enjoy themselves so. Out on the floor they scootch along until they learn to crawl, then before long they are pulling themselves up to chair legs and playpen sides. Life grows more dangerous, for now they can get to dangerous things—the heater, the tablecloth, even that cupboard under the sink where mother keeps those dangerous cleaning chemicals. But locomotion is wonderful, and adults must organize the environment so it is safe, not dangerous.

Happy babies are noisy, at least some of the time. They increasingly use their vocal cords to get attention and to express their excitement. A parent or a caregiver who wishes for silence should think of a deaf child who has never said, heard, or responded to a word. His mother would have given anything to have heard him shout. That day on his third birthday when he was finally fitted with a hearing aid, the therapist quietly said to the mother, "Call your child." The mother said "John." When the child turned toward her, she wept openly. During all those infant months when he had been silent, she had thought of him as a "good baby" and didn't wonder why.

Happy babies are social. They like people and enjoy the games that people play with them. They aren't out to beat the adults, or to control them, or to test them. They give back what they get. If they are given love, they return it. Other human beings are so important to these small bundles of humanity that toys, and television, and propped-up bottles should never replace the human touch and voice in their day. To be happy and secure, they must be loved unconditionally because they are there and because they are ours.

Happy babies are smart. They are constantly exploring their world for the knowledge they need to fill their clean slate. They are doing it through touching, tasting, chewing, seeing, and hearing. You often see them discovering that one action makes something else happen. For example, a baby kicks his crib and the bell on the mobile rings. He stops and the bell stops. He kicks again, the bell rings. A big smile covers his face, for he has learned a relationship that he didn't know existed—kicking makes the bell ring.

Happy babies are sleepers. Perhaps no moment is so moving as to watch a sleeping infant for a while. What deep trust he must have to be so completely relaxed. He tells us that all is well. Can we promise to be true to that trust as we help him grow?

Toddlers   Happiness for a toddler is allowing him to try his wings—to achieve *autonomy*, as psychologist Erik Erikson calls it. A positive behavior is his exploring on his own. He wants to use the tricycle, though he may walk it along instead of pedaling it.

Happiness, too, is getting on high places that sometimes he may be worried about getting down from. He will look and feel like "king of the mountain" and mother will scurry to rescue him lest he tumble down.

Try visualizing yourself as a toddler to understand the pleasures of his life. For example, happiness is getting into things and poking your fingers into things. A carton from the grocery store makes a toy that you can use for days—in and out, out and in you go, sitting down, rising up—a rhythm of exploration. You poke at Grandma's toe through her open-toed shoe and could just as well poke around the electric cord if someone didn't watch out for you.

Happiness is practicing the sounds you know and having people get very excited because you've spoken to them. It probably happens to Daddy first, for you are most likely to say "da-da" first, then

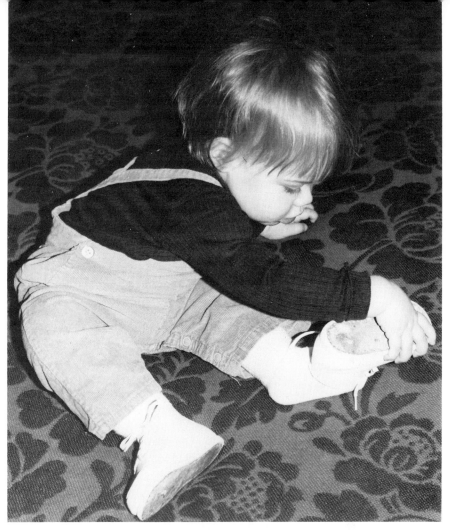

Happiness is working at putting on your own shoe and having someone help you finish the job. (Frances Kertesz, Photographer.)

"mama," and after that other sounds and then real words that you try out. You love doing it. (One mother put the tape recorder by her toddler's bed and recorded the language practice that he carried on long after others thought he was asleep.)

Preschoolers   Action for a preschooler is a positive behavior, the key to healthy development, the sign that the child is growing as he should. Physical action means continuous running, climbing, crawling, and hopping. Perhaps no one ever appreciates all the things

277   *Meaningfulness of Behavior*

Happiness for toddlers is poking your finger into things. (Mary Gray, Photographer.)

the normal child can do until he knows a handicapped child who can't do them.

Sitting still is a preschooler's cup of tea only if he decides to do it—that's why we let him choose his nursery school activity. He knows best what his body needs next. If he decides to look at a book or do a painting, his concentration can be quite intense.

Pretend that you are a preschooler now. Positive behavior is laughing after recovering from the shock of having a turtle put in your face by a teasing boy. Positive behavior is taunting when your best friend tries to hit you with paperwads, "Missed me! You missed me! Now you've gotta kiss me!" Positive behavior is pretending about a big banner seen across the street—"Yeh! It's a big net and it is winding around us. It's got us! We can't get away!"—and having your friends pretend to be caught in the struggle and laugh with you.

Positive behavior is singing into the stethoscope and finding out if you can hear yourself. Positive behavior is making skis out of the hollow ramps, putting your feet in, and walking, and having your

Happiness is working on a project until you get it finished. (Michigan State University Laboratory Preschool, Connie Lisiecki, Photographer.)

buddies laugh at the new discovery that they hadn't seen before. Positive behavior is wanting to throw a rope over a tree limb, then having your friend hold a stool for you while you get high enough to succeed. Positive behavior is hanging by your knees on the jungle gym and having your friend say, "I didn't know you could do that!"

Positive behavior is seeing the chick come out of the egg, hearing the cow "moo" and sheep "baa"— all those things you've been told about but never experienced until now. Positive behavior is playing lotto and knowing which card has the picture that turns up.

Positive behavior is feeling big enough to say "Bye" to Mom and really not caring if she leaves you and goes uptown to shop. Positive behavior is being weighed and having the teacher say "You've gained two pounds." Positive behavior is wrestling with your friend in the grass and knowing you can hold your own but that he won't really hurt you. Positive behavior is feeling relieved that Mom finally bought you some blue jeans like the older boys in the school wear. Positive behavior is being glad when Daddy surprises you by stopping by the school to visit for a while. Positive behavior is doing your job at clean-up time and having the teacher say, "Everybody was really great on clean-up today."

For preschoolers, talking is more interesting than listening. As a teacher, you will frequently hear conversations that make you feel like you've run two interviews together on the tape recorder. Both children talking, neither listening.

Talking and getting an idea across is a positive behavior when the preschooler can tell someone how he feels, like when Jeff whispered to Jimmy, "I like Peggy," or when Junior took Kenny's clay and Kenny shouted, "No! no!" Talking is asking for information, "Teacher, do the moon guys wear helmets, in case they crash on the moon?" Or talking is telling the teacher the most important news before someone else has told her—"I have a new baby sister." Talking is inviting a best friend, "I'm going to take you and Charlie to the rodeo this night." Talking and having someone to listen, talk back, and not say "shut up" are positive interactions for preschoolers.

Positive behavior is Carolyn and Bradley playing house and Bradley going over to Carolyn, putting his arms around her neck, hugging her and kissing her on the cheek. Positive behavior, too, is Carolyn just laughing as they go on playing.

Positive behavior is Clair painting a picture for each of her brothers, or Melanie taking a cookie home to her brother, " 'Cause he doesn't have any cookies."

Positive behavior is Cindy tying Marilyn's shoes when she didn't have any of her own to tie. And Keith swinging alone chanting

Swing, swing
My swing is swinging.
Swing, swing
I'm making it go.

Behavior has meaning, and our job as parents and teachers is to search for that meaning. What do all the things a child does tell us about him? We can't draw conclusions from one or two incidents but must watch him over a period of time before drawing conclusions and making decisions about him. When we sit down after school each day, or at home when the children are safely tucked in, to take stock, we should start with "What positive behavior did we observe today?" Then we can analyze what we did to help or hinder these "happenings." These can be lessons for the tomorrows.

Of course, problems are not ignored—even problems may be positive behavior for some children. How? Well, for example, you might have a child who is quiet and withdrawn, then he gradually grows to trust you and himself and begins to stretch and strain the rules. These may be problems for you, but for that child they signify growth. What do you do? Don't press down hard enough on him to push him back into his shell, for heaven's sake! Ignore him for a while unless he's going to hurt someone, because through acts of self-expression this child is now overcoming a problem. The teacher's goal is to tailor the guidance to children's individual needs. Within a short time, this child will likely be willing to follow the rules.

CONCLUSION

The samples of positive behavior in the preceding sections are only a few of the types and kinds you'll find in any group of healthy children. The various kinds of positive behavior are resources, the human resources that education is trying to develop. There are friendship, love, laughter, curiosity, initiative, language, energy, skill, knowledge, empathy, and sympathy exemplified. There are more examples that you will find. These are real children, normal children, doing normal things, and growing into more competent, worthy individuals each day.

APPLICATIONS

1. Assist with children at home or at school and make two two-minute diary records (an account of everything they do or say) of two young children's activity. Analyze the records by listing each bit of behavior in a positive or negative column. What kinds of behavior do you find in each column? Trade lists with one of your classmates and observe whether you and your friend agree on the rating of behavior. What are your conclusions?
2. Discuss with a mother or a teacher what kinds of behavior she considers positive or good. Summarize the conversation. Do you agree with her position? Discuss with your class.
3. Record three instances when one child appears to give another pleasure. What were the settings in which the behavior occurred? Describe.
4. Discuss with a teacher or a parent the positive behavior you have observed in a child. Report how the adult helped you complete your view of the child.
5. Which children are friends? What do they seem to contribute to each other? Explain.
6. From your records analyze the positive behavior your case-study child has exhibited. Begin to complete your case study.

FOR FURTHER READING

BRYAN, J. H., and P. LONDON. "Altruistic Behavior by Children." *Psychological Bulletin*, Vol. 73, No. 3 (1970), 200–211.

CRUSE, D. B. "Socially Desirable Responses at Ages 3 Through 6." *Child Development*, Vol. 37, No. 4 (1966), 909–916.

HEATHERS, G. "Emotional Dependence and Independence in Nursery School Play." *Journal of Genetic Psychology*, Vol. 87 (1955), 37–58.

KAGAN, J., and H. A. Moss. "The Stability of Passive and Dependent Behavior from Childhood Through Adulthood." *Child Development*, Vol. 31 (1960), 577–591.

Understanding Negative Behavior

Timmy, age four, pounded abusively on the piano. He noted the approaching adult and quit. He said, "Teacher, I can play a song." "Good," she said. "Let me hear it." She listened a while, but had to leave to take care of another child. Timmy lost interest in the piano, walked into the room where three jack-o-lanterns were displayed on the shelves. He rolled them off in one fell swoop. An adult arrived to care for Timmy and restore order to the mess he'd made.

JUST A FEW INSTANCES like this one can make teachers feel that Timmy's whole day is spent in mischief. Teachers may even tend to avoid dealing with him, feeling quite ineffective and hoping that others will step in and cope with him. In this instance, the teachers knew that Timmy's behavior was interfering with the work of the school. He destroyed others' learning environment, he hurt children, and he damaged equipment, though this had been minimal up to this point. Sadly enough, he was beginning to be a scapegoat in the group, for if anything troublesome happened it was easy for children to blame it on Timmy. Something had to be done.

MEANINGFULNESS OF BEHAVIOR

Timmy and other children who knock things over, hit children, and pound pianos abusively are telling us something by their behavior. They are saying as clearly as they know how, "All is not right in my world. Help me."

As Timmy's teacher, you would wisely ask, "Is

this just a bad day for Timmy or does he do these things with regularity?" How would you proceed so you could help Timmy and get your class to function adequately again?

Observation   Observation is a first requirement of learning about and doing something about troublesome behavior. As mentioned earlier, observation helps us appreciate positive behavior. It frequently helps us find the "good" or strengths in troubled children. One teacher began spending time in the observation booth, making notes of Timmy's activities. Where did he play? With whom did he play? What "good" things did he do? When did the blow-ups occur? How often did he really blow up or disturb the learning environment? How often did he really hit others?

In Timmy's case, the teachers observed a very bright little boy. He knew answers to questions, he quickly concluded from clues what was going to happen next. He was much more comfortable when close to an adult, especially the head teacher. She could give him attention and attend to others' needs at the same time more effectively than any of the other adults. The other children tended to be afraid of him.

There is a fallacy that is frequently operating when materials and curricula are designed to zero in on "problem," "disadvantaged," or "handicapped" children—individualized observation is neglected. A narrow focus on the "problem" may ignore the child's very strengths that will help him to correct his difficulty. Whether the difficulty is minor or severe, we should first assess the child's strengths. We should also watch closely and note whether the alleged "problem" is really a problem. Sometimes adults simply have expectations that are unrealistic for the age of the child or expect him to know something that no one has bothered to teach him.

Parent Conference   The head teacher made an appointment to talk to Timmy's mother, whom she knew from other conferences and home visits. They talked about her job, how things were going for Timmy and the baby, and so on. The teacher learned that Timmy's father had recently joined the Army. The teacher wondered how his absence was affecting Timmy. This question opened up the mother's long discussion about Timmy, including the fact that he played with matches. She reported that the babysitter spent the afternoon watching TV and gave Timmy very little attention.

The teacher reported that the adults at school had observed some of the same behavior and told the mother that their present emphasis was on giving him the attention he seemed to be wanting so badly. She pleased the mother with the assessment that Timmy was a bright little boy with answers to questions that other children couldn't answer. They talked about things she might do.

Action   After making notes for a number of days, the teachers met to decide what they might be able to do. They decided for the head teacher to stay near Timmy, stopping his problem behavior firmly if needed. Primarily she was to involve him specifically in activities, giving him the attention he seemed to be craving. She referred to him by name repeatedly so he would know she was thinking of him. She planned activities he particularly enjoyed and let him know that she had done it because he liked those things. If Timmy wandered away, an assistant continued the activity with the group so the head teacher could stay near Timmy. Soon Timmy began acting out less. Other children became more accepting and less fearful of Timmy. He was now getting to show off his bright observations using his keen intelligence. The problems didn't cease, but improvement was evident.

A troubled child like Timmy must be helped, or the entire group will be affected. Some would say that Timmy was getting more than his share of the teacher's time, and that's true. Strangely enough, the children were glad to have him more relaxed and under control. They weren't vying for the teacher's time when she was with him. They willingly accepted help from the other teachers.

Three things helped the situation: (1) observation to be sure what was actually happening, (2) conference with the mother, and (3) staff planning and carrying out of the plan.

AREAS OF TROUBLESOME BEHAVIOR

Negative or troublesome behavior needs discussion lest someone think we don't have our feet planted on the ground of reality.

There are three areas of behavior that we have designated as calling for limits. They are (1) aggressive behavior toward others, (2) destroying the learning environment, and (3) destroying property. We will discuss some typical behavior of young children to illustrate these areas. In addition, several other problems will be discussed that usually are troublesome to the individual child.

Aggressive Behavior Toward Others

Children are learning to get along with other children. They are growing from very self-centered infants to more socialized preschoolers. We have previously discussed some of the kinds of behavior that are positive or acceptable, the kinds that bear repeating and bring rewards from adults.

Aggression isn't all bad. We often speak of the successful businessman as one "aggressive enough to get the accounts." We mean that he moves in without timidity. It can also mean that he pushes others aside in the process, but we may tend to forget this.

Infants occasionally hurt others by pushing too hard or striking another with a hard toy held in wobbly and uncertain grasp. The pushing is often a form of "Hello," a way of greeting for a child short on vocabulary. The striking is seldom done with any malice but more from lack of coordination. It isn't sensible to scold infants for these transgressions. We need only to keep them apart or free from toys or other objects that might be hurtful. They are easily distracted, and a harmful toy can be spirited away quite easily and a soft one put in the child's hands instead.

Toddlers, too, are still short on vocabulary and on social skills. They learn to defend their space with shrieks, which may sound like they are badly hurt when they usually aren't. The shrill shriek serves a purpose. It causes adults to come running and to scold anyone in sight, assuming the "poor baby" was the victim. This technique is successfully used on older siblings. Once the habit is established at home, you will see it practiced in the nursery school.

Physical aggression is usually disruptive in the nursery school. We feel we have to protect other children, and their parents expect us to protect them. We aren't able to go take a bubble bath, as one psychologist told a mother to do when her three children were constantly bickering. The psychologist said, "The children are manipulating you, seeing which one you'll side with. When they fight, go take a bubble bath."

Hitting and Kicking

Very seldom is a preschooler maliciously hitting and kicking. Rather these children strike out because of frustration or because of some interference or assumed interference from another child. The adult must stop the hitting or kicking by restraining the child if necessary, and saying, "I can't let you hit me, it hurts" or "I can't let you kick Jenny, it hurts her." Though it restrains him, the comforting arm on his shoulders also reassures him that you still like him. Continue to attend him until he gets himself under control.

Sometimes a bully terrorizes children almost without a teacher's knowing it. He has a sense of timing, harming others when the adults have their backs turned. Parents have been known to withdraw their children from a school with such a child, and with good reason. Their fearful children do not like school. Teachers should be on the lookout for such occurrences and should listen to parents' complaints.

What are helpful clues to look for? Observe carefully the situation when a particular child strikes out. Is it on the playground where there isn't much adult guidance? If true, provide the extra guidance. Is it when others are in too close proximity and interfere with his play? Then arrange to prevent overcrowded areas. Does the child have words to express his feeling? If not, you can tell him, "Tell Todd that you are using that block."

The child may not know better ways of dealing with interferences than to strike out. He can be helped to learn better ways. Teach him to say, "Jimmy, move over" or "Mike, I'm using that bike." You can also remind him that Jimmy or Mike may not know what he wants when he hits out.

Is there too much pressure on the child at home or at school or both? Are activities scaled too high, making him strain to achieve what he thinks is the expected goal? Are activities of low interest or scaled below his ability, leaving him bored with nothing challenging to do? If these situations exist, work to reduce the pressures or to generate interest both at school and outside the school.

Does the child seem tired or hungry? Fatigue often accompanies outbursts of aggression. The child may not be getting sufficient rest or food. There may be too many children in the group, contributing to crowding, noise, and consequent fatigue. This may also be true of the family. Adjustments can be made in mealtimes and planned rest and naptimes. Parents can be alerted to help with the problem.

What can adults do about hitting or kicking? First, stop the behavior without blame or punishment—neither of these stops negative behavior except in a short-run sense. Second, make adjustments in indirect guidance, arranging the space, schedule, routine, and so on in ways that may more readily fit the children. Third, recognize the child for his strengths and good behavior and avoid making issues over transgressions of rules. In other words, give him attention for his "good" works, not for his "bad." Fourth, give him opportunities to talk out his feelings. Fifth, find a diversion for his energy.

A diversion for hitters is a Bobo clown—a plastic toy that the child can try to knock down repeatedly as it bounces back. Or boxing gloves can be used to hit a bag. Carpentry is a good outlet for children who have aggressive feelings. If you can set them to hammering before some incident triggers hostility, they may pound away and have a good emotional release from the pounding. Of course, you can't give children tools when they are angry unless they can work alone a while and have adult supervision.

Teaching a child to say "I'm sorry" rarely does any good toward stopping aggressive behavior. A child can say "I'm sorry" and really have no feeling in what he is saying.

Biting and Spitting

Biting and spitting are often resorted to in moments of extreme frustration. A child who feels weak, as far as other forms of defending himself are concerned, may bite or spit or both. First, watch closely to see that no one gets hurt. Then observe the time and occasion when the child bites or spits. Determine whether there is something or someone particularly involved. Try to alleviate those situations. Some spitters have been helped by having them spit in the toilet until they are "through." Tell them, "When you are through spitting come out and we'll have no more spitting."

Verbal Aggression

Verbal aggression is preferable to physical aggression—at least the hurt is only psychological. You often hear children say, "I don't like you," "You're stupid," or "No! No! No! I told you I wasn't playing with you, I'm busy." Any of these children could have hit a companion but clobbered him verbally instead. Fortunately, these kinds of ill winds generally blow over quickly, and children go right back to playing together.

Teachers seldom need to check verbal aggression. In fact, they should encourage a child to talk out his rage instead of striking out. Teachers can say, "John, talk instead of hit. Tell Dean you don't want him to take your blocks." In addition, you can verbally reflect his feeling, saying, "It makes you very *angry* when Dean takes your blocks. You *really* don't like it at all." This accepting rather than judgmental comment ("You shouldn't hit Dean") helps the child cope with his feeling of anger. In the meantime you also stop Dean from his infringement on John's territory.

Teasing. Teasing is a form of verbal aggression that develops in the fourth and fifth years as children become skillful with words. Older siblings often tease younger ones, a form of aggression they can get by with, whereas hitting would be punished by parents. Providing other means of achieving attention is usually the solution.

Name-Calling. Name-calling, harsh language, and swearing may also be aggressive. It can be a habit learned at home or in the neighborhood. Somehow even adults who swear feel it should be stopped in preschoolers. This seems to be some kind of double standard operating. Of course, it seems useful to teach the child some new words to replace swearing. However, if children hear the language at home and if it is common even in college dormitories, then nursery school teachers should determine what the language means to the child before moving in to squelch it. Clearly, the words do not mean the same things to the children using them that they do to adults. Guidance offered before tempers flare is usually the best solution.

Destroying the Learning Environment

Acts destructive of the learning environment are disturbing to the children and to the teacher. We should arrange our rooms to help avoid accidental interference with the learning environment. Blocks arranged out of the traffic lanes, puzzles on a table, books in a quiet nook—these are the learning environments for children using those materials. Children thoroughly enjoy knocking down blocks, but it really isn't fair for anyone but the builder to do the task. Therefore, good guidance calls for redirecting wandering children who might interfere with others' projects. They usually need something to do themselves. There is really no substitute for a good, rich program that keeps children so busy with their own activities that they don't have time to interfere with others. If a child wants to be with a child who is already at work, then positive verbal guidance can be used to help him enter the play in an acceptable manner.

Destroying Property

Respect for property should be learned, else there will not be toys for other days. Acts of aggression and neglect with respect to equipment should not be allowed. Of course, there is normal wear and tear on equipment. Paint gets chipped and toys get broken. For example, reasonable concern for driving tricycles without wrecking them or driving them into the walls can be taught. Children who fail to comply with rules simply are ruled off the tricycles until they agree they can follow the rules. Rough play usually occurs in older preschoolers who are capable of understanding the rules and the consequences.

Children can develop pride in their building and playground by helping keep it neat and clean. They can go on litter hunts to pick up the accumulation of materials that blow in or are left around. Helping children appreciate beauty may serve as a countermeasure to those who may disregard the environment and would destroy it.

Other Troublesome Behavior Children, like Timmy in our opening anecdote, may display multiple problems. Besides striking out, Timmy was an attention-seeker.

ATTENTION-SEEKING

Children may behave like Timmy, doing unacceptable acts to get attention—negative attention being better than no attention. They may seek help when they could do a task themselves. They may seek reassurance. Their behavior clearly says, "I want you to notice me." Using children's names frequently in working with them helps a child know you are talking to and noticing him. Greeting children individually each day with special little conversations about something that others don't know about, such as something the teacher learns on a home visit, helps individualize teaching. Keeping groups small so individual attention is the rule, not the exception, also helps.

Denying attention does not help an attention-seeker improve. Ways must be found to allow him to shine legitimately, then he can cast off his attention-seeking devices. Increased self-confidence helps a child feel less need to use attention-seeking devices.

QUIET AND WITHDRAWN BEHAVIOR

Quiet and withdrawn behavior may be the most difficult to deal with. In large groups, quiet and withdrawn children may actually move through the day almost without notice because the aggressive children receive all the teacher's time and energy. In such groups, if you were to ask the teacher for a character sketch of each child, the quiet and withdrawn children are the ones she would likely "forget" or have little to say about.

One quiet child's mother said, "I'd jump for joy if she would stamp her feet and yell, 'No!'" The mother truly seemed to want the child to be more of an extrovert. Perhaps that was not in the child's nature, but the teachers did notice that the child gained confidence as she broadened her skills and interests through the year.

Another child was frequently an observer when other children were active. She was seen, for instance, watching the boys at the carpenter's bench for over fifteen minutes. She sat nearby, watching them intently and laughing at their jokes. Some adults wanted to force her to participate, but she was extremely stubborn if pressed to do something she didn't want to do. Consequently, a more personal method of helping her participate was designed. There was no doubt that she was learning as she watched. Her mother cared for several babies in a mobile home, so it was easy to see why quiet behavior was approved by the parents.

Removing pressure to do certain activities and the reassuring presence of the same adult usually help the withdrawn child cope with the preschool situation. Protection may be necessary to keep others from approaching him too quickly.

Some of these children may need help from their mothers in making the initial adjustment to the nursery school. Mothers may have to bring them for only short periods for several weeks or stay in the classroom with them.

LYING

Lying and fantastic tales are closely related. The preschooler does sometimes deny that he has done misdeeds that at the moment of doing he may not have remembered as wrong. The adult may contribute to lying of this sort by the way questions are asked. The natural inclination is to defend oneself;

therefore, when asked, "Did you dump out the puzzle?" the child may say, "No." He may also report that someone else did it, noting your apparent displeasure. Some "Who did it?" questions simply don't matter that much.

Preschoolers often spin fanciful tales. Some may be designed to get attention or make the child feel powerful. Others may be wish-fulfilling, like the fatherless child who told many stories of the heroic roles his father played. Sometimes it helps to remind a child "That is one of your pretend stories, isn't it?" to help him keep reality in mind. There seems little reason to make him admit it as a lie.

TATTLETALES

Tattletales are troublesome to some teachers. Children who tell on other children are often unpopular with their peers, even in preschool. Parents of a tattletale may be encouraging tattletaling by having older siblings in charge of younger ones. There are obvious times when adults appreciate having problems pointed out to them that they may be unaware of. Hence, there is some ambivalence and resulting confusion regarding a child's telling what peers or siblings are involved in.

One response to a tattletale child is "Don't worry, I'll take care of Mary, if you take care of . . ." (using the child's own name). However, if you respond immediately by going to check on Mary, then the tattletale will receive reward from having reported. One thing that can be said for the tattletales is that they know the rules and can verbalize them, which may be a higher level of conscience than some of their peers have. The adult should help these children to develop more rapport with other children and to receive the teacher's attention in other ways.

THUMBSUCKING, NAILBITING, AND MASTURBATING

Thumbsucking, nailbiting, and masturbating are all habits that may grow out of tension and a need for comfort. They may be devices that relax the child as he goes to sleep. Rather than attempt to deal with the behavior, you should look for the cause of the tension in the child's life. Stopping one behavior usually results in starting another unless the pressure that is causing it is removed. Shaming or calling these behaviors naughty and the like is usually counterproductive. Some other points regarding masturbating are discussed in Chapter 10.

CONCLUSION

These are some of the kinds of problem behavior that teachers will see in classes of normal children. Behavior deviations tell us that a child has problems. Many behavior problems cannot be ignored, for they interfere with other children's safety and learning. The teachers first observe the child over a period of time to be sure that an act is not an unusual one for him. Through discussions with the parents, a teacher can learn whether the behavior occurs at home and what they are doing about it. She can also learn whether home factors may be contributing to the tension that is a part of the problem. Following this study, the teacher will attempt to set the stage for the positive behavior the child can perform to replace his negative behavior. A coordinated plan made with other staff members is desirable so that they are not working at cross purposes. Helping the child to find outlets and to talk over his behavior may be helpful.

In cases of extreme deviance, the teachers should get in touch with behavior advisors in a guidance or mental health clinic. Such a professional might visit the school and offer the staff advice for coping with a troubled child. Persons skilled in behavior modification might be called in.

An inventory of the possible assistance available in the community should be made before alarming the parents. Once the strongest and most reliable source of help has been located, then referral recommendations can be made in a conference with the parents. Parents require both assured and delicate handling if the child is to, in fact, finally get to the agency for treatment. Discussion of problem behavior in their children is something that is very difficult for parents, and taking advice from a variety of agencies does not come easily. Teachers should be very much aware of this fact.

APPLICATIONS

1. Discuss with a mother or a teacher what kinds of behavior she considers negative or "bad." Summarize the conversation. Do you agree with her position?
2. Help with a group of children in a classroom or on a play yard. What are the kinds of behavior you find yourself stopping? What is your basis for deciding to stop a particular kind of behavior?
3. From your memory, recall the types of behavior that your teachers or parents labeled as "naughty." Can you remember any feelings you had then about the way people were reacting to these? Explain.
4. Observe or attempt to recall instances of behavior that the teacher stops. What appear to be her reasons for doing so? Discuss the matter with her if feasible.
5. Report on children who you think have sufficient negative behavior to warrant special attention. Describe the behavior to your class. If these children were your responsibility, what would you do to help them?
6. From your records analyze the negative behavior your case-study child has exhibited. Continue to refine your case study.

FOR FURTHER READING

BERGER, ALLAN S. "Anxiety in Young Children." *Young Children*, Vol. 27, No. 1 (Oct. 1971), 5–11.

FESHBACH, NORMA, and SEYMOUR FESHBACH. "Children's Aggression." *Young Children*, Vol. 26, No. 6 (Aug. 1971), 364–377.

HYMES, JAMES, JR. *Behavior and Misbehavior*. Englewood Cliffs, N.J.: Prentice-Hall, Inc., 1955.

KATZ, LILIAN G. "Condition with Caution." *Young Children*, Vol. 27, No. 5 (June 1972), 277–280.

MOORE, SHIRLEY, and SALLY KILMER. *Contemporary Preschool Education: A Program for Young Children*. New York: John Wiley & Sons, Inc., 1973.

SIBLEY, SALLY A., et al. "Modifying Behavior of Kindergarten Children." *Young Children*, Vol. 25, No. 6 (Aug. 1970), 345–352.

SIGEL, IRVING E., et al. "Social and Emotional Development of Young Children." In Edith Grotberg (Ed.). *Day Care: Resources for Decisions*. Washington, D.C.: Office of Economic Opportunity, 1971.

Communicating with Parents of Preschool Children

"If America's parents are given the place, power, and prestige to enable them to function as guides, companions, and sources of love and discipline for their children, and to have a decisive role in determining the environments and programs in which their children live and grow, the great majority of them will be able to take full advantage of the opportunity to enhance the quality of life both for their children and themselves. Only one caution must be borne in mind. The crucial factor is not how much time is spent with the child but how the time is spent. A child learns, he becomes human, primarily through participation in a challenging activity with those he loves and admires. It is the example, challenge, and reinforcement provided by people who care that enable a child to develop both his ability and his identity. An everyday example of the operation of this principle is the mother who daily talks with her young child and—usually without thinking much about it—responds more warmly when he uses new words and expressions and gradually introduces new and more complex forms which the child in turn adopts. It is in work and play with children, in games, in projects, in shared responsibilities with parents, adults, and older children that the child develops the skills, motives, and qualities of character that enable him to live a life that is gratifying both to himself and those around him. But this can only happen in a society that lets and makes it happen, one in which the needs of families and children become a primary concern not merely of special organizations and interest groups but of all major social institutions—government, industry, business, mass media, communities, neighborhoods,

297

and individual citizens. It is the priorities they set that will determine our children's present and America's future."[1]

THUS PARENTING received emphasis in the 1970 White House Conference on Children. The involvement of parents in preschool programs was an emphasis in the Head Start programs that started in 1965. The parent-cooperative movement has long realized the contribution that parents can make to a preschool program. These groups and many others have emphasized, as was done in Chapter 1 of this book, that parents are resources for their children.

MEETING PARENTS

The first step in communicating with the preschool child's parents is to get acquainted with them. In some families the preschool teacher is the family's first contact with the educational system. Therefore, the preschool gives the parent his first impression regarding how his child is going to be treated in school. If parents have experienced school as an unpleasant, threatening, and unproductive environment in their own student days, they may bring negative feelings with them as they approach the preschool teacher.

As teachers, you will be ready to extend the hand of welcome to parents to let them know that you want to get acquainted and develop a cooperative relationship with them. Even parents with years of experience with school systems, perhaps even teachers themselves, will usually wait for their child's teacher to make the first move of friendship.

Getting acquainted with parents as friendly adults is the first step. You don't have to start right off discussing the program of the nursery school or the problems or pleasures you have with their Sally. You can talk about personal things like hobbies, interests, or the cost of living. Students in training can gain experience with parents on a moment-at-a-time basis

[1] *Report to the President—White House Conference on Children* (Washington, D.C.: Government Printing Office, 1971), p. 241.

Parent groups can participate in policy-making for the center. (University of Houston, Rebecca Hines, Photographer.)

as they greet them at the beginning or end of the day. Parents don't bite. They actually enjoy having someone talk with them about their child. They like to hear about the activities the child enjoys and who his best friends are.

Many parents in this highly mobile society we live in are isolated from their kinship family. They may long for someone with whom they can talk over their concerns about parenting. Therefore, nursery school teachers who are also interested in a parent's child find receptive welcomes when they make efforts to visit and get acquainted. Parents really appreciate someone who will listen as they chat about their children. Two students learned this when they were taking a preschool survey among young parents in married student housing on a university campus. They found a decided tendency among the women to keep the conversation going long beyond the time necessary to answer the survey questions.

Acceptance

Accepting parents as they are is a key to communicating with them. People are different, and parents are all different. If they change, they will have to do the changing themselves. Teachers will be more warmly accepted by parents if they don't try to make them over.

All parents have strengths—good points—and teachers can look for these to help appreciate parents. When teachers get acquainted for the first time with parents from ethnic and social class groups different from their own, they have many new things to learn. Families differ in ways of dealing with their children, with each other, and with outsiders. The teacher must work to understand the ways of the new group, not to change them. She must avoid making judgments about rightness and wrongness of

When parents help on the playground they appreciate the skills their child is learning. (Howard University, Flemmie Kittrell Project, Fred Harris, Photographer.)

their ways. Just because their ways are different from the teacher's doesn't make them wrong.

Hospitality   The nursery and preschool should be considered a supplement to the home. These can be institutions that extend and strengthen the family as well as the child. As such, a cooperative atmosphere is necessary, a give and take that makes the best possible situation for the child and for the family.

The school must be open to visits by parents even before the child is enrolled. Parents are encouraged to shop for preschool services as they do for other consumer services. Therefore, they should be welcomed and allowed to visit the class where their child might attend. Later, the child and parent visit the school to introduce the child to "his school."

Freedom to visit at will without prior appointment indicates openness and honesty. With this policy, parents will feel that your everyday manners are the same as your company manners. It should be easy for parents to drop in to visit when they happen to have a few minutes. Fathers and working mothers especially may find it difficult to arrange for visits but may make a number of short observations if encouraged just to drop in.

CONFERENCES   Numerous conferences will be held over the telephone when parents feel free to call the teacher. These can be very helpful for receiving news of family activity or a crisis that may affect the child in the school. Teachers can also set the stage for calling parents when need arises.

Many short conferences can take place as parents bring their children and pick them up each day. Appointments can be made at that time to tackle problems needing more time.

Longer conferences can be scheduled periodically to guide evaluation of the program for the parent's child. The teacher should organize her thoughts for these conferences so that they can be productive. Conferences may be most useful in getting information from parents, in contrast to giving them information.

301   *Conferences*

HOME VISITS

Home visits are one of the most profitable ways of getting acquainted with children and their parents and of helping them with problems. By meeting on home base, the focus is on parents and child and their concerns. The teacher can meet the other family members and learn incidental information about the child's interests that serves as conversation topics as they meet again in the school. The child feels more secure when he knows the teacher knows where he lives. On occasion she might have to take him there. Parents are not reluctant to have teachers visit when visits are explained as routine procedure that all parents are taking part in. Focusing the conversation primarily on the child and on topics the parents wish to discuss helps avoid any concern about the quality of furnishings. Home visits pay off later in dealing with the child at school. Children are often heard to say, "You came to my house, didn't you, teacher?"

HOME TEACHING

Parents are teachers, too. They are the child's first teachers, and they'll be there long after preschool teachers are outgrown. We must learn to appreciate the opportunities parents have for being learning resources for their child's education. Middle-class parents have long provided their children a wealth of stimulation and experiences that encourage learning. Some researchers have demonstrated the effectiveness of lending toys and books to families and giving ideas about how to use them with their children. Other projects have shown parents how to do learning experiences with a child—teaching him concepts, colors, and the like.

Many parent education programs help parents learn child development principles and help them make applications to their own children. Child Study Clubs, Mothers of Twins Clubs, and Parents Without Partners are examples of self-help associations. The Parent Effectiveness Training (P.E.T.) developed by Thomas Gordon[2] is a promising technique for helping parents talk to and interact with

[2] Thomas Gordon, *P.E.T. Parent Effectiveness Training* (New York: Peter H. Wyden, 1970).

The interactions mothers have with children at home are sandwiched between other responsibilities. (William Mitcham, Michigan State University Staff Photographer.)

their children to build warm personal relations between parents and child.

Parent meetings are one type of parent-teacher interaction. These may be held in small or large groups. Organizers often have difficulty getting working parents to participate. It is understandable that night meetings might be unpopular. When a parent works all day and doesn't see his child, it is difficult to leave him again, perhaps with another stranger, just to go to a meeting. Most successful meetings are those organized by a committee of parents. They plan the type of meeting they desire, issue the invitations, and help with rides and babysitting.

Open houses held at the school inviting the children and their parents to visit the classroom and meet the teacher are popular with some groups. Children enjoy decorating the room for their parents. They may bake cookies and plan a few songs to sing to their parents. Such an event makes another opportunity to see parent-child interaction. Some groups plan family picnics.

PARENT COOPERATIVES

Parent cooperatives are one type of preschool program that specifically involves parents in the operation of the school. A governing board of the parent cooperative sets the policy of the school and hires the teacher. Parents take turns serving as assistants to the teacher. Not only do they receive preschool at reduced rates for their children, but also most parents appreciate the opportunity that participation offers them to learn to work with their child and to further influence the child's development.

Day care groups are also organized as parent cooperatives, especially among parents who have some flexibility in their schedules that allows them time to participate. In both groups parents may organize work parties on evenings or weekends to help with painting or improving the facility or equipment.

Cooperatives often sponsor parent education classes to help parents in their parenting roles. Besides providing useful information, these groups give parents a pleasant social group. They encourage friendships and other human resource exchanges among families, which are especially important for families who may be newcomers in a community.

POLICY-MAKING

In parent cooperatives, Head Start schools, and parent-child centers, parents are elected to the policy-making boards. They help with selection of goals and the distribution of resources. From this experience of active participation in governing, many parents gain confidence in their ability to effect change in social institutions. They then may run for school boards or other elective offices in the community. Parental input helps make programs more accurately reflect the needs of the children they serve.

CONCLUSION

Parenting received special emphasis in the 1970 White House Conference on Children. The possibilities for the preschool to help parents with their parenting role are many. The cooperative nursery schools and Head Start programs have had significant experience in working with parents. At no time in the child's educational experience is a close relationship between home and school more important than during the preschool years. Teachers must work at involving parents and communicating with them. Parents have a great deal that they can offer their child, the teacher, and the school, if they are encouraged to contribute.

APPLICATIONS

1. Visit a parent for the purpose of learning about a child. Before you go, prepare a list of questions that seem appropriate for learning about the child. Check the list with your instructor and get advice about making the appointment.
2. Write a summary of your visit—a "She said, I said" report. Then conclude with a summary of what you learned about the child.
3. Visit the home of your case-study child if you have not yet done so. Incorporate new information into your case study. Refer to earlier chapters and answer any questions that you may have missed. Also, answer more fully those questions where you now have new insights and understanding as a result of your school studies.

FOR FURTHER READING

COHEN, MONROE (Ed.). "Symposium on Parent Centered Education." *Childhood Education*, Vol. 48, No. 3 (Dec. 1971), 114–147.

FEDDERSEN, JOHN, JR. "Establishing an Effective Parent-Teacher Communication System." *Childhood Education*, Vol. 49, No. 2 (Nov. 1972), 75–79.

GORDON, IRA. *Baby Learning Through Baby Play: A Parent's Guide for the First Two Years.* New York: St. Martin's Press, Inc., 1970.

GORDON, THOMAS. *P.E.T. Parent Effectiveness Training.* New York: Peter H. Wyden, Inc., Publisher, 1970.

HILDEBRAND, VERNA. "Parent-Teacher Relations." *The Instructor*, Vol. 78, No. 1 (Sept. 1968), 41.

HILDEBRAND, VERNA. *Introduction to Early Childhood Education.* New York: Macmillan Publishing Co., Inc., 1971.

KNITZER, JANE. "Parental Involvement: The Elixir of Change." In Dennis N. McFadden (Ed.). *Early Childhood Development Programs and Services: Planning for Action.* Washington, D.C.: National Association for the Education of Young Children, 1972.

Marion, Marian C. "Create a Parent-Space—A Place to Stop, Look and Read." *Young Children*, Vol. 28, No. 4 (Apr. 1973), 221–224.

Moore, Evelyn K., and Maurine K. McKinley. "Parent Involvement/Control in Child Development Programs." In Dennis N. McFadden (Ed.). *Early Childhood Development Programs and Services: Planning for Action.* Washington, D.C.: National Association for the Education of Young Children, 1972.

Nimnicht, Glen P., and Edna Brown. "The Toy Lending Library: Parents and Children Learning with Toys." *Young Children*, Vol. 28, No. 2 (Dec. 1972), 110–116.

Streissuth, Ann P., and Helen L. Bee. "Mother-Child Interactions and Cognitive Development in Children." *Young Children*, Vol. 27, No. 3 (Feb. 1972), 154–173.

Evaluating–Who
Needs It?

"Whatcha doing with that book?" inquired five-year-old Mandy, pointing to the little black book carried by Mr. Alonzo, the curriculum coordinator. "I may write in it some time," answered the school official. "Well! If you're not using it, why don'tcha put it away?" remarked Mandy, probably repeating lines she had heard adults use.

MR. ALONZO'S MISSION was evaluation. He visited all classrooms regularly to *examine* and *judge* how the school's stated objectives were being met.

The values of the parents, school, community, nation, and world will influence school programs. Often values are implicit, that is, not specifically indicated. However, better understanding of policies and programs is assured if value judgments are given explicitly, that is, clearly stated.

Values are of major significance and a source of much lively controversy. Lively controversy is a healthy sign in a democratic society and the source of much progress. However, different and changing views in the area of values create fascinating problems for Mr. Alonzo's mission of evaluation.

If there is anything that makes people uncomfortable, it's evaluation. It's scary to have the minister visit unless the house looks just right. You think he's making a judgment about you. Perhaps you wish your mother-in-law would call before she drops in. You think she judges your housekeeping, and you'd at least hurry and get the dishes out of the sink. A teacher becomes "up tight" when she knows the curriculum coordinator is in the building. Or perhaps it's the licensing officer from the depart-

307

ment of social services who is the bogeyman for the child care centers. These individuals are usually making judgments or evaluations of children's programs.

Evaluators are supposed to see if you are meeting some standard. Hopefully, you know what that standard is. Should teachers fear evaluators? Actually, most good teachers are doing a far better job than the criteria for public nursery school and day care standards require. So why should we fret about evaluations?

WHO NEEDS EVALUATION?

Teachers

Teachers should be the first to say, "Of course we need evaluation. We are evaluating all the time, every minute of every day. We make a decision, see the effects of the decision, and make adjustments, even in the immediate situation if necessary, to remedy a situation that doesn't come up to standard. That's evaluation."

Evaluation is nothing more than checking up to see how well you are meeting standards. Teachers evaluate far more often than once a year, or once a term, or once a month, or even once a day. Good teachers are constantly working to do their jobs better. The "better" means that they have some standards to which to compare their performance.

Where do the standards come from? They are established by the profession. They come from national, state, and local licensing and funding agencies. They come from state departments of education and state departments of social services, whichever may have licensing control. Standards come from a parent board in a parent cooperative, a school board in public schools, or a board of directors in a private agency. Typically, these are all minimum standards—the least you can get by with. However, good teachers don't rest comfortably with minimum standards, and when you take a close look at some minimum standards you understand why. Minimum standards really are minimal, and knowledgeable teachers want lots more in their programs for children.

Therefore, teachers who are really professionals set their own high standards for the children's programs. They work to improve their teaching every day, every month, every year. They look constantly for new ideas, new materials, new ways to help children. They read professional journals, which give them new ideas to try—new standards to achieve. They go to school, take courses, read, and study. When you are a true professional, it's your job to improve your profession.

As mentioned earlier, custodial child care, the type that gives only minimum physical care and little or no education, simply must not be allowed to exist in an affluent nation such as ours. We know more and we can afford more. Standards should rise for the sake of present and future generations of children. Teachers have a stake in raising those standards because it's their future, too. They are helping raise the standards when they take stock and improve their own programs every day. They are helping raise standards when they willingly share their ideas with other teachers. They are helping raise standards when they help parents and other citizens recognize the components of high-quality child care programs.

Children   Children need evaluation of their nurseries and preschools. And children, too, evaluate. Children tell us by their behavior how the program is going. They tell us if we've selected equipment and material at the right level by the way they use that equipment and material. They are happy if everything is in pretty good balance, they're grouchy if it is not. You can tell, and parents can tell. Does the child want to go to school, or does someone have to drag him? If he doesn't want to go, then something isn't quite up to standard. But if the children yell at the door, "Let me in," then you can bet that things are pretty much all right.

Children need evaluations of their schools because their whole future is at stake. It is their human resources—skills and knowledge—that aren't being developed if they have a substandard, mediocre program day in and day out for all their preschool years. If their safety is in danger, then children do need someone to say, "Hey, this place is unsafe, you can't keep kids here." In one school the teachers were using rulers on bare behinds to make children obey. That surely doesn't meet your standards, and it didn't meet those of a woman who worked there. She reported it to the agency licensing the school. Those children needed a friend like that woman.

Parents
Parents need evaluation of the preschool. And parents, too, evaluate—as they learn from Johnny or Mary what happened in school today. They ask other parents about the school, too, when they meet them in the grocery or at a ball game. Parents judge how things are going by how happy or reluctant their child is to attend. They can tell how things are going by the new ideas their child brings home, by his paintings, and by the things they see at school. Parents care about their children and are watching and listening to be sure that the place they send their precious little one has a high-quality program.

Parents need evaluation of preschools by outside forces because they may not understand fully what standards ought to be. They are very trusting, sometimes believing that "you couldn't call it a school if it wasn't a good one." Parents may be mislead for a while by fresh paint, bus service, and good advertising. They are sometimes desperate for a place for their child. Society should check up on the people offering child care and nursery school services and be sure that standards are being met. These, indeed, are consumer services as significant as businesses like barber shops, restaurants, and swimming pools that government has inspected for years.

Society
Society needs evaluation of preschool services. As preschools serve more and more children, their influence on future generations grows. Lots of people, professionals, researchers, philosophers, and the like, all need to keep their fingers on the preschool pulse. What types of people are they turning out? What values do they hold? What skills do they have? Certainly in a democratic society we are committed to the development of the human resources of every child. We should always remember that in a democratic society every child is expected to become an

active member of the governing class. Under the democratic ideal, the responsibility for the quality of life—that is, the extent of justice, equity, general welfare, and basic human rights—rests on the shoulders of every individual.

CONCLUSION

Evaluation is needed by children, teachers, parents, and the society to assure that high-quality educational programs are being provided for young children. As more and more young children are cared for in facilities outside the home, the government has an obligation to monitor them just as they do any consumer service.

High-quality programs for young children are services that this country can and must afford. Failure to accept the responsibility for this aspect of modern life will be far more costly. Excellent programs for young children represent investment expenditures that pay a high rate of return.

Responsibility for the future heights that the nation and the world achieve, whether humanitarian, intellectual, aesthetic, industrial, or celestial, rests squarely on the generations to come. Will even our best be good enough?

APPLICATIONS

1. Evaluate the center where you are observing from the viewpoint of a child. Prepare a report.
2. Evaluate the center from the viewpoint of a teacher. Prepare a report.
3. Evaluate the center from the viewpoint of a parent. Prepare a report.
4. Complete your final draft of your case study and discuss it with your instructor.

FOR FURTHER READING

BOURNE, PATRICIA G., et al. *Day Care Nightmare—A Child Centered View of Child Care*. Berkeley, Calif.: University of California, 1970.
FEDDERSEN, JOHN, JR. "Establishing an Effective Parent-Teacher Communication System." *Childhood Education*, Vol. 49, No. 2 (Nov. 1972), 75–79.
FEIN, GRETA G., and ALISON CLARKE-STEWART. *Day Care in Context*. New York: John Wiley & Sons, Inc., 1973.

HILDEBRAND, VERNA. *Introduction to Early Childhood Education.* New York: Macmillan Publishing Co., Inc., 1971.

MENDELSON, ANNA, and RUTH ATLAS. "Early Childhood Assessment: Paper and Pencil for Whom?" *Childhood Education,* Vol. 49, No. 7 (Apr. 1973), 357–361.

MORGAN, GWEN G. "Regulation of Early Childhood Programs." In Dennis N. McFadden (Ed.). *Early Childhood Development Programs and Services: Planning For Action.* Washington, D.C.: National Association for the Education of Young Children, 1972.

MURPHY, LOIS BARCLAY. "The Stranglehold of Norms on the Individual Child." *Childhood Education,* Vol. 49, No. 7 (Apr. 1973), 343–349.

OFFICE OF CHILD DEVELOPMENT. *Guides for Day Care Licensing.* Washington, D.C.: Department of Health, Education, and Welfare, Government Printing Office, 1973.

PRESCOTT, ELIZABETH. "Approaches to Quality in Early Childhood Programs." *Childhood Education,* Vol. 50, No. 3 (Jan. 1974), 125–131.

SMITH, MARILYN, and ROSEMARY GRESY. "A Guide for Collecting and Organizing Information on Early Childhood Programs." *Young Children,* Vol. 27, No. 5 (June 1972), 265–271.

Index of Names

Subject Index